SUPERPOWER

Comparing American and Soviet Foreign Policy

Christer Jönsson

 Frances Pinter (Publishers), London

First published in Great Britain in 1984 by

Frances Pinter (Publishers) Limited
5 Dryden Street, London WC2E 9NW

British Library Cataloguing in Publication Data

Jönsson, Christer
  Superpower
    1. Soviet Union–Foreign relations–United States
    2. United States–Foreign relations–Soviet Union
    3. Soviet Union–Foreign relations, 1975–
    4. United States–Foreign relations, 1981–
    I. Title
    327.47073   E183.8.S65

  ISBN 0-86187-377-7

To Lena and Linus

Typeset by Folio Photosetting, Bristol
Printed by Biddles, Ltd., Guildford

Contents

List of Tables

List of Figures

Acknowledgments

Researchers, like elephants, have long pregnancies. I have been pregnant with this research project for the better part of a decade. The actual date of conception is difficult to pin down. Yet, in retrospect, my confrontation with Thomas Franck's and Edward Weisband's book *Word Politics: Verbal Strategy Among the Superpowers* in the early 1970s planted a seed which would later grow into the research reported in this book.

Necessity, according to an old saying, is the mother of invention. In the contemporary academic world, however, funding is the mother of research. I gratefully acknowledge the parenthood of the Swedish Council for Research in the Humanities and Social Sciences. Without its generous grants from the inception of the project to the publication stage this offspring would never have seen the light of day.

Several colleagues and friends have been helpful in bringing up my progeny from infancy to adolescence, if not maturity. The Department of Political Science at the University of Lund has been a fruitful environment for growth. In particular, Lars-Göran Stenelo and Hans F. Petersson have served as 'godfathers' in the original, benign sense. I have been fortunate enough to be able to draw on the expertise of American specialist Göran Rystad and Soviet specialist Kristian Gerner at the neighbor Department of History. Others who have offered constructive criticism and provided opportunities to discuss my project in seminars include Alexander Dallin, Alexander L. George, Kjell Goldmann, Daniel Heradstveit, Kalevi J. Holsti, Charles W. Kegley, Jeanne Kirk Laux, William C. Potter, Franz Schurmann, Michael J. Shapiro, Jiri Valenta, and Robert S. Walters. During my visit to Moscow in the spring of 1977, members of the USA Institute of the Soviet Academy of Sciences gave generously of their time in interviews.

My descendant has profited from the help and care of several 'nannies.' My research assistant, Ulf Westerlund, provided invaluable services in collecting material and formulating ideas. Inga-Märta Lindgren painstakingly and cheerfully typed consecutive versions of the manuscript. And Frances Pinter encouraged me to slim my hopelessly overweight baby to publishable and readable size.

To all those mentioned — as well as numerous unmentioned helpers — I extend my sincere thanks coupled with the traditional absolution from responsibility for remaining errors and shortcomings.

This book is not the first public appearance of my offspring. Chapter 1 draws on my and Ulf Westerlund's 'Role Theory in Foreign Policy Analysis' in *Cognitive Dynamics and International Politics*, which I edited and Frances Pinter published in 1982. And part of Chapter 2, 'The Ideology of Foreign Policy,' is a slightly revised version of a chapter in Charles W. Kegley and Pat McGowan (eds), *Foreign Policy USA/USSR* (Sage, 1982). Permission to reprint these portions is gratefully acknowledged.

Finally, I owe a special debt of gratitude to my wife Evy and my children Lena and Linus for their graceful acceptance of this progeny as a 'foster child' despite its multifaceted talent for disturbing a quiet and normal family life. To Lena and Linus, whose future depends in large measure on the wisdom of the superpowers, I dedicate this book.

Christer Jönsson

Introduction

D'autant que l'Amérique et la Russie, riches en hommes et en ressources, compactes par leur territoire, naturellement protégées, l'une par d'immense océans, l'autre par sa propre étendue, sont en vertu de leur masse sollicitées à une expansion que, suivant l'éternel usage, se drape du manteau des doctrines, mais qui est en dernier ressort un déferlement de puissance.

[Charles de Gaulle, 1946]

The two superpowers are the biggest international exploiters and oppressors of today. They are the source of a new world war. They both possess large numbers of nuclear weapons. They carry on a keenly contested arms race, station massive forces abroad and set up military bases everywhere, threatening the independence and security of all nations. They both keep subjecting other countries to their control, subversion, interference or aggression. They both exploit other countries economically, plundering their wealth and grabbing their resources.

[Deng Xiaoping, 1974]

We are living in a time when the hegemony of the superpowers grows stronger and stronger. Their power is unparalleled. It is most obvious in the field of weapon technology. But it is also true in the technological, scientific and economic fields. This can mean a threat to the independence of the small nations. . . . Moreover, it is in the essence of *détente* that the superpowers prefer the preservation of status quo to change. It also appears that the leaders of these two states do not object to the strain of conservatism this gives the policy of *détente*. . . . For the sake of *détente*, the superpowers may be so afraid of the consequences of every change that they would rather accept the prolongation of an unjust and dangerous situation.

[Olof Palme, 1974]

Statements such as these have been proliferating in the contemporary world. The idea of parallel features in American and Soviet foreign policy and common superpower interests detrimental to the interests of smaller states, first espoused by de Gaulle's France and expressed in more categorical terms by China in the 1970s, is today frequently referred to by an increasing number of smaller states in different international forums.

If we, however, turn to the academic community, we find that both American and Soviet foreign policy are generally analyzed in terms of idiosyncratic factors and 'tailor-made' models. Each is treated as something unique and extraordinary. Both the United States and the Soviet Union have come to be regarded as antipodal archetypes. And whenever a comparative perspective is applied, the objects of comparison have usually been other Western states in the case of the United States, other communist states in the case of the Soviet Union. In imitation of the old Kipling dictum on the incompatibility of East and West, one might say that 'Soviet studies are Soviet studies and American studies are American studies, and never the twain shall meet.' The co-editors of a rare collection of comparative essays (Kegley and McGowan, 1982: 7–8) put it thus:

> Given the prominence of the United States and the Soviet Union on the world stage, it is not surprising that the foreign policies of these two countries have received so much scholarly attention. Literature that discusses each of these superpower's foreign policies independently is voluminous, if not always objective or incisive. What *is* surprising, in our view, is the extent to which the foreign policies of these powers have largely escaped systematic *comparison*. While many studies of one or the other of these two countries' foreign policies abound, studies that explicitly seek to compare their foreign policies are rare.

To be sure, there is a wealth of works on superpower *relations*, displaying a wide variety of approach, methodology and quality. This body of literature frequently proffers metaphors, suggesting parallels between the American and Soviet predicament. The alarmist imagery of two scorpions in a bottle gained wide currency in the early days of the Cold War. Another variant, which eschews the implication that the superpowers act merely by instinct, pictures the two rivals as playing with fire while sitting on powder kegs or wading in gasoline. Allowing for more calculating behavior still, the United States and the Soviet Union have more recently been compared to chess players, albeit 'chess players in the dark, absorbed in a game they can barely see' (Barnet, 1977: 9).

Such suggestive imagery notwithstanding, relatively few *comparative foreign policy* studies of the two post-war superpowers have been undertaken. There has been no shortage of calls for such studies. For instance, after searching for past parallels to American foreign policy, Ernest May (1968: 342, 344) concludes that 'there may be only one nation in all of history that has had anything like America's post-1945 experience, and that is its contemporary and adversary, the U.S.S.R.;' thus 'the Cold War era in American history is likely to be best understood by comparing American with Soviet experience.' Similarly, William Taubman (1975: 203) suggests that in foreign affairs there has occurred a species of United States–Soviet convergence, reflecting the imperatives of 'superpowerhood,' which has not been sufficiently explored.

Paradoxically enough, the far less compatible *domestic* political systems of the United States and the Soviet Union have been subjected to more comparative studies. In the 1960s theories of convergence of American and Soviet societies flourished. And the landmark study by Zbigniew Brzezinski and Samuel Huntington (1964) devoted only one out of nine chapters to foreign policy phenomena.

In embarking upon a comparative study of superpower foreign policy, one need not suffer from a shortage of material. Two sets of literature and two separate research communities have evolved around American and Soviet foreign policy, with few attempts to build bridges between them. Yet even a perusal of works from these two traditions suggests fruitful points of comparison. In this study I shall draw heavily on extant studies of American and Soviet foreign policy respectively. The principal purpose of this study is precisely to build bridges, to juxtapose and synthesize insights and findings from the two sets of literature. To that extent, my project involves little original research. Such undertakings have never been at a premium in the academic community where the pejorative adjective 'eclectic' is often used to stigmatize efforts at combining results and insights from different disciplines or subdisciplines. In venturing my project I derive encouragement and moral support from one of the greatest 'eclectics' of our time, Arthur Koestler (1975), who argues that the act of creation, including scientific discovery, follows a basic 'bisociative' pattern — the sudden interlocking of two previously unrelated matrices of thought. In the same vein, but on a more modest plane, I submit that the 'bisociation' of the two separate research traditions of American and Soviet studies may contribute to a better understanding of United States, as well as Soviet, external conduct.

'Juxtaposition is not comparison,' admonishes James Rosenau (1974: 14), and a French proverb holds that 'comparaison n'est pas raison' (Faurby, 1976: 159). These formulations go to remind us that besides being juxtaposed, phenomena must also be rendered comparable. Criteria of similarity and dissimilarity have to be developed, and these criteria are inevitably a function of the purpose of the study and the questions being asked.

For the past two decades a new subdiscipline labeled 'comparative foreign policy' has struggled with the theoretical and methodological problems of comparative analysis of elusive foreign policy phenomena. Many of the solutions suggested by this subdiscipline are not readily applicable to — and have in fact tended to preclude — a focused comparison of American and Soviet foreign policy. Yet this sub-discipline constitutes another natural point of reference for my undertaking. The subsequent discussion will therefore be inter-spersed with references to, and a critical review of, comparative foreign policy.

The problem of 'many variables, small N,' common to social sciences, applies *a fortiori* to the comparative study of foreign policy. Whereas the number of states whose foreign policy one can usefully compare is limited, the number of conceivable explanatory factors seems almost boundless. The favoured solution within the sub-discipline has been to 'maximise N,' to increase the number of cases as much as possible in order to allow statistical treatment and across-the-board comparisons. The aim has been nomothetic, yet generalized statements about foreign policy phenomena valid through time and across space have not emerged from these endeavors. A recent review of the comparative foreign policy subfield, therefore, prescribes reduction of the level of generality and more focused comparisons as a way to avoid 'quantitative ignorance' and 'methodological myopia' (Kegley, 1980: 19–20, 27–8).

An alternative solution to the 'many variables, small N' dilemma, suggested by Arend Lijphart, is the 'comparable-cases strategy' of 'testing hypothesized empirical relationships among variables on the basis of the same logic that guides the statistical method, but in which the cases are selected in such a way as to minimize the variance of the control variables' (Lijphart, 1975: 164).

To single out the foreign policies of the United States and the Soviet Union for comparative analysis seems to represent a step in that direction, insofar as it apparently rests on the notion, whether explicit or implicit, that these two represent 'comparable cases.' At a minimum, we tend to place the United States and the Soviet Union in the same 'superpower' category, distinguishing them from other states in the contemporary international system.

Apart from the superpower factor, however, the United States and the Soviet Union are routinely considered to be dissimilar on most other background variables. And yet in international forums public statements alleging increasing similarities between American and Soviet foreign policy, common hegemonial interests, and even nascent superpower condominium, abound. At the very least, this dissonance suggests a need to make more rigorous comparisons and to take a harder look at the factors explaining superpower behavior than has been done previously. A better understanding of the determinants of superpower foreign policy (where do the similarities and dissimilarities reside?) is, in effect, a necessary antecedent to 'minimizing the variance of the control variables' on which the 'comparable-cases' strategy hinges. The first task I set before myself in this work is therefore to make an attempt at comparing relevant background variables and uncovering 'causal chains' accounting for superpower behavior. In the absence of solid theory, this undertaking necessarily assumes a rather speculative character.

The hypothesized 'causal chains' will be 'tested' (in the weak sense of probing their plausibility) in three case studies. To cover the whole gamut of superpower external conduct in the post-war era would, of course, be a Sisyphean task. Therefore I have singled out for scrutiny American and Soviet behavior in three well-documented issue-areas which loom large in political statements alleging superpower parallelism and condominium and which extend over the entire post-war period: (1) aid relations with the Third World, (2) crisis management in the Middle East, and (3) nuclear nonproliferation.

This means that several important aspects of US–Soviet relations — such as the arms race, arms control efforts, and alliance politics — will only be treated tangentially. For one thing, these omissions pertain to aspects which suffer from no dearth of literature. Moreover, it will be recalled that my primary concern is the comparative analysis of American and Soviet foreign policy in different areas and on different issues — which may, or may not, involve direct or indirect US–Soviet interaction — rather than US–Soviet *relations per se*. And since political allegations about 'superpower politics' go beyond the obvious parallelisms deriving from the nuclear deterrence relationship, I have chosen foreign policy issues with other immediate targets than the other superpower.

Political statements comparing the external conduct of the two superpowers imply a set of pertinent research questions. The United States and the Soviet Union are said to (1) display similar behavior in foreign affairs; (2) be extremely and equally powerful, and (3) establish a kind of superpower 'condominium.' These are obviously assumptions in need of more systematic research. Once we reformulate these assumptions as research questions, a number of corollary questions and problems of definition arise.

(1) *Do the two superpowers behave similarly in foreign affairs?* It is a matter of controversy whether the United States and the Soviet Union are to be regarded as 'most different' or 'most similar' systems (cf. Przeworski and Teune, 1970: 31–43), and whether a comparative analysis of superpower foreign policy implies uncovering similarities hidden under apparent divergencies or looking for dissimilarities behind apparent likenesses. At least three different clear-cut positions along the similarity–dissimilarity continuum can be distinguished: at one extreme are those who argue that the United States and the Soviet Union are antipodes with regard to both foreign policy and background factors. This is, for example, the position taken by Albert Weeks (1970: 22):

> In foreign policy few, if any, current comparison-makers have found or even sought any meaningful likenesses between the two countries, aside from the visible accoutrements of the superpower status of the bipolar leviathans. Instead, one may find numerous differences in their political instrumentalities and environments, not to mention differing geopolitical and historically determined circumstances. These in turn react upon the foreign policies of the two countries, often in the direction of aggravating their mutual divergence.

Others maintain that whereas there may be similarities in the foreign policy behavior of the two superpowers, the factors explaining that behavior are quite different. For instance, Soviet foreign affairs specialist Georgi Arbatov (1974: 8) implies as much when he states that 'both states, for all their differences in social structure and all their profound ideological and political contradictions, do have . . . areas of parallel or coincident interests on many major problems.' Finally, the other extreme position considers American and Soviet external conduct as well as its sources to be essentially similar. The Chinese have propagated that line in the 1970s, contending that the parallels in superpower behavior in world politics flow from their common 'state-monopoly capitalist' character.

The answer to the similarity/dissimilarity issue depends to a considerable extent on the way foreign policy and its sources are conceptualized and operationalized. First, is foreign policy to be operationalized in terms of discrete actions or in terms of long-term trends, configurations, profiles, grand designs, and overarching objectives (cf. e.g., Hermann, 1972a: 72–4)? Most comparative foreign policy research has come to rely on so-called events data (where events are understood as discrete, non-routine actions above and beyond the normal flow of transactions and the data bases are newspaper indexes or other chronologies). I am, however, interested in long-term *patterns* of superpower foreign policy behavior and its sources which I shall attempt to uncover by drawing on extant analytical literature.

Further, in comparative foreign policy research there has been a tendency to rely on *remote*, structural explanatory variables which lend themselves to quantification and the use of statistical techniques. Correlations between foreign policy events and structural variables such as political or economic system are typically examined without much regard — theoretically or empirically — to the process whereby these variables might be converted or translated into foreign policy decisions and actions. Put differently, volition plays a minor role in the basically deterministic schemes of comparative foreign policy. The subdiscipline has, in fact, been accused of using deterministic logic for indeterminate phenomena. The mounting criticism of the prevalent deterministic and mechanistic modes of analysis has entailed calls for the need to 'bring men back in.' For instance, Charles Kegley (1980: 25) writes thus:

> The kinds of conditions and factors crying most for measurement are ones conventionally ignored because they are difficult to tap. Included here are mental states of central decision-makers, psychological and perceptual variables, and, yes, even the political processes that have been black-boxed so routinely.

In my search for sources of similarities and dissimilarities of superpower external conduct I shall emphasize more *proximate* explanations connected with cognitive and decision-making processes, while employing some of the variable categories suggested by comparative foreign policy students.

(2) *Are the two superpowers equally powerful?* Again, different answers have been given to this question. Among those who answer in the

negative, some argue that one or the other superpower is superior, others argue that the power of both superpowers is limited — that the superpowers are impotent rather than omnipotent. Moreover, the 'balance of power' has been assessed differently at different points in time. To mention but two prominent examples, the Chinese have during the 1970s changed their estimate from one of equally powerful superpowers to one of increasing Soviet superiority, whereas French commentaries have consistently tended to emphasize American superiority.

To research the controversial question of American and Soviet power is admittedly extremely difficult. In fact, to political scientists the concept of power represents a notorious stumbling-block. While there is general agreement that power is a pivotal concept in the study of politics, there is far less consensus concerning the actual meaning of the concept. Without delving too deeply into the perennial conceptual debate, I shall adhere to the the common distinction betwen *potential* power and *exercised* power and try to answer the question of relative American and Soviet power in two steps. First, a comparison of superpower capabilities will be undertaken in Chapter 3. While yielding a rough estimate of potential power, such an analysis provides no firm basis for conclusions about the successful exercise of power which implies the mobilization of relevant capabilities and involves a communication process with complex psychological dimensions (cf. Jönsson, 1979b). The relative ability of the super-powers to 'get other actors to do something these would not otherwise do' — to adopt Robert Dahl's (1957) oft-quoted definition of power — will be scrutinized in the three case studies (Chapters 4–6). In each case this will include an inquiry into the objectives of the involved actors and the messages 'encoded' and transmitted by the super-powers and received and 'decoded' by the influencees.

Finally, power is a relational concept. Since the exercise of power is a process involving two or more actors, there is a manifest possibility of reciprocity. Thus, when a superpower tries to exercise power over another state, it enters a relationship which opens the door for attempts by that state to exercise power over the superpower. An inquiry into the power of the United States and the Soviet Union must therefore take possible reciprocal influence attempts into account.

(3) *Has a superpower 'condominium' been established?*   This question, like the two foregoing, is highly controversial. Both the United States and the Soviet Union vigorously deny charges of tacit or behind-the-

scenes collaboration. Even among those who maintain that a superpower condominium is emerging, there are disagreements as to its sources and motive forces. One school of thought views condominium as a reflection of the superpowers' preponderant power and offensive designs. The Chinese have, for example, depicted the superpowers as 'nuclear overlords' who want the rest of the world to 'kneel down on the ground and obey orders meekly' (cf. Jönsson, 1979a: 122). Amaury de Riencourt (1968: 338) argues that the United States and the Soviet Union 'have been, for years, building the chessboard and defining the rules of this new worldwide game, rules and regulations forged during the numerous international crises; the chessboard is now about completed and the rules set.' And Jean Carral (1971: 248–57) sees the superpowers acting jointly as global 'monopolists' in an international class struggle, where the European nations constitute the 'middle class' and Third World efforts at unity represent 'trade unionism.'

Others, however, consider US–Soviet condominium efforts to be a defensive response to their declining power. Consider, for example, Ronald Steel's (1977: 47) diagnosis:

> Like generals of two mutinous armies, they are becoming aware of the fact that, although they are on opposite sides, the problems they face are strikingly similar, and that what is to the advantage of one is not necessarily to the disadvantage of the other. Indeed, their interests in many cases are surprisingly parallel. Trying to maintain a nuclear balance, keeping restless allies in check, paying blackmail to the underdeveloped nations, and seeking to prevent Third World revolutions from spilling over into conflagrations that might involve them, the super-powers are being drawn together into an unacknowledged, and still rather embarrassing, cooperation.

The term condominium evokes associations in the direction of international order and norms. In recent years international 'norms' or 'rules of the game' have received renewed attention among students of international politics (see e.g., Kratochwil, 1978; Cohen, 1980, 1981). International politics scholars have tried to identify sets of rules constituting 'international order' in the traditionalist vocabulary, or 'regimes,' in the vernacular of modernists belonging to the 'interdependence' school of thought.

International order has been defined as 'a pattern of activity that sustains the elementary or primary goals of the society of states' (Bull,

1977: 8; cf Kratochwil, 1978: 19). International regimes are defined as 'principles, norms, rules, and decision-making procedures around which actor expectations converge in a given issue-area' (Krasner, 1982: 185; cf. Keohane and Nye, 1977: 19; Haas, 1980: 358; Young, 1980: 332). In other words, whereas international order is a concept denoting a universal set of norms valid for all facets of international politics, the term regime refers to delimited issue-areas and has been applied primarily to politico-economic issue-areas. Yet the two concepts are not always easily separable. For instance, the nineteenth-century Concert of Europe has been analyzed both as an international order (se e.g., Cohen, 1981: 5) and a 'security regime' (Jervis, 1982: 362–8).

Just as typologies of international order generally include the notion of a great power 'directorate' (see e.g., Cohen, 1981: 3–5), so 'hegemony' has been a major concern of scholars analyzing international politico-economic regimes (cf. Keohane, 1980). Superpower 'condominium' could obviously be a subclass of either of these categories, although students of regimes might prefer synonymous terms such as 'duopoly' or 'dual hegemony.'

Condominium is originally a legal concept, denoting a type of arrangement which includes (1) formal association of two or more subjects of international law, and (2) joint exercise of authority within a particular territory (Holbraad, 1971: 2). International rules of the game can, in general, be considered as existing along a spectrum of formality. Raymond Cohen (1980, 1981), for example, proposes a classification ranging from tacit understandings, at the one extreme, to international treaties, at the other. The contemporary notion of a US–Soviet condominium, in particular, is mostly conceived of as an informal understanding rather than an arrangement defined in legal terms. At this opposite end of the spectrum of formality, the dual components of condominium can be reformulated as (1) partnership, or a high degree of collaboration on major issues of international politics, and (2) a high degree of joint exercise of power *vis-à-vis* other states and joint control over major issues of international politics.

To summarize, my inquiry falls at the intersection of, and hopefully contributes to, three different discourses: (1) political statements alleging superpower foreign policy parallels; (2) the academic sub-discipline of comparative foreign policy; and (3) the specialized studies of American and Soviet foreign policy, respectively. From the political discourse I have derived my overriding research questions; my analytical framework has grown out of a critical review of comparative foreign policy studies; and the case literature on American and Soviet external conduct has provided the chief empirical input.

A final caveat is warranted before setting out on an inquiry guided by the three questions outlined above. By restricting my comparison to American and Soviet foreign policy, I shall not be able to draw any firm conclusions as to how the external conduct of the two super-powers compares with that of other states or types of states. It is obvious that some of the similarities between American and Soviet foreign policy are generic rather than unique for the two superpowers. By treating each superpower as unique, we have been blinded to points of comparison not only with the rival superpower but also with other states. However, this broader comparison falls outside the pur-view of this study.

PART I: SOURCES OF AMERICAN AND SOVIET FOREIGN POLICY

1 The Nature of 'Superpower'

Comparative methodologists constantly remind us that two objects being compared must necessarily be of the same class. Classification — an 'either-or' procedure — must precede comparison — a 'more-or-less' procedure (cf. e.g., Kalleberg, 1966: 74–6; McGowan, 1975: 71–2). The reason why the foreign policies of the United States and the Soviet Union suggest themselves as objects for comparison is precisely that we tend to place these two countries in the same 'superpower' class. Understanding the nature of 'superpowerhood' is therefore antecedent to comparison.

'Superpower' obviously connotes a special *status* within the international system. In other words, it presupposes that the international system, like other social systems, is stratified. Despite the long-lived legal illusion of a world of 'sovereign and equal' states, most contemporary observers and practitioners of international politics proceed from notions of a stratified international system.

Different observers may conceive of varying numbers of pegs in the international pecking order. One common categorization distinguishes between superpowers, great powers, middle powers, and small powers (see e.g., Brecher *et al.*, 1969: 90). A more differentiated version is Steven Spiegel's (1972) division into superpowers, secondary powers, middle powers, minor powers, regional states, microstates, and dependent states. The examples could be multiplied, but suffice it here to note a common feature of these and other conceptualizations: a 'superpower' category at the top of the international hierarchy is commonly reserved for the United States and the Soviet Union.

To limit the superpower class to these two countries only is not entirely uncontroversial. In fact, William Fox (1944), who first coined the term, included Great Britain among the superpowers. To many of his contemporaries, however, it was obvious that the British Empire was eclipsed by the two non-European victors of World War II. Bertrand Russell, for instance, in 1945 stated that 'there are only two major Powers in the world at present, namely the United States and the Soviet Republic' (quoted in Fisher, 1946: 5–6). Having achieved an almost axiomatic character in subsequent decades, this notion is today again being challenged. China, Japan and a unified Western Europe are frequently portrayed as candidates for 'superpowerhood.'

Such ambiguities and disagreements stem in large measure from the fact that the basis for international stratification is seldom explicit. Very often status is understood in terms of *capabilities*. Likewise, most definitions of 'superpower,' whether explicit or implicit, are couched in terms of capabilities. Their second-strike nuclear-missile capability is then the main factor distinguishing the American and Soviet superpowers from other states in the contemporary international system. The superpowers rank high on other capability indices as well, but only in the sphere of military force are their capabilities unrivaled. Already before the advent of the nuclear age, Fox (1944: 21) defined superpower as 'great power plus great mobility of power.' Even if 'neither the possession of nuclear power nor being one of the polar powers in a two-power world was essential to the original notion of super-power' (Fox, 1980: 420), the development and amassment of nuclear weapons and intercontinental missiles in the United States and the Soviet Union signify unprecedented geographical accessibility and global reach. In the words of one caustic characterization, 'a super power is one able to wreck half the world, and committed upon conditions to do so' (Burns, 1971: xi).

Others maintain that the Soviet Union and the United States are superpowers rather by virtue of their combination of capabilities (cf. e.g., Brecher *et al.*, 1969: 90). However, they usually fail to address the aggregation problem: how are we, for instance, to weigh economic capabilities *vis-à-vis* military capabilities? The question then also arises whether the superpower status of the Soviet Union is based on other than military capabilities; and the borderline between superpowers and other states becomes blurred.

In other social systems, stratification is commonly based on *ascribed* status. Though less common, such notions have been applied to the international system as well. One major theoretical and empirical focus of contemporary international politics research has been the relationship between 'status inconsistency' and conflict. 'Status inconsistency' has then been operationalized by measuring discrepancies or inconsistencies between state rankings according to ascribed status (using scales based on diplomatic representation and prestige) and rankings on certain capability attributes such as population, urbanization, military expenditure, and industrial production (cf. Romagna, 1978: 2–3).

Superpower status, too, has been defined in ascriptive terms. Consider, for example, Hedley Bull's (1971: 143) conceptualization:

A country which is a great power is one that is recognised by other states to have a certain status in the international hierarchy. Such a state is entitled to have a voice in the resolution of issues that are not its immediate concern; it is expected to take a leading part in the affairs of the international system as a whole; it is, in other words, not merely the depository of a certain degree of armed strength, but the bearer of certain special rights and duties. To speak of great powers (or, in present day terms, of super powers) is already to presuppose the existence of an international society in which these states are 'great responsibles.'

A further elaboration of the ascriptive perspective is to define status in terms of *roles*. Again, while most common in studies of other social systems, this approach has been employed by some students of the international system. David Wilkinson (1969: 4–13) constructed a typology of world roles distinguishing among the roles of 'first, second, and third parties' in international relations, roughly corresponding to great powers, great power allies, and nonaligned states respectively. In a seminal article, Kalevi Holsti (1970) focused on national role conceptions. A state's self-defined *role conceptions* and the *role prescriptions* emanating from other actors in the external environment are regarded by Holsti as determining the state's *status* (denoting a rough estimate of the state's ranking in the international system) and hence influencing the state's foreign policy behavior, or *role performance* Drawing on Holsti, Naomi Wish has attempted to correlate national attributes, national role conceptions, and foreign policy behavior (Wish, 1977, 1980) and has suggested the use of national role conceptions in examining changes in the international system over time (Wish, 1978). Stephen Walker (1979) tested congruity among role conceptions, role expectations, and role enactment in dyadic and triadic 'role sets' involving the United States and the Soviet Union.

In keeping with these conceptualizations, I suggest that the status concept 'superpower' be interpreted in terms of role rather than capability. In other words, what makes the United States and the Soviet Union superpowers is ultimately the fact that we all *conceive* of them as such. This is not to say that perceptions and ascribed status are totally separable from capabilities. 'Even after you give the squirrel a certificate which says he is quite as big as any elephant, he is still going to be smaller, and all the squirrels will know it and all the elephants will know it' (Samuel Grafton, as quoted in Fox, 1980: 418).

To speak of American and Soviet — or, for that matter, superpower — roles strikes a familiar chord among most readers of foreign policy statements and commentaries.

In the first years of this Administration we outlined a new American role. In 1970, we implemented policies which embody our new purpose. . . . It will take many years to shape the new American role. The transition from the past is under way but far from completed. [Nixon, 1971: 3, 7]

The Soviet leadership now appears once again to be engaged in a wide-ranging and fundamental re-examination of the Soviet Union's role and purpose in the international community, stemming from Moscow's status as a global power whose capabilities and reach continue to grow at a time when her prestige and role within the world communist movement appears to be shrinking and under challenge or attack from China, Eastern Europe, Western Europe and the Third World. [Aspaturian, 1980b: 695]

Only the super powers are today in the full sense great powers, and the role they play in world politics is one they have inherited from the former European great powers. [Bull, 1971: 143]

As these quotes indicate, the term 'role' looms large in the vernacular of foreign policy decision-makers, commentators and scholars alike. While frequently used, the word is seldom given any precise meaning. Yet there exists in the social sciences a set of concepts and theories associated with the term 'role.' A brief digression into some generic key concepts of the role language therefore seems warranted at this stage of the discussion.

As with most prevalent concepts, there exists no agreed definition of the concept of role. For instance, role analysts differ as to whether 'role' should include only the norms applicable to a position or also non-normative expectations and conceptions. (Turner, 1968: 553). Theodore Sarbin's (1968: 546) definitions of role as 'the behavior expected of the occupant of a given position or status' seems wide enough to mediate this controversy. *Role expectations* are essential in this conceptualization.

Role expectations are a conglomerate of the actor's own (ego's) role conceptions as well as those of other actors (alter's). Unless alter's role conceptions constitute highly authoritative and very specific pre-scriptions, there is seldom a one-to-one correspondence between ego's and alter's role conceptions (Walker, 1979: 177). Role ambiguity or role dissensus (Biddle, 1979: 195) may thus result from ego's and alter's divergent role expectations.

A particular social position involves not a single associated role but an array of associated roles. The fact that actors typically engage in multiple role-taking along with the possibilities of role ambiguities and contradictions noted above may create *role strains*.

Two conclusions following from this brief excursion into the vernacular of role theory merit attention. First, role theory addresses itself to *continuities* and *patterns* rather than to small samples of behavior or events, yet role concepts are flexible enough to be applicable to social systems with varying degrees of permanence and fluidity. In Heinz Eulau's (1963: 42) words, 'the structure of role relationships is not only patterned but fluid.' This is of obvious importance for the relevance of role perspectives to the international political system which is generally regarded to be less structured than other social systems.

Second, role indicators could obviously be either actions (role performance) or cognitions (role conceptions). Among psycho-logically-oriented role analysts there has been a marked tendency to rely on performance indicators, and 'despite their importance, few role analysts have given much attention to symbolic records of behavior' (Thomas and Biddle, 1966b: 28). To some extent, political scientists differ in this respect. For example, Heinz Eulau (1963: 44) and Alexander George (1968: 9–10) both find it preferable to focus on ego's and alter's role expectations.

Similarly, those who have applied role concepts to the international context have, first, been interested in long-term *patterns* of foreign policy rather than discrete actions or events. Holsti (1970: 307) argues that 'because the notion of national role suggests general orientations and continuing types of commitments, actions, and functions, it has a level of generality appropriate for both foreign policy theories or frameworks, and systems studies.' Wish (1977: 13) similarly sees in national role conceptions 'a very powerful tool for explaining variations in many types of foreign policy behavior.'

Second, in their reconstructions of national roles these analysts have relied on *perceptual* variables, using *verbal* statements as indicators. The possibility of correlating national roles and action — or 'rhetoric and behavior' (Walker, 1979) — while suggested by Holsti, is actually probed by Wish and Walker.

My understanding of national roles and status coincides roughly with Holsti's (cf. Figure 1).

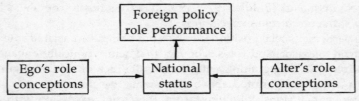

Fig. 1. National roles and foreign policy

Of course, one has to be mindful of the imperfect congruence between the international political system and other types of social systems normally referred to in role theory. To use the theatrical analogy on which the role perspective rests, there is no 'director,' the 'script' is ambiguous and allows much leeway, and the 'audience' is heterogeneous in the international arena. The international political system is frequently described as anarchic. The norms, or role prescriptions, emanating from the environment are weak. The relative lack of normative direction from the international environment has led Holsti (1970) to concentrate on self-defined (ego's) role conceptions at the expense of alter's role prescriptions. Yet he is careful to point out that the difference between the international and other social systems is one of degree rather than kind and that his choice is one of research expedience:

> To argue that in the international context role prescriptions of the alter are relatively primitive does not mean that they are non-existent or that their impact is necessarily negligible, even in crisis situations. . . . While we must acknowledge that the alter or external environment is relevant to foreign policy analysis, this study will consider it a constant. [Holsti, 1970: 244]

The observation that several smaller states tend to express ideas of parallel features in American and Soviet foreign policy strongly suggests that externally derived (alter's) role conceptions be included in an inquiry into superpower roles. I do agree, however, with Holsti about the limited *normative* content of such statements and therefore prefer to speak of alter's role *conceptions* rather than prescriptions, as in Holsti's framework.

States, like other social actors, typically perform *multiple* roles. Holsti (1970: 260–73), for instance, identifies seventeen different role conceptions in his cross-national survey, and finds that no state in his sample conceives of only a single national role. As a first attempt to uncover the *combination* of role conceptions which make up the 'superpower role,' the 1946–75 records of the general political debates of the UN General Assembly were analyzed in order to identify ego's (the United States and the Soviet Union) as well as alter's (other UN members) role conceptions (cf. Jönsson and Westerlund, 1982).

Drawing on Holsti's (1970) classification, Wish's (1977) extension of the approach, and a preliminary reading of the UN material, fifteen relevant role conceptions were distinguished (cf. Table 1).

Table 1: Superpower role conceptions

Promoter of universal values
Violator of universal values
Promoter of own value system
Preventer of other superpower's values
Model
Developer
Liberator
Liberation supporter
Regional protector
Bloc leader
Exploiter
Intervener
War instigator
Mediator
Protector of own state

Those role conceptions that the two superpowers have in common can be said to constitute the 'superpower role' (cf. Figure 2).

How did the superpower role evolve and how similar/different were American and Soviet roles perceived to be in the post-war era?

As can be seen in Table 2, there is a considerable degree of parallelism in prevalent American and Soviet role conceptions. The only marked deviations (italicized in the table) are the appearance of 'protector of own state' among Soviet role conceptions — which seems

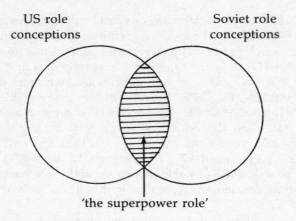

Fig. 2. The superpower role

Table 2:　The six most frequent ego's role conceptions of the United
States and the Soviet Union, 1946–75

Rank	USA			Soviet Union		
1	Promoter of universal values	54	(42%)	Promoter of universal values	74	(52%)
2	Regional protector	22	(17%)	Liberation supporter	22	(15%)
3	Liberation supporter	18	(14%)	Regional protector	18	(12%)
4	Developer	18	(14%)	Promoter of own values	14	(10%)
5	Promoter of own values	11	(8%)	*Protector of own state*	8	(6%)
6	*Mediator*	6	(5%)	Developer	7	(5%)
	Total	129	(100%)	Total	143	(100%)

natural considering the comparatively more exposed geopolitical
situation of the Soviet Union — and of 'mediator' among American
role conceptions — instances which occur in the 1970s. But the overall
picture confirms the impression that the two superpowers are
'drawing closer in their definition of their respective roles in the world'
(Barnet, 1977: 170), that American and Soviet policy-makers have
'tended to perceive their nations as performing international functions
which were quite similar' (Wish, 1980: 550).

The US–Soviet parallels extend to alter's role conceptions as well,
although the ascribed superpower roles differ from the superpower's
own conceptions (cf. Table 3).

Table 3: The six most frequent ascribed US and Soviet roles, 1946–75

	USA			Soviet Union		
1	Violator of universal values	144	(37%)	Violator of universal values	91	(44%)
2	Intervener	96	(25%)	Intervener	45	(22%)
3	Exploiter	69	(18%)	Exploiter	23	(11%)
4	War instigator	56	(14%)	Promoter of universal values	23	(11%)
5	Developer	12	(3%)	War instigator	19	(9%)
6	Promoter of universal values	11	(3%)	Developer	7	(3%)
	Total	388	(100%)	Total	208	(100%)

A breakdown of the data on alter's role conceptions points to 1956 as a watershed (cf. Table 4).

Table 4: The three most frequent ascribed superpower (US and Soviet) roles, by five-year periods

	1946-50	1951-5	1956-60	1961-5	1966-70	1971-6	Total
	%	%	%	%	%	%	%
Violator of universal values	9 (3.8)	11 (4.7)	42 (17.9)	34 (14.5)	109 (46.4)	30 (12.8)	235 (100)
Intervener	9 (6.4)	10 (7.0)	28 (19.9)	37 (26.2)	37 (26.2)	20 (14.2)	141 (100)
Exploiter	7 (7.6)	10 (10.9)	13 (14.1)	18 (19.6)	26 (28.3)	18 (19.6)	92 (100)
Total	25 (5.3)	31 (6.6)	83 (17.7)	89 (19.0)	172 (36.8)	68 (14.5)	468 (100)

The year 1956 saw the dramatic crises of Suez and Hungary. And, in Raymond Aron's (1974: 54–5) words, 'it was only in 1956, with the two simultaneous crises in central Europe and the Middle East, that Europeans became fully aware of their subordination to their own Big Brother and the price to be paid for the security ensured them by a power more powerful than themselves.' It became apparent that there were only two superpowers in the post-war world, and the US–Soviet collusion in the Suez crisis was perceived by many as a first indication of nascent superpower condominium. Since then two distinct

perspectives can be identified among alter's superpower role conceptions (cf. Figure 3).

		Attitudes and role expectations, the Soviet Union	
		positive	negative
Attitudes and role expectations, the United States	positive	superpower perspective	Cold War perspective
	negative	Cold War perspective	superpower perspective

Fig. 3. Alter's role conceptions: different perspectives

On the one hand, the Cold War perspective — in which positive
attitudes and role expectations toward one superpower are coupled
with negative attitudes and role expectations toward the other — has
persisted. On the other hand, a superpower perspective has gained
strength, lumping the United States and the Soviet Union together in
terms of attitudes and role expectations. There are two main variants
of this superpower perspective: either one assesses both superpowers
in equally positive terms, or in equally negative terms. The former
perspective was, for example, expressed by Nehru's India in the late
1950s and early 1960s. Both superpowers were conceived of as
'developers,' and co-operation between the two was expected to bring
positive yields for smaller states (cf. Gupta, 1971). The latter perspective, which attributes more negative roles to the two superpowers and
sees negative implications of their collaboration — *détente* entails
entente — has gradually come to predominate, as the UN data indicate.
'Equidistance' has become a catchword to describe the attitudes of
many nonaligned nations toward the superpowers. Even though the
Cold War and superpower perspectives are incompatible, one may
find traces of differing perspectives in individual statements and assessments. For instance, one recent study (Petersson, 1982: 27–41)
demonstrates that the different perspectives have coexisted in almost
equal strength in Swedish public opinion throughout the 1970s.

How can these — admittedly tentative and inconclusive —
indicators of common superpower role conceptions be interpreted? I
shall argue in favor of one interpretation which stresses the tendency
among Soviet policy-makers to emulate American roles in their quest

for recognized superpower status. In other words, American foreign policy behavior provides precedents for Soviet conceptions of the superpower role. The United States is thus the principal 'role referent' for the Soviet Union.

Thomas Franck and Edward Weisband (1972) have observed what they label an 'echo phenomenon' in American and Soviet verbal strategies in conflicts within each superpower's region. Noting that American verbal strategy in the early 1960s — especially in connection with the 1965 intervention in the Dominican Republic — helped pave the way for reciprocal conceptions by the Soviet Union in the 1968 invasion of Czechoslovakia, they conclude that 'the verbal strategy of a superpower in a specific crisis, even if meant only to justify one instance of conduct, can be picked up by the other side and used in reciprocal circumstances to its own advantage' (Franck and Weisband, 1972: 128). Moreover, according to the ubiquitous principle of reciprocity, 'something one superpower has previously asserted by word and/or deed tends to inhibit it from preventing the other superpower from subsequently asserting the same right' (Franck and Weisband, 1972: 129). As I shall try to demonstrate, this reasoning could be broadened to encompass superpower role conception in the post-war era.

America's position as 'role referent' dates back to the end of World War II. The United States emerged from the war strong and vigorous, the Soviet Union weak and crippled. The performance of the Red Army during the war and Stalin's policy in Europe in the years after the war combined to create exaggerated estimates of Soviet power, not least in the United States (see e.g., Yergin, 1978: 270–1). Hence, the Soviet Union was conceived of as a superpower 'before she acquired any of the dimensions of a global power' (Windsor, 1979: 2). Only in the latter part of the 1950s, with the transition from Stalin to Khrushchev, did the Soviet Union shift from a regional to a global perspective and exhibit any readiness to enact the superpower role. And, as Helmut Sonnenfeldt and William Hyland (1979: 11) observe, 'in the course of adopting a global policy, the USSR was gradually transforming her techniques in ways that drew on the expertise of her only true global competitor, the United States.'

Several factors contribute to the Soviet propensity to emulate American roles. First, Soviet leaders are extremely status-conscious. Averell Harriman in 1949 cabled the State Department: 'Being new rich with a lingering inferiority complex and feeling gauche uncertainty in international society, Russia is inordinately sensitive re appearance as well as substance of prestige' (quoted in Dunn, 1981: 415). Soviet concern about status has not abated since then. In Philip Windsor's (1979: 8) words, 'it is very hard to underestimate the anxiety to gain acceptance, the need to demonstrate equality, which have been so characteristic of the Soviet leadership and are likely to remain so.'

In addition, Soviet attitudes toward the United States have always been peculiar and contradictory.

> The Soviet view of the United States is inherently ambiguous. The United States is the object of both envy and scorn; the enemy to fight, expose and pillory — and the model to emulate, catch up with and overtake. [Dallin, 1979: 13]

These contradictions are graphically illustrated by the Soviet historians N.V. Sivachev and N.N. Yakovlev (1979: 255) who in a recent book write that 'the notion of "two superpowers" is alien to Soviet foreign policy in principle,' only to note a few sentences later 'the significance of Soviet–American relations for improving the international situation.' Witness also the concluding paragraph of their book:

> We are resolutely against the 'superpower' concept. But it has been the obvious truth that our two great nations share too much responsibility in international relations, in preserving world peace, to allow unscrupulous, irresponsible, and vested interest groups to distract them from fulfilling truly historical tasks. [Sivachev and Yakovlev, 1979: 269]

In short, the United States has consistently been the principal referent and object of comparison, against which Soviet achievements in various fields can be measured. This is no less true of international affairs, where the Soviet Union's international status has come to hinge to such a great extent on its relationship with the United States.

Soviet status-consciousness, combined with the tendency to look to America, have created an evident yearning to achieve equality and gain global credentials, to be treated as a superpower on a par with the United States. A pervasive element in Soviet international conduct ever since the Khrushchev period has thus been the quest for recognition — especially by the United States — of its superpower status. Soviet spokesmen have made increasingly insistent claims that the Soviet Union, by virtue of its superpower status, has an equal right to global presence. Foreign Minister Andrei Gromyko in the wake of the Cuban missile crisis in 1962 declared that 'history has so developed that without mutual understanding between the USSR and the USA not a single serious international conflict can be settled, agreement cannot be reached on a single important international problem' (CDSP, 1963: 11). In his speech before the Supreme Soviet in 1969, Gromyko reaffirmed the Soviet intention to enact the superpower role with greater self-confidence: 'It is natural . . . that the Soviet Union, which as a major world power has extensive international ties, cannot adopt a passive attitude toward events which might be territorially remote but affect our security and the security of our friends' (quoted in Kulski, 1973: 27). Gromyko's tone at the Twentyfourth Party Congress in 1971 was more assertive still: 'Today there is no question of any significance which can be decided without the Soviet Union or in opposition to it' (quoted in Aspaturian, 1980a: 1).

While begun under Khrushchev, the Soviet quest for recognized superpower status became especially evident in the Brezhnev era. By any measure, Soviet capabilities had vastly increased between 1945 and 1965. Yet,

> despite her enormous gains in power, the Soviet Union remained obsessed by the notion of inequality. She still saw the United States as an established world power and herself merely as an aspiring one. [Sonnenfeldt and Hyland, 1979: 14]

Khrushchev's successors 'believed that the USSR was entitled to . . . be treated and respected as a super-power; and that this role should be given formal recognition through treaties and understandings, above all with the United States' (Sonnenfeldt and Hyland, 1979: 15). The Soviet leadership was determined that the USSR should have her rights of global access, presence and influence acknowledged internationally. In recent years the Soviets have made oblique public contentions — and have openly admitted in private — that strategic parity implies an 'equal right to meddle in third areas' (cf. Dallin, 1980b: 57). For instance, the Soviet Ambassador to France, S.V. Chervonenko, made a speech in the wake of the Afghanistan invasion in which he claimed that Soviet equality with the United States entailed an equal right for the Soviet Union to be consulted and involved everywhere in the world on all major issues. This contention contained an implicit threat of intervention to sustain such a right (cf. Aspaturian, 1980a: 17).

If the quest for equal superpower status has been an element of continuity in Soviet international conduct over the past few decades, other states have obviously not been persistently forthcoming in recognizing Soviet equality with the United States. In particular, the rival superpower has been slow and inconsistent in granting the Soviet Union superpower status.

> Soviet commentators point out that the build-up of the Soviet navy, armour and combat aircraft, and recent Soviet missile programmes, have all been natural products and parts of the Soviet acquisition of global parity and super-power status. Why, they ask, should the United States retain control of the seas as well as superiority in strategic weapons? According to the Soviet perspective, Washington has continued to resist the logical implications of parity, refusing to acknowledge that the USSR is equally entitled to a presence far away from her shores, to a global navy and to a voice in all international disputes — in short, that she is entitled to act much as the United States has been acting all along. [Dallin, 1979: 18]

Recurrent complaints in Soviet commentaries about American failures to recognize parity bear witness to the fact that American recognition is considered to be of vital importance to the Soviet Union:

> Soviet writers implicitly recognize that the equality which they so passionately cherish remains essentially an ascriptive one. Although they express confidence that the impersonal but objective forces of history will render it permanent, and thus free Soviet equality from its dependence upon American recognition, they are aware that for the time being it is not. [Aspaturian, 1980a: 9].

The historical record shows little readiness among successive administrations in Washington to grant the USSR equal status. Roosevelt's abortive hopes for continued wartime collaboration and equally abortive Grand Design for a great power consortium ('the Four Policemen') appeared to imply a form of recognition. FDR is also held in great regard by Soviet commentators for his 'farsightedness' and 'instinctive presentiment of the future' (cf. Schwartz, 1978: 44).

Another 'deviant case' is Kennedy after the Cuban missile crisis. The peaceful resolution of that confrontation, the American University speech — which Khrushchev labeled 'the greatest speech by any American President since Roosevelt' (Schlesinger, 1965: 826) — and the nuclear test ban treaty have earned him a favorable reputation in the Soviet Union. This rests in large measure on the perception that Kennedy, in Khrushchev's (1974: 513) own words, 'was realistic enough to see that now the might of the socialist world equaled that of the capitalist world.'

If these early indications of American willingness to bestow equality upon the Soviet Union were implicit and ephemeral, the Nixon-Kissinger years displayed a unique congruence of American and Soviet conceptions of the Soviet Unon's world role the SALT accord, the 1972 Basic Principles Agreement, and the 1973 Agreement on the Prevention of Nuclear War all seemed to imply formal American recognition of Soviet superpower status and parity with the United States. Soviet spokesmen were clearly pleased, and the Nixon administration won recognition as an 'acceptable partner' (Arbatov, 1973).

> The Nixon administration was, indeed, given high marks for its 'sober' attitude towards the Soviet Union. The very essence of its 'realism' consisted in its willingness to accept the USSR on its own terms, to treat Moscow as an equal, and to recognize the legitimacy of Soviet interests. [Schwartz, 1978: 123]

The major Soviet apprehension was that Nixon's China policy might imply that the conferred equality was to be shared with China — a theme conspicuously avoided by Soviet writers (Aspaturian, 1980a: 5).

With the advent of the Carter administration the congruence of role conceptions was disrupted. Cultivation of the 'special' US–Soviet relationship was no longer assigned top priority. Carter's emphasis on human rights involved criticism of Soviet policy toward dissidents and constraints on emigration. In Moscow this was seen as an attempt to 'lecture' the Soviet Union which was, in effect, to treat it as a second-class power rather than an equal superpower. Moreover, the Carter administration's criticism of Soviet behavior in Africa and, in particular, Afghanistan implied an unwillingness to treat the USSR as a superpower (cf. Aspaturian, 1980a: 4–5; Schwartz, 1980: 10–12). Carter was perceived by the Soviets to be 'applying a double-standard — condemning Moscow for behaving much as the United States itself has behaved — thus rejecting the Soviet claim to equal treatment and superpower status' (Schwartz, 1980: 13).

The Reagan administration thus far has a mixed record in this regard. On the one hand, it is obviously more willing to put US–Soviet relations at the top of the foreign policy agenda and to recognize the Soviet Union as a *military* superpower. On the other hand, the anti-Soviet tenor and the emphasis on Soviet internal weaknesses point in the opposite direction.

To summarize, in this chapter I have argued in favor of a conceptualization of superpower status in terms of roles. The similarities in American and Soviet role conceptions (ego's and alter's) are great enough to suggest the existence of a 'superpower role.' The congruence of role conceptions, it has been argued, is largely the result of the Soviet Union emulating the United States — the 'role referent.'

Moreover, the 'superpower role' seems to be fairly consistent over time. To be sure, in the early 1970s there was much talk about an American search for a new world role. For one thing, this entailed temporary American recognition of a symmetrical role for the Soviet Union, as we have seen. Apart from that, it involved acute role strain between 'preventer of other superpower's values' — as codified in the containment doctrine — and 'promoter of universal values.' At home and abroad doubts accumulated as to whether containment of communism could justify American actions in Vietnam which were seen as violations of basic international norms and values. Yet after the American withdrawal from Vietnam and the Soviet 'superpower role performance' in Afghanistan the traditional American role conceptions have gradually been restored.

Role is rarely posited as the sole explanatory factor in any behavioral science. In comparative foreign policy analysis, it seems reasonable to regard national role conceptions as intervening variables mediating the impact of traditional background factors or 'sources' on foreign policy behavior. Wish (1977: 134) finds support in her data for the assumption that foreign policy is 'the result of the indirect effects of national attributes which have been mediated by national role conceptions.' Rather than determine behavior, national roles are thus assumed to limit the range of foreign policy behavior, insofar as certain types of behavior are associated with certain roles.

Similarly, I proceed from the assumption that the 'superpower role' constitutes an intervening variable which mediates the impact of other sources and narrows the range of American and Soviet external conduct (cf. Figure 4).

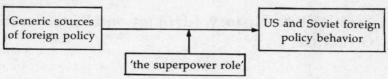

Fig.4. The 'superpower role' as intervening variable

Having identified superpower status and role as the lowest common denominator, I shall therefore turn next to a scrutiny of explanatory factors commonly singled out in comparative foreign policy studies as applied to the United States and the Soviet Union. The guiding question will be: What kinds of foreign policy similarities and differences between the superpowers can be expected on the basis of these background or source variables?

2 Similarities: History, Ideology and Bureaucratic Structure

Introduction

In the contemporary study of foreign policy, independent variables have been posited at different levels of analysis. Specifically, the balance between external and internal, or foreign and domestic, determinants of foreign policy has been the subject of a perennial debate among scholars. While the traditional 'billiard-ball' model of international politics black-boxes the inner dynamics of state decisions and actions, there has been a tendency recently to overemphasize the domestic determinants of foreign policy. To strike a balance between the two extremes is not unproblematic, as envisaged early by James Rosenau (1966: 31):

> To identify factors is not to trace their influence. . . . To recognize that foreign policy is shaped by internal as well as external factors is not to comprehend how the two intermix or to indicate the conditions under which one predominates over the other.

In their attempts at uncovering — deductively or inductively — the interrelationship and relative potency of independent variables, comparative foreign policy analysts have frequently relied, more or less explicitly, on an 'additive model' (Goldmann, 1975). That is, they have proceeded from the assumption that the identified variables contribute independently to explaining foreign policy and that each variable or variable cluster can be studied separately and then added together.

It seems more realistic, however, to assume that independent variables do interact and affect foreign policy jointly. Reliance on such 'multiplicative' (Goldmann, 1975) or 'nonadditive' models implies focusing on the complex *interplay* between explanatory variables. The interconnectedness of explanatory variables may presumably amplify, abate, or transform their isolated effects. *Synergism* is a term commonly used to denote such interconnectedness in ecological and medical contexts.

Statistical techniques doubtless exist for analyses of this kind. Yet the kind of data students of foreign policy have recourse to for the most part seem too 'soft' to lend themselves to these sophisticated techniques. Illuminative in this regard is the fact that most statistical studies in the subfield of comparative foreign policy have dealt primarily with dichotomized background variables (large/small states, open/closed political systems, developed/underdeveloped economic systems, etc.)

We are thus left with the technically less sophisticated method of 'mental experiments' where the researcher, through mental rehearsals, varies critical variables in order to estimate variance in outcomes (George, 1979: 105). My subsequent analysis will thus take the form of, first, constructing 'schemes of conceivable effects' (Stenelo, 1972) noted in the specialized literature on American and Soviet foreign policy and, then, trying to uncover 'linkages' between explanatory variables. My choice of variables rests chiefly on two considerations: (a) the chosen variables should tap all conceivable levels of analysis, and (b) they should have been considered pertinent in former studies of foreign policy. The six possible determinants of American and Soviet foreign policy that I have singled out are: (1) capabilities; (2) historical factors; (3) ideology; (4) political system; (5) social and economic system, and (6) the international system.

Instead of treating these variable clusters separately and analyzing all conceivable effects at length, this and the next chapter are organized so as to reflect the second step of identifying prominent 'causal chains.' Thus, the remainder of this chapter will focus on those interrelated factors which point in the direction of similar superpower behavior. In the following chapter the focus is redirected toward those factors which may account for differences in American and Soviet conduct. It should be recalled that the factors singled out are treated only in their capacity as *independent variables*. In other words, no comprehensive treatment of, say, the American and Soviet ideologies and political systems will be found — only the aspects deemed relevant for the explanation of foreign policy behavior will be scrutinized.

In the remainder of this chapter I shall argue that historical, ideological and bureaucratic background factors constitute one prominent 'causal chain' accounting for similarities in superpower conduct.

History

The historical dimension is all too often neglected in comparative foreign policy studies. Turning to history in search of explanations of superpower foreign policy after World War II implies looking for pre-war patterns of American and Soviet history.

'History' as an explanatory variable may be conceived in two principally different ways. Either history is understood as an inexorable force above and beyond human control, or it is seen to assume significance through the 'lessons of history' that policy-makers perceive and act upon. In the former perspective, man is the tool of history; in the latter, history is the tool of man.

Ideas of historical inevitability have been applied not least to America and Russia. Already in 1790 Baron Melchior von Grimm, in a letter to Catherine II, foresaw an inescapable development toward American and Russian domination of the world.

> Two empires will then share all the advantages of civilisation, of the power of genius, of letters, of arts, of arms and industry: Russia on the eastern side and America . . . on the western side, and we other peoples of the nucleus will be too degraded, too debased, to know otherwise than by a vague and stupid tradition what we have been. [quoted in Dukes, 1970: 9]

Half a decade later, Friedrich List predicted that the natural course of history would in a hundred years time produce two antagonistic giants, Russia and America, which would become 'the two most successful nations on earth' (Hölzle, 1953: 152–3). Around the same time, Alexis de Tocqueville expressed similar notions of historical inevitability:

> There are, at the present time, two great nations in the world which seem to tend toward the same end, although they started from different points: I allude to the Russians and the Americans. . . . All other nations seem to have nearly reached their natural limits, and only to be charged with the maintenance of their power; but these are still in the act of growth; all the others are stopped, or continue to advance with extreme difficulty; these are proceeding with ease and with celerity along a path to which the human eye can assign no term. . . . Their starting point is different, and their courses are not the same; yet each of them seems to be marked out by the will of

Heaven to sway the destinies of half the globe. [quoted in Dukes, 1970: 49]

Similarly, more recent adherents of historical inevitability point to long-term historical trends in accounting for the emergence of the two global superpowers after World War II.

The alternative perspective on historical explanation, which focuses on policy-makers' perceptions of historical events and patterns, is in keeping with my professed preference for proximate over remote causes. In Ernest May's (1973: ix) apt summary,

> framers of foreign policy are often influenced by beliefs about what history teaches or portends. Sometimes, they perceive problems in terms of analogies from the past. Sometimes, they envision the future either as foreshadowed by historical parallels or as following a straight line from what has recently gone before.

In drawing 'lessons' from the past, policy-makers may thus either resort to *analogies* or make linear *projections* of historical trends. These 'lessons,' which presumably have a crucial impact on decision-making, can be derived from domestic as well as international historical experiences. In the following I shall attempt to trace events and trends in American and Russian domestic as well as international history and the historical 'lessons' foreign policy decision-makers may have drawn from these.

Domestic History

American and Russian domestic historical developments have both taken place in a big continental setting, with a relatively small ratio of the population to the size of the territory (Szeftel, 1964: 380). Both have a long history of 'latitudinal' expansion from relatively small and isolated 'cradle areas' — the East Coast in the United States, and the area around Moscow in Russia. Hostile neighbors and physical obstacles such as mountains and rivers necessitated development within the 'cradle area' until the population had grown sufficiently large for expansion. The Russians moved east beyond the Ural Mountains and the Volga into Siberia toward the end of the sixteenth century; the Americans passed the Appalachian Mountains and the Mississippi in their westward drive toward the end of the eighteenth century. The formative history of the two superpowers-to-be thus consisted of migration, colonization, and territorial expansion in opposite directions, both destined for the Pacific Ocean (cf. Parker, 1972: 23–6).

Space, territorial expansion, and moving frontiers represent common factors in American and Russian historical development. The main historical 'lesson' derived from these experiences has been a mutual belief in a historical destiny or mission, which will be treated in greater detail in the following chapter on foreign policy ideology.

Yet these similarities should not obscure significant dissimilarities in the geographical setting of American and Soviet history. The most obvious one concerns the external security of the two nations. In Joseph Lieberman's (1970: 400) succinct formulation:

> America was blessed with natural barriers. To its east and its west, two great oceans have provided security from attack. Russia, on the other hand, is exposed. Sitting on a vast plain, there is nothing of military consequence separating Russia from Asia to the east and Europe to the west. Russian history from its beginning to our time is characterized by continuous military assaults, particularly from the west. The Huns, the Bulgars, the Avars, the Khazars, the Magyars, the Pechenegs, the Tartars, the Polish, the Swedish, the Turks, the French, and finally the Germans — each of these nations came in their turn to threaten, attack, and often conquer Russia.

The constant exposure to attack and the long history of successive invasions have had a profound impact on the Russian political system. To survive in their hostile environment, the Russians were compelled to mass together under strong leadership and became accustomed to rule by a powerful, highly centralized autocracy. In order to be constantly prepared for military defense and to command the men and resources necessary to protect the state, the autocratic government had to exercise complete control (cf e.g., Schwartz, 1975: 75; Lieberman, 1970: 401). This heritage has left an obvious imprint on the communist rule of Soviet Russia as well.

Besides its indirect influence via the political system, the Russian history of insecurity and successive invasions has also had a direct impact on foreign policy through the historical 'lessons' drawn by Russian policy-makers. Xenophobia and a 'national sense of insecurity' have become part of the Russian heritage, and traditional Russian as well as contemporary Soviet policy-makers have tended to view the outside world with a sense of mistrust and suspicion and to stress the need for constant preparedness and vigilance (cf. Schwartz, 1975: 76–7).

Another difference is that which exists between a land-locked or 'continental' nation (Russia) and a seaward-looking or 'maritime' nation (the United States). Both may be equally prone to expand. 'A featureless plain does not compel but facilitates broad conquests and large states, much as an insular realm invites to commerce and perhaps overseas expansion' (Wesson, 1974: vii). Yet while maritime nations throughout history have displayed great mobility and fast expansion, continental nations have tended to develop and expand more slowly. W.H. Parker (1972: 28–9) sees in the emergence of today's superpowers a recurrence on a global scale of earlier European history. He suggests an analogy betwen contemporary Europe and ancient Greece (both having lost their previous command of the sea and their colonial areas), between the United States and Rome (both trying to unite and dominate seaward-looking and ocean-communicating peoples), and between the USSR and the transalpine Gauls and Germans (both having long been regarded as backward and 'barbarian,' having had to fight climatic and physical obstacles, and thus having developed more slowly). Parker furthermore contends that history indicates that continental nations, in spite of their slower initial development, eventually surpass maritime nations.

On the other hand, George Liska (1980: 58–9), who argues that 'the ancient land-sea power division antedates even that between Sparta and Athens,' holds that sea power was only temporarily eclipsed by the land-rooted feudal political economy but has successfully challenged land power again in modern Europe and the con-temporary world. Historically, however, 'the land-sea power conflicts tended to erode both of the changing parties to it and to be ultimately resolved by the unevenly timed, but finally reciprocal, dispossession of both' (Liska, 1980: 63).

Beyond such speculative notions of historical inevitability, the difference between the maritime United States and the continental Russia has had an impact on the economic systems of the two countries. While maritime nations tend to engage in external trade, the economic activity of continental nations consists less of trade and more of the exploitation of natural resources within their boundaries. Hence this difference in geographical setting may have an indirect impact on foreign policy via the economic system (cf. below, Chapter 3).

Both Russia and the United States were populated by migrations of European peoples, though at different times and for different reasons. Toward the middle of the nineteenth century the population structure of both countries had assumed a multinational character (cf. Hölzle,

1953: 155), and in the minds of Americans and Russians this tended to reinforce ideas about the universal application of their own models.

International History

In considering the effects of international historical experience upon contemporary foreign policy, it seems logical to proceed from a review of early Russian-American relations.

In 1809 Russia and the United States opened diplomatic relations. This symbolic action sealed the 'curious and incongruous friendship' (Bailey, 1950: 1) between the two countries which was to persist for more than a century. 'Our attachment to the United States is obstinate, more obstinate than you are aware of,' wrote Count Rumiantsov to John Quincy Adams in 1810 (quoted in Williams, 1952: 3). And in 1862 the American Secretary of State William Henry Seward said of Russia: 'She has our friendship, in every case, in preference to any other European power, simply because she always wishes us well, and leaves us to conduct our affairs as we think best' (quoted in Bailey, 1950: 70).

Not only Western but also Soviet historians have noted the long history of peaceful and friendly Russian–American relations. V.A. Valkov (1965: 7–8), for instance, writes thus:

> The history of the development of Russian–American relations is remarkable, insofar that for a protracted period — from the time of the US Declaration of Independence up to the end of the nineteenth century — these relations were friendly. On several occasions Russia showed her support of the United States in difficult periods. She was on the side of the American people at the time of their struggle for independence at the end of the eighteenth century, in the course of the war between England and the US in 1812–1814, and also during the Civil War betwen the North and the South in the 1860s. The American people, on their part, nourished sincere sympathy for the Russian people, especially during the invasion of Russia by Napoleon's army and the Crimean War.

The Civil War period probably marked the high point of Russian–American sympathy. While technically neutral like all the powers of the world, Russia — unlike, for instance, France and Britain — was conspicuously friendly toward the Northerners (cf. Bailey, 1950: 70). Russia's moral and diplomatic support undoubtedly helped to discourage British and French interventions on behalf of the

Confederacy. In late 1863 the Russians sent two squadrons of their Pacific and Baltic fleets on unannounced visits to American ports. Though primarily a move in the growing conflict between Russia and Britain–France as a result of the coincident uprising against Russian rule in Poland — sending the ships to the United States would keep them from being bottled up in Russian ports and give them a convenient base from which to harass British and French shipping in the event of war — these visits were seen as signs of Russian support for the Union and created pro-Russian euphoria in the North (cf. Gaddis, 1978: 21–3; Weeks, 1970: 76–8).

What were the reasons behind the long history of friendly relations between tsarist, despotic Russia and the young, fervently anti-autocratic American republic? Thomas Bailey (1950: 347–8) provides a succinct answer:

There were common foes, notably Britain; there were common problems, such as freedom of the seas. Neither nation was vibrantly aggressive, though Pan-Slavism and Manifest Destiny provided something of a spark, in limited areas and for limited periods. Each nation sprawled over an enormous land mass; each saw relatively little of the other at close range; and each could expand without impinging upon the domain of the other.

The latter point is amplified by Albert Weeks (1970: 69):

Geography has played a curiously positive role in promoting cordiality in Russian and American relations. The very remoteness of the two countries from each other has precluded any direct confrontation or clash. They have never met as enemies on the field of battle, thus avoiding the Scriptural injunction against being 'dipped in the blood of thine enemies.'

John Lewis Gaddis (1978: 17–23) emphasizes the mutual interest in preserving the European balance of power, citing the frequent theme of seeking good relations with Washington as a counterweight to London in Russian diplomatic correspondence.

The smoothly reached transfer of Alaska in 1867 could be seen as 'one more milestone in the display of traditional friendship between Russia and America for most of the nineteenth century' (Weeks, 1970: 79). Yet William Appleman Williams (1952: 23) singles out the sale of Alaska as 'the great divide in the contour of American–Russian relations:'

For the United States it marked the final advance on the continent prior to a large-scale effort to penetrate the markets of Asia. To Russia it was the symbol of a decision to concentrate on the effort to gain an Asiatic outlet on the Pacific. Both decisions reflected the increased tempo of industrialization in each nation.

To Parker (1972: 29), the history of Alaska, the only territory to have been under the sovereignty of both superpowers, illustrates 'the effect of stagnation in Russia and dynamism in America.' While 'the eastward human flow from Russia was diverted westwards to the battlefields of Europe,' the American westward drive continued unsapped.

In any event, the late nineteenth century saw a gradual change of climate in Russian–American relations, as the two expanding countries stood face to face across the Pacific. There had been earlier skirmishes between American and Russian interests in the American Pacific coastal areas and Hawaii (cf. Hölzle, 1953: 82–91), but now Russian and American expansionism began to clash in the Far East. The United States reached East Asia via Guam, Hawaii, and the Philippines; the Russians by way of Siberia. The two clashed directly over Manchuria. The gradually improving American relations with Britain were viewed by the Russians as detrimental to their own interests, at the same time as the United States came to see Russia as the chief threat to the Far Eastern balance of power (cf. Gaddis, 1978: 27–41).

Yet the traditional friendship was not completely ruptured. Russian–American relations were 'swinging between good and poor' (Weeks, 1970: 87). The Soviet historians Nikolai Sivachev and Nikolai Yakovlev (1979: 18) admonish that 'one should not exaggerate the degree and importance of Russian–American conflicts at the turn of the century, inflate them artificially, or dramatize them artificially, as many American historians have done during the years of the cold war.' The great discontinuity in Russian–American relations occurred as a result of the Bolshevik revolution in Russia in 1917. In fact, the change from apparent friendship to overt confrontation was so abrupt as to suggest the irrelevance of earlier history to the subsequent development of Russian–American relations. Henry Roberts (1962: 586), for one, maintains that *'at the level of foreign policy* Russian–American relations have undergone a decisive change in character in the course of the last fifty years, a change that is not to be explained by their earlier experience *on this level.'* According to Roberts, the terms of contemporary Soviet–American relations were in large measure shaped by the initial confrontation between Wilsonian America and Leninist Russia in the years 1917–19.

Yet, 'American attitudes toward Communist Russia, from 1917 to 1941, ran through cycles of hysteria, ignorance, indifference, and wishful thinking' (Bailey, 1950: 348); and American policy toward the Soviet Union was ambivalent, on the one hand deploring and having as little as possible to do with its government, on the other hand promoting trade and investment opportunities for American business-men (Gaddis, 1978: 98–105). Similarly, Soviet policy toward the United States in the inter-war years displayed considerable ambiguity, stemming from the stress on the monolithic nature of capitalism, on the one hand, and the desire to encourage 'contradictions' within the capitalist camp, on the other (Gaddis, 1978: 87–93); and Soviet hostility toward the United States did not crystallize until after World War II (cf. Barghoorn, 1950: 103–5). In the inter-war period, 'the attention of the Soviet Union, like that of the United States, was mainly directed inwards' (Dukes, 1970: 107). It might even be argued that each country drew on the experience of the other during this period. For example, in FDR's New Deal 'a leaf or two were taken out of the Soviet book,' at the same time as American models loomed large in Stalin's schemes for economic development (Dukes, 1970: 113–14; cf. Parker, 1972: 37).

Only as a result of the radical changes in international power relations and technology after World War II did the United States and the Soviet Union emerge as rival superpowers. Hence there are many who would argue that the earlier history of Russian–American relations is irrelevant to an understanding of contemporary American and Soviet foreign policy. Yet, if we understand historical explanation in terms of historical 'lessons' rather than historical inevitability, this argument needs to be qualified. For 'lessons' of the past were indeed invoked by makers of foreign policy in the wake of World War II.

> The breakdown of the European state system, and the rejection of its conventions by both the Soviet Union and the United States, left decision-makers on both sides without reliable guides as to the other's motives. Under such circumstances the most useful inference guidance devices seemed to be the lessons of history. [Kratochwil, 1978: 6]

The lessons actually drawn depended on whether the policy-makers relied on analogies or projections of long-term trends and, in the latter case, where the time-cut was made. Immediately after the war there were those, particularly in the United States but presumably also in the Soviet Union, who projected the record of Russian–American friendship over the long term into the future (cf. Weeks, 1970: 93–4). The Russian–American Pitirim Sorokin (1944) may be taken as a representative and illuminative example of this view. Referring to the 'uninterrupted peace' between America and Russia made possible by 'the lack of any serious clash between the vital interests or basic values of the two countries' and facilitated by 'the mutual mental, cultural, and social congeniality of the two nations,' Sorokin (1944: 19) concluded:

> Throughout the entire history of the United States, Russia has been its best friend. If the respective governments do not commit the stupidest blunders, Russia will constitute in the future our best and most important ally. In the interest of both nations and of humanity at large, the most whole-hearted co-operation is not only possible and desirable but essential. The chances for such co-operation between Russia and the United States are better, and those of an armed conflict are slighter, than the respective chances in the relations of either of these countries and any other great power.

Harold Fisher (1946), in the same way, argued that the similarities between the United States and the Soviet Union outweighed the dissimilarities and that US–Soviet political and economic co-operation was not only necessary but also highly probable in view of the fact that the two countries had never in history waged war on each other. No doubt there were key policy-makers reasoning along parallel lines with Sorokin and Fisher, at least in the United States. One might infer from certain Soviet statements around the same time that similar historical 'lessons' were drawn by some policy-makers in the USSR as well. Barghoorn (1950: 6), for instance, reports that the mayor of Vladivostok told him in May, 1946: 'American and Russian troops have never fired on one another.' In the Soviet Union as well as the United States such long-term projections from the history of Russian–American relations were reinforced by recent experiences of wartime unity and co-operation. The conclusion of a February 1944 *Pravda* editorial that 'the union of three great powers has not only its historical yesterday and its victorious today but also its great tomorrow' (Barghoorn, 1950: 103) was shared by many in both superpowers.

Yet on both sides these optimistic projections were soon overshadowed by other historical 'lessons' drawing on short-term trends and analogies with recent traumatic events. The short-term trends referred to dated back no longer than to 1917. To Americans, Soviet expansion into Eastern Europe in 1944–5 raised the old specter of world revolution. And Russians could see a trend of American perfidy and hostility running from the participation of American armies in the 1918–19 invasion to overthrow the Bolshevik revolution in Russia, via the long delay in fulfilling the promise of a second front in World War II, to the failure to recognize Soviet security interests in Eastern Europe.

These short-term projections could be buttressed by analogies with recent wartime experiences. In planning for the post-war future, decision-makers on both sides tried to prevent another World War II. Analogies with the events of the 1930s leading to war thus easily suggested themselves (cf. e.g., May, 1973: Chapter 2; Gaddis, 1972: 1–3). These analogies often envisaged the other superpower in the role of the defeated common enemies.

The Munich Conference and the Molotov–Ribbentrop Pact taught both victorious superpowers similar lessons: concessions to, or appeasement of, the enemy is a disastrous policy. It does not make the enemy more conciliatory, it does not even buy time. It only whets the enemy's appetite and leads to further demands and aggression. In the evolving Cold War, this lesson was gradually applied to the redefined enemy, that is the other superpower, thereby obstructing mutual concessions and adding to mutual feelings of irreconcilable conflict.

> Thus, considering only the 'lessons' of the immediate past, both powers had reason to be unyielding and suspicious. While 'no more Munichs' was the guiding principle for a good many American actions from Truman to Johnson, fear of being double-crossed again and awareness of the great damages inflicted by the war must have figured prominently in the calculus of Soviet leaders. [Kratochwil, 1978: 62]

In addition, the lesson of the need for constant vigilance and preparedness was forcefully driven home by the surprise attacks which drew the United States and the Soviet Union into the war. Just as the parallel of Pearl Harbor was often cited in debates over the necessity and level of military preparedness in the United States during the Cold War, so the lack of military readiness at the time of the German invasion has become the standard warning example in Soviet discourse. Thus, the grim expectation derived from short-term trends and analogies with recent events came to dominate foreign policy-making on both sides during the Cold War.

The Ideology of Foreign Policy

The very word ideology evokes divergent associations in the United States and the Soviet Union. In America it has a pejorative, in Soviet discourse a favorable, connotation. While American foreign policy is usually characterized as 'pragmatic' rather than dogmatic,[1] ideology both inside and outside the USSR is assumed to be an important motive force of Soviet foreign policy. And whereas the social sciences operating within the American context have been influenced by the American contempt for ideology, Soviet theorists and practitioners view ideology as a general social-political phenomenon, present in all societies. It may be considered 'one of the minor ironies of modern intellectual history that the term "ideology" has itself become thoroughly ideologized' (Geertz, 1964: 47).[2]

This has, of course, not been conducive to conceptual clarity. 'Ideology' remains an elusive term. In trying to pin down its meaning, I have proceeded from the broad notion that 'within every operative society there must be some creed — a set of beliefs and values, traditions and purposes — which links both the institutional networks and the emotional affinities of the members into some transcendental whole' (Bell, 1970: 105). In order to qualify as an *ideology*, such a creed has to meet certain criteria. The following can be singled out as prominent among the existing variety of conceptualizations:

(1) *High level of generality.* Being comprehensive and located high on the abstraction ladder (Sartori, 1969: 410), ideologies cover a wide range of objects (Shils, 1968: 66). (2) *Integrated character.* Ideology serves to 'relate different aspects of social life: the moral, the economic, the political' (Weisband, 1973: 7); it 'bridges the emotional gap between things as they are and as one would have them be' (Geertz, 1964: 55); and it links theory with action (Brzezinzki, 1967: 132; Sartori, 1969: 399). (3) *Simplicity.* Ideologies center around one or a few prominent values (Shils, 1968: 66). 'Ends' rather than 'means' constitute the central elements (Sartori, 1969: 410). (4) *Affect.* Ideologies are characterized by 'strong affect' (Sartori, 1969: 405); 'their acceptance and promulgation are accompanied by highly affective overtones' (Shils, 1968: 66). (5) *Permanence.* Ideology is a

'closed cognitive structure' (Sartori, 1969: 404–5) resistant to change and innovation (Shils, 1968: 66). (6) *Social nature*. As a 'general system of beliefs held in common by the members of a collectivity' (Parsons, 1951: 349) or an 'action program suitable for mass consumption' (Brzezinski, 1967: 5), ideology entails 'the conversion of ideas into social levers' (Bell, 1962: 400). Ideology is an instrument of political mobilization (Sartori, 1969: 411), and the unity of social groups rests to a significant degree on common ideological orientations (Geertz, 1964: 55).

The focus of this inquiry is on the beliefs *relevant to foreign policy*. One question that immediately arises is whether both superpowers have discernible foreign policy ideologies, or rather whether there does, contrary to the conventional wisdom, exist such a thing as an American foreign policy ideology. Louis Hartz (1955: 59) has argued that 'American pragmatism has always been deceptive because, glacierlike, it has rested on miles of submerged conviction.' The fact that American ideological beliefs have largely remained unrecognized may well be a tribute to the force of their general acceptance rather than an indication of their lesser importance (Weisband, 1973: 61). In fact, there are those who suggest that ideology may be a more potent determining factor in American than in Soviet policy.

> Granted, American ideas are less overt than Soviet ideology, less systematic, less dogmatic, and certainly not embodied in any institution like the Communist Party of the Soviet Union. But is American ideology any less influential for being different? Is it not in fact more influential as a guide to action because, in contrast to the Soviet case, it is not generally perceived as ideology, because it is less crude and therefore more widely credited, because in a democratic system it is 'fed back' from masses to leaders in elections which the latter stand to lose as well as win? [Taubman, 1975: 197–8]

If we do accept that ideology is a pervasive phenomenon encompassing both the United States and the Soviet Union, the next question is whether the two are comparable. Again, the conventional wisdom holds that they are not. American liberalism is seen as the antidote to Soviet Marxism–Leninism. And if we limit the focus to manifest 'isms' — as students of ideology have tended to do — the premises and conclusions of the American and Soviet ideologies are no doubt divergent. But in matters of external policy, American liberalism and Soviet Marxism–Leninism provide inadequate or incomplete analytical prisms and guides to action. Other ideological beliefs which are not directly derived from liberalism and Marxism–Leninism appear to guide decision makers in Washington and Moscow. In the following I shall attempt to untangle some basic ideological tenets (i.e. tenets which meet our criteria of generality, integration, simplicity, affect, permanence, and broad following) that have been woven into the fabric of American and Soviet foreign policy rhetoric. It will be argued that the antipodal character of Soviet and American ideological beliefs generally obscures the compatibility of basic but less manifest ideological beliefs pertaining to foreign policy in particular.

Paradise on Earth

Ideology, it has been argued, is a response to the cultural strain that results when 'a political system begins to free itself from the immediate governance of received tradition' (Geertz, 1964: 63–4). The loss of orientation and conceptual confusion arising from the irrelevance or repudiation of the established images of political order gives rise to ideological activity. This notion applies well to the genesis of American and Soviet foreign policy ideologies.

> Most of the older states evolved. The United States of America and the Union of Soviet Socialist Republics were declared into existence, each by a group of men. Each group had definite ideas about the nature of the state they were creating. [Rapoport, 1971: 9]

In each case there was a strong sense of uniqueness and a stated intention to break away from the established international system. There were feelings of superiority and distinctiveness from other states which fostered not only extensive self-glorification but also an urge to universalize their domestic achievements. Americans and Soviets alike regarded themselves as members of 'redeemed' societies with a mission of redemption to others.

Two seemingly contradictory foreign policy orientations flow from these attitudes: *withdrawal* — a rejection of the world's complexity; and *globalism* — a wish to end complexity by reforming the world. The contradiction is more apparent than real. The seventeenth-century French philosopher Lallemant argued that 'the more inward we are, the more we may undertake outward activities' (quoted in Stillman and Pfaff, 1966: 168). Similarly, globalism is withdrawal turned inside out — moral separateness and the belief in a special destiny, projected outward into the world. Both represent 'a romantic retreat from the real world' (Steel, 1977: 333). 'An absolute national morality,' argued Hartz (1955: 286), 'is inspired either to withdraw from "alien" things or to transform them: it cannot live in comfort constantly by their side.'

The prevailing trend among inquiries into American and Soviet foreign policy has been to emphasize one of these orientations while either denying the other or discarding it as an aberration. Just as debates over, and analyses of, American foreign policy have typically been conducted in terms of isolationsism *versus* globalism/interventionism, so Soviet foreign policy has generally been discussed in terms of nation-building and national protection *versus* world communism. To posit these tendencies as opposites obscures more than it reveals. They might rather be seen as different manifestations of the same sense of uniqueness and moral superiority.

The theme of a special 'mission' and a supernatural calling pervades American political thought.

> Perhaps no theme has ever dominated the minds of the leaders of this nation to the same extent as the idea that America occupies a unique place and has a special destiny among the nations of the earth. It is an idea which characterizes not simply flamboyant orations but pervades the writings of critical philosophers and distinguished historians and social scientists. No period of our history has been free from its seductive influence. [Burns, 1957: 5–6]

For almost three decades the theme of a unique, even divine, American world role has recurred. The Puritan Jonathan Edwards claimed that Providence intended America to be the renovator of the world (Bloomfield, 1974: 62). On the eve of the American revolution, Thomas Paine wrote that 'the cause of America is in great measure the cause of all mankind' (Crabb, 1976: 34), and George Washington in his Farewell Address stressed America's duty to set an example to mankind. Ralph Waldo Emerson concluded that 'our whole history appears to be a last effort of Divine Providence on behalf of the human race' (Williams, 1980: 87). The late eighteenth century saw the emergence of the idea of 'God's American Israel' with Thomas Jefferson among its most prominent proponents (Weinberg, 1958: 39–

40). Being the chosen people, Americans provided, in Abraham Lincoln's highflying words, 'hope to all the world, for all future time' (Bloomfield, 1974: 62; Crabb, 1976: 34). In 1952 President Truman declared that, under his administration, America had 'finally stepped into the leadership which Almighty God intended us to assume a generation ago' (Burns, 1957: 14).

The belief that American values are universal and that American history provides a prototypical example acquired a 'nearly theological intensity' and, according to Edmund Stillman and William Pfaff (1966: 23) 'it is no exaggeration to label it an American ideology.' Isolationism has its roots in this sense of moral superiority.

It was as if, by founding the Republic, Americans had made a new covenant with God. No political policy was ever closer than isolationism to the deep sources of a nation's understanding of its role in the world. That role was not really political. Though it was political in form, it was understood to be a moral role. We were participants in a great moral experiment, the creation of a new kind of political community. [Stillman and Pfaff, 1966: 16–17]

The creation of a New World meant turning away from Europe, the Old World. Owing its existence largely to inter-European conflicts, the United States repudiated the national rivalries and aristocratic diplomatic practices of Europe. America was viewed as 'a particular treasure to be preserved from the world's corruption' (Stillman and Pfaff, 1966: 17). And, in the words of William Appleman Williams (1980: 53), 'the faith in America's uniqueness coupled with the failure of others to copy the perfect revolution generated a deep sense of being *alone*.'

It was, however, a short step from the vision of America as a treasured universal model to the belief that the outside world should be made to conform more closely to that model — to activate the *Exemplum Americanum* into the *Pax Americana* (Bartlett, 1974: 1–2).

Embodying an absolute moral ethos, 'Americanism,' once it is driven on to the world stage by events, is inspired willy-nilly to reconstruct the very alien things it tries to avoid. [Hartz, 1955: 286]

In other words, internationalism in America has commonly taken the form of interventionism (Burns, 1957: 268). The interventionist or expansionist urge was apparent from the beginning of the nation's history. While turning her back on Europe, America's 'manifest destiny' did not stop at the Pacific or the Caribbean Sea. Already in 1787, John Adams maintained that the new republic was 'destined' to extend its rule over the entire northern part of the hemisphere (Weinberg, 1958: 40; Parenti, 1971: 8), and in a moment of political ecstacy he wrote in 1813 that the republic 'will last forever, govern the globe, and introduce the perfection of man' (Bloomfield, 1974: 62). In the 1840s the prolific and influential publicist John O'Sullivan preached the unlimited potential for American expansion: 'who will, who can,' he demanded, 'set limits to our onward march?' (O'Connor, 1969: 67) While O'Sullivan and his contemporaries primarily envisioned hemispheric expansion, such limits were, by the turn of the century, seen as too narrow by many Americans. One vocal exponent of interventionist policy, Admiral Mahan, argued that just as religions which rejected missionary enterprise were doomed to decay, so with nations that failed to look beyond their borders (Burns, 1957: 271). In 1899 the President of Ohio Wesleyan University declared: 'We imagine that God has called us to the rulership of the world. He sends us as He sent His well-beloved son, to serve the world and thus to rule the world' (Rystad, 1975: 47). And in the twentieth century the globalization of America's moral mission became official policy when Woodrow Wilson sought to impose upon the United States the prodigious task of 'making the world safe for democracy.'

In brief, American self-righteousness from the early days of the new republic wore a Janus face. Max Lerner (1958: 888, 920) speaks of 'the twin impulses of expansionism and self-sufficiency' which are 'inseparable not only from the fabric of the civilization but from each other.' And Hartz (1955: 38) formulates it thus:

> We have been able to dream of ourselves as emancipators of the world at the very moment that we have withdrawn from it. We have been able to see ourselves as saviors at the very moment that we have been isolationists.

Soviet ideology, though internationalist in character, shares with American ideology its roots in a sense of uniqueness. The notion of a historical mission dates back to the earliest days of Muscovy (see e.g., Ulam, 1968: 5; Wesson, 1974: 14). In Russian religious thought there was a streak of Messianic universalism. Moscow claimed a unique position among Christian nations, seeing itself as the 'Third Rome' with the obligation to spread the gospel of the Orthodox Church throughout the world (see e.g., Schwartz, 1975: 75–6). With the creation of the Soviet Union, the mission became secular but the sense of uniqueness remained.

> Firm in their conviction regarding the 'scientific' validity of the doctrines of Marx and Lenin, the Soviet leaders share old Russia's pretensions regarding the universal validity of official – then Orthodox, now Communist — faith. Like the rulers of Old Muscovy, they tend to see themselves as the bearers of a unique message and the center of a new, higher civilization. Now as in the past, Moscow proclaims itself as an example to all peoples. [Schwartz, 1975: 82]

With regard to the residue of traditional Russian beliefs in Soviet ideology, Adam Ulam (1962: 39) has observed:

> Communism, a materialistic and rationalist philosophy with international roots and pretensions, appears today to many as just another emanation of Russian imperialism of the nineteenth century, of nationalism and Panslavism founded, among other things, upon a semi-mystical if not obscurantist notion of the uniqueness of Russian society and the special historic mission of the Slavs.

Noting the persistent coexistence of eversion and inversion orientations in Russian and Soviet foreign policy thinking, Walter Clemens (1978: 41, 52) concludes that 'historic tendencies associated with Slavophilic introversion and pan-Slavic expansion live on.' Similarly, Ulam (1981: 5) maintains that 'nationalism in this peculiar, partly defensive, and partly aggressive form has . . . been the strongest element in Russian political culture, permeating the radical as well as the liberal and conservative camps.'

The common denominator of these traditions has been the tendency to 'contrast "our" inherent superiority with "their" soulless materialism and hypocrisy' (Ulam, 1962: 43–4). As in the American case, 'they' meant chiefly Western Europe. The Russians have been perenially preoccupied with discussions on Russia versus the 'West.' And the contempt of the Bolshevik leaders for the existing Europe-centered international system matched and surpassed that of the American Founding Fathers. Trotsky, in publishing secret diplomatic documents in 1917, noted that 'the struggle against the imperialism which is exhausting and destroying the peoples of Europe is at the same time a struggle against capitalist diplomacy, which has cause enough to fear the light of day' (Goldwin *et al.*, 1959: 100). And Lenin (1967: 18) in 1918 described the European great powers in the following terms: 'While the German robbers broke all records in war atrocities, the British have broken all records not only in the number of colonies they have grabbed, but also in the subtlety of their disgusting hypocrisy.'

From its creation, the Soviet Union was perceived to have the dualistic character of a prototypical state based upon new concepts and principles, on the one hand, and a revolutionary power, on the other. And like in America, two different foreign policy orientations have flowed from the conviction of being a chosen people: globalism and withdrawal. The faith in Russia as the herald of a universal teaching (Christianity, communism) has inspired missionary tendencies as well as self-absorption and a lack of concern for life abroad.

The early Bolshevik leaders were predominantly internationalist in outlook. They regarded themselves not as citizens of Russia but as leaders of the world revolution. However, once the new Soviet state was created and it became increasingly obvious that the expected world revolution would not occur in the foreseeable future, there was a tendency to elevate the Russian revolution and the Soviet Union to *the* models of global transformation. 'When we came to power,' said Lenin in 1918, 'our task . . . was to retain that power, that torch of socialism, so that it might scatter as many sparks as possible to add to the growing flames of socialist revolution' (Goldwin *et al.*, 1959: 110).

The view of the Soviet Union as 'the prototype of the new society of the future of all mankind' (CPSU Party Program of 1961, quoted in Schwartz, 1975: 112) was, in a way reminiscent of the American experience, reinforced by the polyethnic character of the new state. Just as Americans regarded the 'melting pot' character of their own republic as a testimony to its universal applicability, so the multinational Eurasian composition 'gave to the Soviet Union the glow of an incipient, genuine universalism' (Aspaturian, 1971: 25).

The universalist example of the Soviet Union had to be protected and consolidated in a hostile environment, and gradually the active promotion of world revolution gave way to notions of non-participation in international relations and withdrawal to consolidate the new Soviet Republic. While Lenin considered revolution in Europe essential to the survival of the Bolshevik revolution, he also realized that the survival of the Bolshevik regime was essential to the success of world revolution. The withdrawal tendencies were evident already in Lenin's approach at Brest-Litovsk and were later rendered explicit in Stalin's famous doctrine of 'socialism in one country.' Stalin thus made a virtue out of what was necessity for Lenin (Schwartz, 1975: 109). In the polemics with the 'world revolution now' faction headed by Leon Trotsky, Stalin triumphed, and for a long time loyalty to the Soviet Union became the touchstone of 'proletarian inter-nationalism.' 'An internationalist,' said Stalin, 'is he who uncon-ditionally, without hestitation and without provisos, is ready to defend the USSR because the USSR is the base of the revolutionary movement, and to defend the advance of this movement is impossible without defending the USSR' (quoted in Aspaturian, 1971: 96). Concomitantly, Russian patriotism and Russian history were increas-ingly invoked by Soviet policy-makers. The internationalism of the old Bolsheviks thus never had the opportunity to establish itself in the minds of ordinary Russians. 'As the old generation of Marxist intellectuals was obliterated under Stalin in the thirties, those remaining were the peasants and workers with their minds steeped in traditional Russian forms, on the one hand, and a new generation of Party cadres and technicians socialized with the help of a deliberate revitalization of the same Russian forms, on the other' (Gerner, 1980: 61).

A crucial difference between the evolution of the American and Soviet ideologies of foreign policy concerns the sense of threat from the environment. Whereas American ideas developed under con-ditions of relative security and absence of threats from the outside world, the doctrines of the new Soviet state — as well as those of traditional Russia — were formed against the background of an acute sense of threat and insecurity. Unlike Russia, the frontier, in American experience, has mainly been associated with opportunity, not with security (cf. Bartlett, 1974: 180).

Hence differing views on the harmonious/conflictual character of international politics have arisen. Americans have tended to exag-gerate the harmonious elements and to regard conflicts as temporary aberrations. According to Stanley Hoffmann (1968: 123), this involves a 'sin of transposition'; it is the 'liberal ethos writ large' or 'the liberal society superimposed on a state of nature.' Soviet ideology, on the other hand, emphasized the conflict elements of international politics:

short of the global victory of communism, harmony cannot prevail. The Soviet view of international politics, like the American, is derived from, and coincides with, their experience of intra-state relations. It is the class struggle writ large or 'internationalized' with the USSR replacing the 'proletariat' and the capitalist nations (especially the United States) replacing the 'bourgeoisie' (cf. Schwartz, 1975: 100–1). The economic roots of the two diverging world views are evident, the liberal vision of a harmonious nation and a harmonious world of free enterprise and free trade vs. the Marxist vision of domestic and global conflict between irreconcilable economic interests.

Paradise in One Region

If the early foreign policy orientations of the United States evolved from withdrawal toward increasing interventionism, those of the Soviet Union described the opposite trajectory, from interventionism toward increasing withdrawal. Yet both were soon to find a convenient niche between globalism and self-sufficiency in the idea of regional hegemony.

The Monroe Doctrine epitomizes this stage in the development of American foreign policy ideology. The notion of two politically and morally as well as geographically separate hemispheres germinated well before James Monroe's message to Congress in 1823 (cf. e.g., Weinberg, 1958: 63–4) which, however, rendered it into an ideological norm. The isolationist impulse was evident in the Monroe Doctrine. European colonization and territorial expansion in the Western hemisphere were interdicted, and in return the United States pledged to refrain from interfering in intra-European politics. This part of the message reflects the American aversion to Old World political values and politics (cf. Crabb, 1976: 37).

Yet President Monroe's warning that the United States would consider any attempt by European powers to intervene in the hemisphere 'dangerous to our peace and safety' and 'the manifestation of an unfriendly disposition toward the United States' (Crabb, 1976: 303) also implied a commitment to an interventionist position. The meaning of self-protection was enlarged, and the defense of North America came to be regarded as an adequate motive for expansion (cf. Weinberg, 1958: 388–9). Thus the Monroe Doctrine became a source of 'self-defensive expansionism' (Weinberg, 1958: 396). Polk's restatement of the Doctrine in 1845, by banning European intrusion by any means, be it diplomatic or military, broadened the basis for possible American intervention (cf. Weisband, 1973: 24–5; Weinberg,

1958: 396). And the right of intervention was given a candid and extreme formulation in President Theodore Roosevelt's famous 1904 'corollary' to the Monroe Doctrine (quoted in Weisband, 1973: 31 and Weinberg, 1958: 428):

> Chronic wrongdoing, or an impotence which results in a general loosening of the ties of civilized society, may in America, as elsehwere, ultimately require intervention by some civilized nation, and in the Western Hemisphere the adherence of the United States to the Monroe Doctrine may force the United States, however reluctantly, in flagrant cases of wrongdoing and impotence, to the exercise of an international police power.

No longer was intervention limited to self-protective measures, nor was it restricted to legally recognized conditions, but it could be based on broad moral criteria (Weinberg, 1958: 428).

The early history of the Soviet, like the American, young republic was one of growth by annexation and assimilation of successive geographic layers. The Soviet constitution of 1918 established the RSFSR (Russian Soviet Federated Socialist Republic). In 1924, under the second Soviet constitution, the Ukranian, Belorussian and Transcaucasian SSRs were added to the original RSFSR. And by 1936, when the third constitution was inaugurated, the USSR consisted of eleven union republics (Triska and Finley, 1968: 14–15). The territorial expansion, in effect, amounted to a reconstitution of the old tsarist empire under Soviet rule. And although the internationalist ambitions of the Soviet leaders ostensibly followed class and party lines rather than geographic boundaries, they had an apparent regional focus on Russia's neighbors in Europe. That was where the world revolution was expected to be triggered off, and that was where coalitions with national communists were sought.

The creation of the Communist International, Comintern, in 1919 provided a framework for, or a vision of, regional co-operation under the principle of 'proletarian internationalism.' Comintern was, in Lenin's words, to be the 'forerunner of the international republic of Soviets' (Korey, 1969: 52–3). The invitation spoke of the need for a central organ with the function of 'subordinating the interests of the movement in each country to the common interest of the international revolution' (Korey, 1969: 53). In practice, the Comintern imitated the Soviet government and party pattern of organization, and the interest of the world revolution and 'proletarian internationalism' came increasingly to be identified with the interests of the Soviet Union.

Among the early Comintern leaders, the idea that an eventual 'socialist commonwealth' would put limitations on the national sovereignty of its members loomed large, and so did the belief that the members of the commonwealth would have a moral right to intervene militarily to further the world revolution or protect an already established communist regime (Korey, 1969: 55–6). Thus, like in America, a doctrine of 'just wars' or ethically asymmetric wars evolved. This notion was a radical departure from the prevailing European, Clausewitzian conception of wars, according to which all wars were equally 'just' and all belligerence equally 'right' (Rapoport, 1971: 48–50, 56–7).

The 'socialist commonwealth' did, however, not materialize until after World War II, when eight European (Poland, German Democratic Republic, Czechoslovakia, Albania, Bulgaria, Hungary, Rumania, and Yugoslavia) and later four Asian (China, North Korea, North Vietnam, and Outer Mongolia) party-states came into existence. In a sense, the old expansionist-cum-isolationist Pan-Slavic dreams of a regional empire sealed off from the rest of the world had finally come true, albeit under different premises.[3]

Stalin's isolationism had to be abandoned, and the phrases 'people's democracy' and 'socialist internationalism' were coined to denote the ensuing 'new type' of regimes and relationships. 'Socialist internationalism' and 'people's democracy' alike were seen as imperfect reflections of, or steps on the road to, 'proletarian internationalism' and the Soviet model respectively. Thus the idea of the USSR as the center of an ideologically rather than territorially based coalition survived. 'Socialism in one country' was replaced by 'socialism in one region' (Triska and Finley, 1968: 14–18). The interests of the 'socialist commonwealth' were ostensibly above those of any individual party-state although, as before, there was a tendency to define system interests compatibly with Soviet interests.

Serpent in Paradise

If the compatibility of American and Soviet foreign policy ideologies had hitherto been latent, the onset of the Cold War revealed and crystallized the similarities of the two 'social myths' (Wheeler, 1960; Niebuhr, 1964) at the same time as it blinded the two sides to these similarities.

First of all, the Cold War entailed a clear identification of the enemy. Mutual rivalry and animosity transcended the previously shared contempt for the diffuse 'Old World.' This identification of one another as the main enemy came gradually, via frustrated expectations of post-war collaboration and via perceived associations and analogies with their mutual wartime enemy, Germany, on both sides.

Similarities between Nazi Germany and Soviet Russia had been articulated by Americans both before and after World War II and 'once Russia was designated the "enemy" byAmerican leaders, Americans transferred their hatred for Hitler's Germany to Stalin's Russia with considerable ease and persuasion' (Adler and Paterson, 1970: 1046). 'Totalitarianism' became a convenient formula to rationalize this metamorphosis (cf. Adler and Paterson, 1970; Spiro and Barber, 1971). Similarly, the notion that the United States was replacing Germany on the global scene and that fascism and liberal democracy were merely the same beast in other guises was being voiced in the Soviet Union (cf. Barghoorn, 1950: 104, 181, 183–4; Aron, 1974: 37). 'Imperialism' came to play a role in Soviet ideology similar to that of 'totalitarianism' in American ideology. As Thomas Larson (1978: 160) has noted, 'just as the totalitarian formula served American policy needs in the post-war years, so the imperialism concept fitted to a tee the needs of Soviet policy.'

For the United States and the Soviet Union alike, the enemies thus identified were not really states but 'conspiracies disguised as states.' Having been the beneficiary of relatively sympathetic Soviet attitudes during the war, the United States came, after Roosevelt's death, increasingly to be regarded, in Soviet parlance, as the incarnation of evil, cynical, global imperialism. And to Americans, the Soviet Union became identified with world communism. When American leaders 'trying to make sense of the new world emerging from the smoke of war looked into Stalin's face they saw Hitler. They had underestimated one dictator by ignoring *Mein Kampf*. To avoid making the same mistake, they dabbled in Marx and Lenin' (Barnet, 1977: 66).

Both sides thus found themselves fighting 'isms' rather than nations and inferring the intentions of the adversary not so much from what they *did* as from what they *were* (imperialists/communists). For both superpowers the struggle began at home. The search for internal subversion to account for errors in policy became a prominent feature of the American and Soviet political scenes in the late 1940s and early 1950s (cf. Ulam, 1971: 141).

The former difference in perceived threats from the environment was furthermore abated with the advent of atomic weapons and mutual deterrence. No longer could Americans be confident of military invulnerability and impermeability; the Soviet sense of threat, on the other hand, gradually became less acute. As a result, both modified their views on harmony and conflict in the international system. The American belief in natural harmony of interests between nations and peace as a normal condition was no longer tenable, and the Americans learned to accept war and conflict as integral features of world politics. In Walter Lippmann's words (quoted in Yergin, 1978: 194), 'the ideal of peace' and the 'unearned security' of America's geographical position had up to then 'diverted our attention from the idea of national security.' After World War II 'national security' became a 'Commanding Idea' of American foreign policy, according to which an adverse turn of events anywhere in the world might endanger the United States (Yergin, 1978: 193–220). The Soviet zero-sum image of world politics also underwent gradual modification, as manifested in Khrushchev's 1956 declaration that war was no longer inevitable and his proclamation of 'peaceful coexistence' as the general foreign policy line of the USSR. World politics was henceforth described as conflict-cum-collaboration.

The mutual identification of an ideological enemy in combination with the alleviation of the sense of insecurity in the Soviet case and the deprivation of the sense of security in the American case unleashed the missionary zeal of both foreign policy ideologies. Having long articulated what they were fighting *for*, both now had a clearer vision of what they were fighting *against.* In addition to stating what and who will win, the ideologies became explicit as to who will ultimately lose. The enemy furthermore provided an external scapegoat to blame for any temporary failure to realize ideological goals, and concretely revealed the face of 'sin' (Wheeler, 1960: 180). If the crusading spirit had previously been restrained by a Soviet lack of means and an American lack of need to intervene abroad, the post-war situation elicited a fresh sense of threat *along with* opportunity in both countries. As a result, isolationism and withdrawal gave way to globalism and interventionism. The traditional confidence in the supreme virtue of their own example was reinforced by the conception of the social system of the adversary as the embodiment of vice.

At the height of the cold war both sides used the rhetoric of disease to describe the system of the other. Communism was a virus, a social sickness, a disease of the body politic. Capitalism, bourgeois culture, was a source of contamination, cancer, rot. [Barnet, 1977: 73]

Thus, in the post-war American and Soviet global interventionism one recognizes the old theme of moral separateness, the belief in the special goodness of the American/Soviet system.

In American foreign policy ideology, the Truman Doctrine epitomizes the new direction as well as the continuity with the past. In the words of Robert Tucker (1968: 52), 'the Truman Doctrine in our age applies to the world the principles embodied in the doctrine of Monroe.' Just as the Monroe Doctrine was designed to set the New World apart from the Old, so its twentieth-century counterpart was meant to draw the lines between the communist and the 'free' world.

Yet now the boundaries were drawn along *ideological* rather than geographical lines. The Truman Doctrine involved 'the containment of an ideology' (Steel, 1977: 22). Even if Greece and Turkey were the immediate targets of the Truman Doctrine, it provided a rationale for a policy of global intervention against communism. And the Korean War in 1950 heralded the globalization of the doctrine.

The American ardor for drawing lines of demarcation in the spirit of the Truman Doctrine paralleled the simultaneous crystallization of the Soviet 'two-camp' thesis. Zhdanov, speaking at the meeting establishing Cominform half a year after the proclamation of the Truman Doctrine, represented international politics as a struggle between two camps. The Soviet Union and the new people's democracies constituted the socialist camp opposing the imperialist camp led by the United States and supported by its 'satellites' Great Britain and France. Whereas the imperialist camp was described as decaying and aggressive, the forces of socialism were ascendant (cf. Barghoorn, 1950: 103–4). From then on the thesis of an all-out global struggle between the two camps, between good and evil, the forces of the past and those of the future, was to dominate Soviet discourse. This represented a reversion to Marxist-Leninist orthodoxy in striking contrast to the optimistic views on great power co-operation immediately after the war (cf. Barghoorn, 1950: 102–3).

The identification of an ideological enemy also contributed to rigidifying American and Soviet regionalist ideas. As demonstrated by Thomas Franck and Edward Weisband (1972), the two superpowers have enunciated strikingly parallel regional doctrines. The 'Brezhnev Doctrine' — called by Adam Ulam (1974:6) 'the Monroe Doctrine of the Communist world' — and the 'Johnson Doctrine' both contain notions of limited sovereignty (cf. below, Chapter 5). The Dominican Republic in 1965 and Czechoslovakia in 1968 became prominent test cases of these doctrines, which recall to a considerable extent, and in a perverted manner, the regional hegemony ideas embedded in the Monroe Doctrine and the Comintern.

In brief, the Cold War imprisoned Soviet and American foreign policy in ideological straitjackets. The foundations of the foreign policy ideologies of the superpowers were, as we have seen, already laid during their early history. In the post-war era they crystallized into curiously symmetrical models.

Political Systems

The American and Soviet political systems are generally regarded as antipodes. To Americans, the United States represents the archetypal 'democratic, pluralist' system; the Soviet Union the archetypal 'totalitarian, autocratic' system. To Russians, the American political system is the tool of exploitative monopoly capital, whereas the Soviet political system represents the interests of the entire toiling people. In Soviet terminology, the USSR is therefore labeled 'democratic' and the United states 'undemocratic.' The only common ground is thus the mutual conviction that the two political systems are too far apart to allow meaningful comparison.

And if we limit the comparison to the political systems *per se*, the differences are indeed great and conspicuous (cf. e.g., Brzezinski and Huntington, 1964: Chapters 2–4). However, if the main focus, as in this inquiry, is on the interrelation between domestic political systems and foreign policy behavior, the picture becomes more blurred.

The Relation Between Political System and Foreign Policy

Scholars have long argued about the effects of variations in political systems on the conduct of foreign policy. One frequently asserted view holds that the American pluralist system renders the consistent and effective pursuit of foreign policy difficult.

From Tocqueville to Carl Friedrich and Walter Lippmann, observers have pointed out that the requirements of success in world affairs contradict the inclinations of democracy, especially when those inclinations are unchecked by pre-democratic traditions and institutions, un-selfdisciplined and undisciplined by political parties, as in the United States. Secrecy, cold rationality, experience, continuity — the requisites of foreign policy — are antithetical to democratic policy. [Hoffmann, 1968: 219]

The corollary of this view is, of course, that an autocracy like the Soviet Union is better fitted to formulate and execute a consistent foreign policy.

Another frequently heard argument concerns differences in diplomatic styles.

> Those who rely on peaceful persuasion, and who must, at the same time, tolerate their defeated opponents by their side, will instinctively transfer the same attitude to their partners in international relations; they will (as a rule) prefer to persuade rather than to coerce, and will (again as a rule) bring a readiness 'to live and let live' to the conference table. If the representatives of top men in a totalitarian power were to show the same attitudes, they would be schizophrenics. [Hermens, 1959: 442–3].

Carried to its extreme, this view linking democracy with persuasion and totalitarianism with coercion implies that democratic states are prone to pursue peaceful foreign policies, while totalitarian states tend to be aggressive and expansionist.

While assertions like these about the different foreign policies flowing from variations in political systems abound, little evidence has been adduced in support. Nor have latter-day students of comparative foreign policy been able to establish any unequivocal correlation between type of polity and the external behavior of states (cf. McGowan and Shapiro, 1973: 94–5, 104). Empirical research on the relationship between pluralist and autocratic or 'open' and 'closed' polities, on the one hand, and foreign policy, on the other, has been limited and sketchy, and the results have been inconclusive and partly contradictory (see e.g., Salmore and Salmore, 1978: 110).

Actors at the Apex

Why, then, is it so hard to point to any decisive conclusions concerning the effect of political systems upon foreign policy behavior? One answer is offered by traditional scholarship on foreign policy and international politics. In William Wallace's (1971: 40) formulation:

> The conventional wisdom of academic interpretation, it would be fair to say, remains that foreign policy is an elite process, dominated by the executive, in all developed states.

In other words, regardless of variations in political systems, executive decision-makers are assumed to act more freely in matters of foreign policy as opposed to domestic policy.

What about executive dominance in the making of American and Soviet foreign policy? It could be argued that neither the notion of pluralist pressures in 'open' states like the United States nor the notion of unrestrained dictatorship in 'closed' states like the USSR coincide with the actual character of foreign policy decision-making in these two countries.

The gradual concentration of foreign policy decision-making power in the 'imperial presidency' in the United States has been noted and analyzed by several observers (cf. Schlesinger, 1974; de Riencourt, 1968: xi, 75; Schurmann, 1974: 20–2). The common core of their arguments is that there is a close connection between global involvement and the centralization of foreign policy decision-making authority in Washington.

If analysts of the United States have uncovered elements of centralization behind a pluralist facade, recent developments in Soviet studies point to pluralist elements or 'cracks' in the monolith. The 'totalitarian' model, which long dominated Western Sovietology, has gradually given way to the 'conflict school,' which regards intra-elite conflict as a crucial feature of Soviet politics. Struggles over power and policy are seen to be going on continuously behind the Kremlin facade of unity. On matters of foreign policy there are, in all probability, fewer participants in the struggle, than on domestic issues. Jerry Hough (1980: 109–13), for instance, identifies an inner circle of the foreign policy establishment in early 1980 consisting of fifteen persons.

Thus, the American and Soviet foreign policy decision-making systems seem to have moved away from the 'pluralist' and 'autocratic' ideal types, respectively, toward an 'oligarchic' intermediary. The general conclusion that Soviet leadership is less omnipotent and American leadership less restrained than the 'totalitarian' and 'pluralist' models assume points to the need for including levels below the apex in a comprehensive analysis of the interrelationships between political systems and foreign policy. The Soviet and American political systems alike are neither 'topless' nor 'bottomless.' Policy initiatives do not necessarily 'trickle down' in the Soviet Union and 'bubble up' in the United States (Brzezinski and Huntington, 1964: 203–8).

Actors Below the Apex

As a reaction to traditional 'unitary actor' explanations of foreign policy, scholars have in recent years begun to take more serious note of the bureaucratic setting of foreign policy decisions. The 'bureaucratic politics' model sees foreign policy not as the result of rational calculations and coherent strategies but rather as the outcome of bargaining between several interdependent organizational actors with separable objectives and parochial priorities.

While this model has been applied primarily to American foreign policy, recent developments in Sovietology parallel the 'bureaucratic politics' approach to the study of decision-making in Washington (cf. Horelick *et al.*, 1975: 36–41). Interestingly, Soviet Americanists seem comfortable with the 'bureaucratic politics' approach which they feel has brought American analysis to a more realistic appreciation of their own political system (Schwartz, 1978: 61). And the principal bureaucratic participants in the bargaining over foreign policy are identical in the two superpowers: the 'military–industrial complex,' the diplomatic establishment, and the intelligence community.

The 'military–industrial complex.' During World War II both the American and the Soviet military were catapulted to a position in command of vast human and material resources and emerged from the war with enhanced power and prestige. The symbolic partnership between the military and the defence industry — the so-called military–industrial complex — is another legacy of World War II. Although the label has, ever since President Eisenhower's famous Farewell Address in 1961, been attached primarily to the United States, C. Wright Mills argues in his classic, *The Power Elite* (1956), that the concept applies to both capitalist and socialist states.

Indeed, certain dissimilarities notwithstanding, there are in both superpowers powerful bureaucratic coalitions wanting 'a bigger bang for the buck' or 'more rubble for the ruble' (Rapoport, 1971: 214). In addition to the military and defense industry, the coalition is sometimes said to include scientists engaged in defense-related research and development in both countries, legislators whose districts benefit from defense procurement in the American case (cf. Rosen, 1973: 2), and professional party *apparatchki* and ideologues stressing the interdependency between security, heavy industry, and ideological orthodoxy in the Soviet case (cf. Aspaturian, 1972).

The linkages between the military and the defense industry are perhaps more conspicuous in the United States where some two thousand retired military officers serve as executives of major military contractors (Schiller and Phillips, 1970: 9; Lieberson, 1973: 63). While personal links of this kind are lacking in the USSR, the fact that Dmitri F. Ustinov, whose whole career has been in the Soviet defense industry, was appointed Minister of Defense in 1976 testifies to close military-industrial linkages there as well. On the other hand, Soviet defense industry is more insulated from the rest of society and subjected to less outside review. It constitutes a privileged 'economy within an economy' with remarkably little spillover into the non-defense sectors (Aspaturian, 1972: 18; Lee, 1972: 74; Agursky and Adomeit, 1979: 110). In recent years the aphorism 'the United States *has* a military–industrial complex, the USSR *is* a military–industrial complex' has gained ground in the West. The Soviet complex is located within the political structure itself, its requirements enjoy top priority, and it is the beneficiary of a massive concentration of resources — including high-quality manpower (Agursky and Adomeit, 1979: 107–9; Alexander, 1979: 22). Soviet defense-industry leaders constitute a group characterized by great continuity, cohesion, and political access (Aspaturian, 1972: 13–19; Morozow, 1971: 96–8; Alexander, 1979: 23).

One crucial difference between the American and Soviet defense industries concerns the fact that profit is not a driving force for Soviet armament managers. For Marxists in East and West, who see the military–industrial complex as but an agent of corporate capitalism and imperialism, this circumstance altogether excludes the possibility of a *Soviet* military–industrial complex. Only in the United States — and other capitalist countries — can the organic inseparability and mutual reinforcement of the military, economic and political structures be found of which the military–industrial complex is one symptom — according to this line of thought (cf. Schiller and Phillips, 1970: 26; DuBoff, 1970: 112).

One counter-argument is provided by John Kenneth Galbraith (1973): American defense industries, like other large American corporations, belong to the 'planning system' where power rests not with the owners but with the 'technostructure' or managers whose overriding goal is organizational growth rather than profit. In this sense, American and Soviet defense industry are essentially similar. Furthermore, if the military–industrial complex is understood as a subtle interplay and coincidence of interests and perceptions rather than as a conspiracy (cf. Rosen, 1973: 24), possible differences in economic incentives lose some of their significance.

How, then, does the existence of a military–industrial complex affect foreign policy? The relationship between the military and defense industry is based on a general identity of interest in the production of weaponry. The need for arms arises out of a sense of threat. Having taken root in the fruitful climate of the Cold War and been fertilized by the natural inclination of bureaucracy to expand, the military–industrial complex can be expected to have a continued interest in the maintenance of international tensions and be highly sensitive to external threats.

How influential is the military–industrial complex? Many attempts at answering this question focus on the accumulation of vast human and material resources which have ostensibly transformed the military–industrial complex from the servants into the masters of foreign policy. However, the influence of the military–industrial complex on matters of foreign policy derives less from 'the absolute power of life and death invested in the few individuals at the controls of the vast military machines' (Rapoport, 1971: 11) than from a mutuality of attitudes and perceptions with foreign policy decision-makers. The Cold War, which is the *raison d'être* of the military-industrial complex, entailed the adoption of military frameworks for thinking by other foreign policy elites, and the traditional semantic barriers between 'political' and 'military' functions were eroded (cf. Barnet, 1973: 28). The strong position of the military-industrial complex seems to rest primarily on the resonance of its way of thinking, rather than direct expression of its self-interest through crude lobbying (Rosen, 1973: 24).

This also means that there is 'a considerable degree of harmony of interest between the complexes of the opposing sides, as both desire to maintain a state of conflict' (Rosen, 1973: 3). Each complex needs the other to justify its existence, and each tacitly protects the other. The 'tacit co-operation' between the two influential military–industrial complexes has contributed to what George Kennan (1982: 35) has labeled a 'militarization of concept and behavior' in US–Soviet relations.

The diplomatic establishment. Both post-war superpowers are, in Hans Morgenthau's (1966: 549) words, 'newcomers in diplomacy.' From the Jacksonian era on, he maintains, the brilliant American diplomacy of the formative years disappeared. When the need for an active

American foreign policy again became manifest in the late 1930s, there was only a mediocre foreign service to build on, and the State Department exerted a subordinate influence on the foreign policy shaped by Roosevelt.

Similarly, Richard Barnet (1973: 25) argues that 'the Monroe Doctrine, which marked the divorce of America from European politics, also marked the shift of American diplomacy from cosmopolitanism to parochialism. In most of the world the American ambassador limited his role to that of a reporter or a scout for commercial opportunities. The State Department in Washington devoted its energies principally to economic, consular, and trade matters.' Even as late as 1948 the Department had only 336 officers out of a total of 5,906 dealing with political questions. The State Department's prestige and power declined further during the war. Roosevelt frequently ignored the Department, and at the same time its ranks were depleted as many foreign service offices were drafted. The decline of the State Department coincided with the rise of the military (Barnet, 1973: 26–7; cf. de Riencourt, 1968: 104–5).

On the Soviet side, the October Revolution entailed the birth of a diplomatic service 'without an umbilical connection with the old Tsarist diplomatic establishment' (Aspaturian, 1971: 622). When Leon Trotsky reluctantly accepted the office of Foreign Commissar, he boasted, 'I will issue a few revolutionary proclamations to the people of the world, and then close up shop.' On his only visit to the Foreign Ministry, he assembled the personnel in a hall and asked those supporting the new regime to divide to the left and those not, to the right. As none chose the left, Trotsky fired them all on the spot and later dismissed summarily all the members of the Russian foreign service abroad if they would not pledge loyalty to the new regime (Aspaturian, 1971: 598, 623).

The expected world revolution, which would have rendered Soviet diplomacy superfluous, did not materialize, and Trotsky's successor, Georgi Chicherin, had to organize a new diplomatic service from scratch when he took office in 1918. When Chicherin was removed in 1929, Maxim Litvinov inherited a re-established and remarkably competent corps of diplomats. Litvinov, however, came to preside over the virtual liquidation of the diplomatic establishment in Stalin's purges between 1937 and 1939. Almost all of Litvinov's ambassadors and ministers were either executed or imprisoned. Again, a new foreign service had to be erected upon the ruins of the old, and under the direction of Vyacheslav Molotov the vacancies left by the purges were filled by young and inexperienced personnel drawn from other departments, especially the Secret Police (See Aspaturian, 1971: 622–32).

Thus, the two giants emerged from World War II with strengthened and prestigious military establishments but crippled and weakened diplomatic establishments. This internal balance of power has no doubt left its mark on American and Soviet foreign policy after World War II. Though gradually rebuilt, the diplomatic establishments in both the United States and the Soviet Union constitute poor power bases, display little coherence, and have been effectively subordinated to the White House and the Politburo, respectively.

The intelligence community. In addition to implementing policies already decided upon, the diplomatic establishment also takes part in the foreign policy-making process, mainly by providing necessary information on which to base decisions. In the latter function diplomats are, however, not alone. The need for better intelligence was promptly recognized in both superpowers after World War II. This was largely the by-product of recent pivotal events when both were taken by surprise: Pearl Harbor and the German attack on the Soviet Union. These traumatic experiences taught the lesson of keeping both unrelentingly vigilant and well-informed. Unprecedented intelligence networks were built up in the wake of the war — in the United States more or less from scratch, in the Soviet Union upon the firm foundation of the Secret Police.

The Soviet intelligence effort is centralized through two organizations, the KGB (*Komitet Gosudarstvennoy Bezopasnosti*) and its military counterpart, the GRU (*Glavnoye Razvedyvatelnoye Upravleniye*). The KGB is also responsible for the internal security of the Soviet Union. The organizational picture is more fragmented and complicated in the United States, where some ten different organizations collect and co-ordinate foreign intelligence. Dominant among these is the Central Intelligence Agency (CIA), created in 1947. Unlike its Soviet counterpart, the KGB, the responsibilities of the CIA do not include internal security, which falls primarily under the Federal Bureau of Investigation (FBI). The Defense Intelligence Agency (DIA) is the American counterpart of the GRU.

While the KGB methods of safeguarding internal security are in striking contrast to American ones, the KGB and the CIA perform their foreign intelligence functions in similar ways. The CIA and the KGB alike maintain formidable international networks. CIA stations abroad are usually housed in American embassies, and in many cases the CIA station chief has longer experience, better contacts, and more money to spend than the ambassador. When President Kennedy took office, the CIA had almost as many officers engaged in intelligence activites abroad as the State Department had for the whole range of its activities (cf. Hilsman, 1967: 67, 77). Soviet embassies abroad contain no official intelligence personnel. Yet it is a well-known fact that a large number of intelligence officers operate under cover designations at the sizeable Soviet missions (see e.g., Triska and Finley, 1968: 48–51). According to one estimate, 60 percent of the Soviet officials stationed outside the USSR are actually career officers of either the KGB or GRU (Cyrus Sulzberger, *New York Times*, June 20, 1966, quoted in Barghoorn, 1971: 121). In addition, the CIA finances and controls a number of 'proprietary corporations,' especially air charter companies, around the world (see Marchetti and Marks, 1974: 146–64); and a large portion of Soviet staff members of Tass, Aeroflot, Novosti, Amtorg, and Soviet commercial delegations abroad are KGB or GRU officers (see Barron, 1974: 27).

The massive deployment of CIA and KGB personnel abroad serves not only to obtain intelligence but also to conduct clandestine operations around the world. The organizations constitute the covert-action arms of American and Soviet foreign policy (for detailed examples, see Marchetti and Marks, 1974; Barron, 1974; and Crozier, 1969: 305–18).

To summarize the discussion thus far, both the American and the Soviet foreign policy-making systems can be described as 'oligarchic,' including an element of bargaining between a limited number of relevant bureaucracies. Among some Sovietologists who are critical of the traditional monolithic conception there has been a tendency to exaggerate the pluralist element of Soviet foreign policy-making; conversely, certain students of American foreign policy-making have reacted to the prevalent pluralistic conception by adopting C. Wright Mills' notion of a 'ruling elite.' Thus, Richard Barnet (1973: 48) speaks of 'a national security elite remarkable for its cohesiveness, consistency and, above all persistence;' and John Donovan (1974) refers to 'a small, closely-knit group of civilian militants.' Whereas adherents of the 'ruling elite' model — whether applied to the United States or the Soviet Union — tend to focus on the shared ideological beliefs of policy-makers, advocates of the 'bureaucratic politics' model point to evidence of bureaucratic competition and tugs-of-war over concrete foreign policy issues. There may be some scope for compromise between the two extremes. For instance, Jiri Valenta (1979: 4, 5), a proponent of the 'bureaucratic politics' approach to Soviet foreign policy decision-making, admits that 'like their American counterparts, Soviet leaders share a certain set of images of national security' yet 'differ on how various issues should be approached and resolved.' And John Donovan (1974: 277), who subscribes to an 'establishment orchestration' model of US policy-making, concedes:

> Bureaucratic politics exists — of this we may be sure — and there is enough there to keep a generation of empiricists busily engaged. Unfortunately, incrementalism may reveal little about the purposes and objectives toward which the process moves — or about the purposes and objectives whose accomplishment the process impedes and obstructs.

The conclusion that suggests itself is that an analysis of foreign policy-making needs to take into account the nexus between actors and ideas. And it is my contention that this nexus constitutes a central link in a 'causal chain' accounting for similarities in American and Soviet foreign policy.

Potential Similarities: Summary

The preceding analysis has suggested several factors which combine to create similarities in the outlook and conduct of the contemporary superpowers. Hugeness and territorial expansion forged ideological beliefs in a historical mission. Whereas this sense of uniqueness traditionally manifested itself in either globalism or withdrawal, a number of circumstances at the end of World War II conspired to strengthen the globalist tendency among both superpowers. The predominant historical 'lessons' of the war concerned 'appeasement' and 'preparedness.' Both superpowers emerged from the war convinced never again to make concessions to the enemy and never again to be caught militarily unprepared. As expectations of post-war collaboration were frustrated and both sides came to perceive associations and analogies between the other superpower and the wartime enemy, these lessons were applied to US–Soviet relations in particular. The mutual identification of the other superpower as the ideological enemy unleashed the missionary zeal and added to American and Soviet foreign policy beliefs a clearer vision of what they were figthing against. At the same time, both emerged from the war with strengthened and prestigious military establishments but crippled and weakened diplomatic establishments. The ideological and institutional foundation was thus laid for 'national security establishments' which resemble each other in terms of both composition and outlook. Their globalist orientation and stress on military might were reinforced by technological developments dramatizing the need for preparedness in the wake of World War II.

Let me dwell for a moment on the nexus between actors and ideas in American and Soviet foreign policy decision-making. As we have seen, some analysts emphasize the cohesiveness, others the bureaucratic factionalism, of the superpower foreign policy establishments. A realistic point of departure seems to be that just as the top leadership may be divided on policy issues, so the bureaucracies below the apex are not necessarily internally monolithic and homogeneous entities, either in the United States or in the Soviet Union. Intra-bureaucracy conflict and inter-bureaucracy collaboration are dual possibilities to be taken into account. Policy issues tend to give rise to coalitions or 'groupings', cutting across formal institutional lines.

In the case of American foreign policy decision-making, Roger Hilsman (1967: 550–5), a participant-observer of the Kennedy administration, holds that every major issue of foreign policy gives rise to rival policies sponsored by different groups or advocates, frequently forming 'entirely informal alliances that cut across departmental or institutional lines.' Similar conclusions have been drawn with regard to Soviet policy-making. Franklyn Griffiths (1971: 342) argues that 'if we look for patterns of articulation on specific issues, as opposed to the conflicting articulations that arise from specific formal groups, we find signs of shared outlooks and claims which cut across formal groups.' His view is shared by Jiri Valenta (1979: 17): 'In Soviet politics, coalitions (also known as 'blocs' or 'factions') seem to be loose, issue-oriented, heterogeneous alliances of convenience among different subgroups for a temporary common purpose.'

As these quotations imply, the conventional wisdom has been that such groupings are *ad hoc* constellations, varying from issue to issue. Yet the foregoing analysis of historical 'lessons' and foreign policy ideologies suggests broader patterns of divergent foreign policy beliefs according to which groupings can be distinguished in both superpowers.

First, the mutual sense of uniqueness and separateness can give rise to *globalist* as well as *particularist* self-images. Globalists and particularists share the moral superiority but differ in policy conclusions. Globalists desire actively to remake the world in their own image and to eradicate the vices of which the adversary is the symbol; particularists want to perfect their own nation so that it stands out as an irresistible model to the rest of the world.

In other words, whereas globalists have a predominantly external policy orientation, for particularists internal (or regional) interests take precedence over international ones. Globalists tend to stress the instability and/or relevance, particularists the stability and/or irrelevance, of the international environment. To globalists, all international situations are of equal concern, while particularists are more prone to make gradations of central-peripheral concerns. Globalists tend to asssess other countries primarily by their stance on international issues, in particular the superpower confrontation; to particularists, on the other hand, the most important criterion is the extent to which other countries adhere to the American or Soviet models and ideals. In terms of the role conceptions discussed in Chapter 1, globalists emphasize such roles as promoters of own value systems, preventers of other superpowers' values, and liberators for their own nation; whereas for particularists roles such as model and regional protector are of overriding importance.

Another dimension, suggested by the preceding analysis, concerns perceptions of the rival superpower. As we have seen, the historical record may suggest 'lessons' of either US–Soviet hostility or of friendship. By the same token, different schools of though have evolved in both superpowers as to how to assess the opponent. On the one hand, there is the 'orthodox' and widespread 'enemy image' of the other superpower. On the other hand, a more modified and nuanced image has evolved under the impact of the interdependence created by the US–Soviet 'thermonuclear duopoly,' where mutual survival becomes a common interest. Thus, in both superpowers a 'dual image' of the other has been articulated, according to which the US–Soviet relationship is one of conflict cum co-operation and certain conciliatory behavior can be expected from the opponent. The contradictions inherent in this image are usually solved by reference to different groups within the other superpower, embodying conciliatory tendencies and residual aggressiveness, respectively. Thus, while the enemy image is associated with Cold War thinking, the dual image underlies *détente*. Adherents to the enemy image tend to ascribe such roles as violator of universal values and war instigator to the other superpower, whereas the dual image allows for more limited roles, such as protector of own state or regional protector. The differences between the two divergent clusters of images may be summarized thus:

Table 5: Enemy and dual images

	Enemy image	Dual image
Re superpower relations	Conflict	Conflict-cum-collaboration
Re nature of adversary	Aggressive	Aggressive and conciliatory
Re plurality within adversary	Unitary actor	Aggressive and conciliatory groups

In the Soviet Union, struggles between adherents of these two principal images can be traced back to Lenin's days (cf. Griffiths, 1967) and reappear to become even more prevalent in the late 1950s after the Stalinist hiatus. Now, as in the 1920s, proponents of the dual image argue that Soviet conduct should be geared to strengthening the conciliatory or 'realist' forces with whom the Soviet Union might enter into certain co-operation and agreements. Adherents of the enemy image, on the other hand, deny the significance of internal differences within the United States and favor an intransigent stance *vis-à-vis* the invariably aggressive American imperialists (cf. Jönsson, 1982a).

In the United States, the divergence between the two sets of images also dates back to the inter-war years. Daniel Yergin (1978) makes a distinction between the 'Riga axioms' and the 'Yalta axioms.' Associated with the diplomats at the US Mission in Riga and the 'Soviet Service' of the State Department during the inter-war period, the 'Riga axioms' amounted to an enemy image of the adversary, 'an image of the Soviet Union as a world revolutionary state, denying the possibilities of coexistence, committed to unrelenting ideological warfare, powered by a messianic drive for world mastery' (Yergin, 1978: 11). Through most of the inter-war years, before the problem of the Soviet Union had moved to the fore, the 'Riga axioms' held sway. But by the mid-1940s another interpretation competed for hegemony in the American policy elite. The 'Yalta axioms,' associated with President Roosevelt and his loyal followers and epitomized by their 'lessons' of the 1945 Yalta Conference, assumed less coherence and purposefulness in the Kremlin's behavior in international politics than the 'Riga axioms.' The Soviet Union was seen to behave like a traditional great power within the international system, rather than trying to overthrow it. 'Business-like relations,' including agreements and even joint action, were possible with such a state. Just as Khrushchev's espousal of the dual image of the United States in the 1960s hinged on experiences from, and included advocacy of, high-level personal contacts, so did Roosevelt's dual image of the Soviet Union.

The cleavage between the enemy image and the dual image of the USSR has persisted and became particularly manifest in the wake of the Vietnam War. Several observers (cf. Roskin, 1974; Holsti, 1979; Holsti and Rosenau, 1980) have come to emphasize the distinction between 'Cold War' and 'Post-Cold War' beliefs among American policy-makers. Cold War beliefs center on the strong and persistent expansionist motivations of a monolithic Soviet bloc and consider the confrontation between the Soviet Union and its allies, on the one hand, and the non-communist nations, on the other, as the over-arching reality of the global system. Disorder and violence within the Third World are attributed to communist influence. Post-Cold War beliefs, by contrast, view communism as a divided movement and the Soviet Union as an established status quo-oriented nation. Threats to national security are seen to arise increasingly from issues that have little if anything to do with communism, and nationalism is regarded as being a stronger force than communism in the Third World. Whereas Michael Roskin (1974) argues that the difference in outlook is generational in character, Ole Holsti's and James Rosenau's extensive survey of a broad sample of the American foreign policy leadership suggests that these cleavages exist within generations as well as between them (cf. Holsti, 1979: 357; Holsti and Rosenau, 1979: 55).

Both in the United States and the Soviet Union the dialogue between the enemy and dual images has perhaps been most manifest among influential academic foreign affairs specialists. The Soviet revival of the dual image in the late 1950s seems to have originated in the foreign affairs intelligentsia of IMEMO (Institute of World Economy and International Relations) (see Zimmerman, 1969: 211–41; Jönsson, 1979a: 152–61). Whereas the foreign affairs intelligentsia continues to be divided (cf. Husband, 1979), the chief caretakers of the dual image legacy have turned out to be the *amerikanisty* of the USA Institute, created in 1967 (see Schwartz, 1978). Similarly, William Welch (1970) has demonstrated the continued coexistence of the enemy and dual images among American Sovietologists, with the dual image becoming more common toward the late 1960s.

It should be added that the two distinct sets of images of the rival superpower in the United States and the Soviet Union are not mutually independent but derive justification from, and serve as 'external pacers' for, each other.

> What we have in fact is not merely a pattern of mirror images, which have been pointed out repeatedly in the literature on Soviet–American relations, but what may properly be called (though neither side likes to hear it said) tacit alliance between adversaries. [Dallin, 1981: 385]

Combining the two dimensions discussed above, we can single out four distinct sets of ideas bearing on superpower foreign policy decision-making (cf. Figure 5).

| | | Images of the adversary | |
		Enemy image	Dual image
Self-images	Globalism	(1)	(2)
	Particularism	(3)	(4)

Fig. 5. Superpower foreign policy 'currents'

The cells in this matrix represent, as it were, 'tendencies' (Griffiths, 1971) or 'currents' (Schurmann, 1974: 30–9) to which groupings must adhere in order to be relevant to foreign policy-making in the United States and the Soviet Union. Cell (1) represents a current which views international issues and actors as integral parts of the global East-West confrontation and supports those forces working to one's own advantage or the other superpower's disadvantage. In current (2) issues and actors are assessed primarily in terms of how they affect East-West *détente* and the ability of one's own superpower to enact its global superpower role without risking open confrontation with the other superpower. Adherents of current (3) emphasize the role of model for their own nation and see support for those forces which really follow that model as the best way to long-term victory over the enemy superpower. Cell (4) represents a low profile current emphasizing the avoidance of superpower confrontation and focusing on internal problems.

These currents are not inextricably linked to specific individuals or groups. As noted above, different policy issues give rise to different groupings, and the same individual or group may give voice to different currents on different issues. The point is that articulations of political participants will ultimately be influential only to the extent that they form part of these currents. Seen from a different angle, each foreign policy needs to acquire *legitimacy* (cf. Trout, 1975; George, 1980a). In order to be legitimized, Soviet and American foreign policy must adhere to one of these currents.

Thus, while expressions of all four currents can be found in both superpowers throughout the post-war period, their strength has varied. In the years immediately after World War II globalism gradually took precedence over particularism and the enemy image prevailed over the dual image. World War II — a global war, unlike World War I — had made isolationism meaningless. The war itself, and the events leading up to the war, had taught the American and Soviet leaders 'that international events moved in simple chain reactions, that all points on a map were equally close, and that every event was of equal import' (Yergin, 1978: 198). Also, in the unfamiliar and uncertain post-war situation, the enemy image provided a clearer framework than the more ambiguous dual image. As immediate post-war events were seen on both sides to confirm the enemy image, the dual image came increasingly to be associated with 'appeasement.' Thus, policy-making in both superpowers tended toward cell (1) in our matrix.

The amalgam of enemy images and globalism yielded powerful 'domino theories.' The basic assumption of the inherent aggressiveness of the adversary in combination with a belief in the historical mission of one's own nation and the mortal danger of retreat produced the metaphor of 'a row of falling dominoes,' in American rhetorics, and that of preventing the 'contagion' of imperialism, in Soviet rhetorics, to justify interventionism around the globe.

Once a foreign policy achieves a degree of legitimacy, it becomes difficult to replace that policy. A new foreign policy will require new legitimation (George, 1980a: 248). This is facilitated by the demonstrated failure of legitimate policies. The perceived dangers of superpower confrontation have occasionally brought the dual image to the fore. After the Cuban missile crisis in 1962 the dual image prevailed both in the United States and in the Soviet Union. Similarly, the Nixon-Kissinger initiatives in the early 1970s to get out of the Vietnam imbroglio entailed a resurgence of the dual image in both superpowers. Yet the triumph of the dual image proved to be temporary and frail in both instances. The burden of proof is always heavier for the inherently contradictory dual image which, in contrast to the enemy image, is easily falsifiable. The enemy image tends to be self-confirming and thus to give rise to vicious circles of self-fulfilling prophecies. Any kind of behavior by the adversary is taken to validate the belief. Conciliatory gestures are perceived as traps, whereas anything that appears threatening is seen as revealing the true nature of the adversary. Hence, 'the outstanding bureaucratic casualties of the Cold War have all been men who took modest risks to promote conciliation rather than confrontation' (Barnet, 1973: 111).

In the wake of the Vietnam War the long-dormant conflict between globalism and isolationism again surfaced in the United States. This dimension is also central to the cleavage between 'Cold War' and 'Post-Cold War' beliefs referred to above. 'Post-Cold War' axioms include the belief that pressing domestic requirements should have priority over foreign affairs (see e.g., Holsti and Rosenau, 1980: 267). As demonstrated by a survey of American leaders, 'George McGovern's plea, "come home America," although clearly not a formula upon which to ride into the White House . . ., nevertheless strikes a responsive chord among a not insignificant element in the United States' (Holsti, 1979: 348–9). Yet post-Vietnam isolationism neither spread widely nor lived long. There has been no corresponding traumatic experience for the Soviet Union which has elicited a re-emergence of isolationist sentiments. One can only speculate whether prolonged Soviet pressures and frustrations in Afghanistan may, in the longer run, have this impact.

In brief, the above analysis leads us to expect American and Soviet foreign policy to oscillate within the same spectrum and to tend toward similar 'globalism/enemy image' currents. These similarities flow from the interplay of historical 'lessons,' ideological beliefs, and decision-making structures.

Notes

1. Zbigniew Brzezinski (1967: 6) even considers the United States *'dogmatically undogmatic.'*
2. An example in point is the comparative analysis of American and Soviet 'political ideas' in Brzezinski and Huntington (1964: 24). Admitting that 'in some respects they perform the same political function,' the authors confine the term *ideology* to Soviet political ideas and prefer to speak of American *political beliefs.*
3. Alexander Yanov (1977) testifies to the continuity with older Russian thought and predicts the resurrection of a 'Neo-Byzantine' orientation of political thought in the Soviet Union, a strategy of imperial isolation geared toward restoring order and discipline to the Soviet 'bloc' rather than conquering or subjugating the 'rotten West.'

3 Differences: Potential Influence

Introduction

The previous chapter focused on certain aspects of the historical background, ideology and bureaucratic structure of the two super-powers which point in the direction of possible foreign policy similarities. This should not be taken to imply that the impact of these background factors is inevitable and unequivocal. There are other aspects of these background factors where the United States and the USSR differ, some of which were noted intermittently in the preceding analysis. For instance, the Russian historical experiences of insecurity and successive invasions contrast with the relative security and absence of outside threats enjoyed by America. Though modified in the nuclear age, the resulting differences in the sense of threat and views on the harmonious/conflictual character of international politics have not been wholly eradicated.

Another — not entirely unrelated — difference concerns the political systems of the two superpowers. Although the foreign policy-making structures are similar, the two political systems obviously differ in terms of *accountability*. Whereas the American political leadership is accountable to the electorate at regular intervals, the Soviet leadership is not directly responsible before, and derives no legitimation from, the public. Furthermore, the American President is accountable to Congress. While the foreign policy role of Congress was for a long time negligible, Vietnam and Watergate ushered in a period of Congressional assertiveness in external affairs, challenging the 'imperial presidency' (cf. e.g., Franck and Weisband, 1979; Rystad, 1981). No corresponding 'checks and balances' exist in the Soviet policy-making system. In the Soviet case, 'ideology substitutes for the sanction of periodic popular approval, and a leadership struggle substitutes for the constitutional transfer of power' (Rakowska-Harmstone, 1976: 52). The effects of this difference are succinctly summarized by Brzezinski and Huntington (1964: 184):

The crucial differences in the two systems are that the American succession struggle occurs before the office is vacant, much of it takes place outside the operating components of the political system, and it has a formal conclusion with a regularized transfer of power. The Soviet struggle, in contrast, occurs after the office is vacant, even if it begins beforehand; it pervades the political system; and it has no formal conclusion.

The constitutional transfer of power in the United States entails transparency and openness, whereas the Byzantine power struggle in the USSR entails extraordinary secrecy. The foreign policy implications of these contrasts are less than clear. On the one hand, they raise the age-old issue of whether autocracies are better fitted to play the essentially undemocratic games of international politics where secrecy and continuity are at a premium. On the other hand, one could argue that the peculiarities of the American and the Soviet political systems may have somewhat symmetrical foreign policy impacts, inasmuch as they tend to complicate for others the conduct of relations with either superpower and the understanding of either's intentions. The fragmentation of authority, and the variety of expressed foreign policy views often makes it 'hard for the foreign representative to know who speaks for the American government as a whole and with whom it might be useful for him to speak' (Kennan, 1982: 30). These difficulties are compounded in election years. No less are the frustrations experienced by outsiders as a result of the uncertainty about the ups and downs of the perennial succession struggle in the Kremlin and the extraordinary Soviet passion for secrecy which 'prevents the Soviet authorities from revealing to outsiders even those aspects of their own motivation which, if revealed, would be reassuring to others and would redound to their own credit' (Kennan, 1982: 31).

The differences in accountability, in turn, entail differences in leadership *turnover*. American constitutionalized succession ensures a relatively rapid and regular turnover rate in the highest offices. The lack of regulated succession makes for less regular turnover in Soviet political leadership. Turnover accelerates during succession struggles and subsides in periods of consolidation. At the end of the Stalin period one could speak of a 'permanent purge' (Brzezinski, 1956). Under Khrushchev, the major upheaval was the purge of the 'anti-party group' in 1957 which drastically changed top-level leadership. After Khrushchev's fall, however, turnover rates have taken a sharp downturn. As a result, the average age of the full members of the Politburo has risen from 58 in 1966 to 70 in 1980 (Hough, 1980: 61). In

1978 the average age of the top Soviet leadership (including the Politburo, the Secretariat, the Presidium of the Council of Ministers, and the Presidium of the Supreme Soviet) was 65 years (Bialer, 1978: 189). And an incredible 89 percent of the living full members of the 1971 Central Committee were re-elected in 1976 (Hough, 1980: 63). The slow turnover applies to the foreign policy establishment as well. Of the fifteen persons identified as the inner core of top foreign policy officials in 1980, six had held their jobs for at least twenty years and another three had served in their posts for a decade or longer (Hough, 1980: 110–12).

In the context of foreign policy decision-making, turnover is significant for at least two reasons (cf. Brzezinski and Huntington, 1964: 173). First, differences in tenure may entail differences in power. Second, the rate of turnover may affect the way in which office holders are prepared for, and experienced in, their jobs. It could, for example, be argued that the power position of Soviet Politburo members is enhanced by their long tenure. And Soviet leaders have frequently reacted to less understood and/or liked aspects of the external conduct of newly inaugurated American presidents by referring to their 'inexperience' in foreign affairs.

It is difficult to assess the overall impact of such US–Soviet leadership differences on foreign policy. The present Soviet leadership's advantage in terms of experience may, for example, be offset by their advanced age and/or internal leadership struggles. In any event, the discussion of these basic dissimilarities in political system raises the question of relative American and Soviet power. In the remainder of this chapter I shall attempt to identify a 'causal chain' bearing upon the potential global influence of the superpowers. My argument turns on the differential impacts of capabilities, socio-economic systems, and the international system.

Capabilities

Because 'feasible goals of foreign policy must be matched by appropriate material and nonmaterial resources' (Knorr, 1975: 38), explanations of foreign policy behavior in terms of state *capabilities* have gained wide currency. Capabilities are commonly conceived of as more or less tangible state attributes. Although different authors include different attributes among state capabilities, there seems to be general consensus around a 'conventional cluster' (Petrén, 1976: 44) of capabilities, including the economic resources, geography, population, and military forces of a state. Traditionally, military capabilities have been considered to be of overriding importance; they provide the *ultima ratio* of states in their relations with each other.

As we have seen, most conceptions of 'superpower' focus on the global reach ensuing from the military might of the United States and of the Soviet Unon. It is therefore natural to begin a comparison of superpower capabilities with a brief overview of military capabilities. The brevity is prompted, partly, by the abundance of detailed treatments in the extant literature; partly, by my contention that excessive preoccupation with the military might of the superpowers tends to obscure significant differences in non-military capabilities.

Military Capabilities

Before 1945 there had been little similarity between American and Soviet military structures. Whereas the United States relied heavily on naval and air power, the standing army was the strongest element in Soviet forces.

> Technologically, therefore, the United States emerged from the war far better equipped than the Soviet Union for the ensuing military competition. At the war's end it possessed the capability of making atomic bombs and a means of delivery on distant targets, plus a navy that could reach the shores of any adversary. The USSR had no such ultimate weapon, no suitable delivery vehicle for such a weapon even if it had it, and no navy capable of distant operations. [Larson, 1978: 170]

For all its losses, the Soviet Union emerged from World War II as the strongest military power in Europe. Yet in terms of overall strength it was surpassed by the United States which had suffered no wartime damage to its economy or civilian population. The Soviets developed a nuclear capability with surprising speed, exploding their first atomic device in August 1949 and testing their first hydrogen bomb less than four years later, in September 1953. Despite Soviet nuclear achievements, the American superiority grew in the mid-1950s, as the United States expanded its nuclear stockpile and deployed large numbers of long-range bombers under the Strategic Air Command (SAC). The Soviet launching of Sputnik in 1957 heralded a Soviet lead in intercontinental ballistic missile (ICBM) technology and thus appeared to mark a new turning point in the strategic balance. The 'missile gap,' however, proved to be illusory, as the Soviet Union failed to convert its head start in missile technology into an operational missile force. Instead, Sputnik triggered intensified American efforts in the ICBM field which resulted in a marked American superiority which was to last into the early 1970s, when rough strategic parity between the superpowers seems to have been attained.

In the 1950s 'the United States on very short notice could have destroyed as much of the Soviet industry and population as it willed, secure in the belief that the Soviet retaliation against the United States would have been trifling' (Dinerstein, 1968: 39); however, sometime in the early or mid-1960s the Soviet nuclear-missile force acquired survivable, second-strike capability (cf. Schwartz, 1975: 53).

Since the mid-1950s, the two superpowers have together accounted for between 60 and 70 percent of the world total military expenditure. While the arms race between the superpowers was basically quantitative in the first two post-war decades, the subsequent stages of this race have been primarily qualitative. The superpowers are engaged in a technological race, focusing on what is called in civil life 'product improvement' rather than multiplication of existing weapons. This requires, above all, massive and ever-increasing inputs of research and development which further accentuate and widen the gap between the superpowers and the rest of the world. It has been estimated that during the 1960s the United States and the USSR together accounted for about 85 percent of the world's military research and development (SIPRI, 1976: 184).

The tremendous military superiority of the two superpowers applies to conventional forces as well. In terms of deployed manpower, China leads the two superpowers — 4.75 million men in 1981 as compared with 3.67 million in the USSR and 2.05 million in the United States (IISS, 1981: 112–13). Yet, in terms of another vital factor in power equations — the flexibility and mobility required to project forces abroad — American and Soviet superiority stand out clearly. The United States has traditionally derived global reach from its naval strength, designed to support American and allied forces overseas and to secure sealanes for commercial shipping. Since the mid-1960s, the Soviet Union has challenged American control of the seas by expanding the size and flexibility of Soviet naval forces and by developing amphibious landing capabilities. In the 1962–72 period the Soviet Union constructed over three times as many naval ships as did the United States, and today the Soviet navy 'shows the flag' over the oceans of the world (cf. Cline, 1975: 81–3). In addition, both superpowers have developed formidable airlift capabilities. Hence, the two superpowers alone can project their military power anywhere in the world, whereas other states have regional rather than global reach.

Divergent estimates of relative American and Soviet military strength abound. The diversity and complexity of present-day superpower weapons systems allow for a bewildering variety of comparisons. The USSR leads the United States in terms of numerical nuclear delivery vehicle strength and overall throw-weight, whereas American strategic forces are generally considered superior in accuracy, diversity and numbers of separately targetable nuclear warheads. Thus, two recent American and Soviet 'white books' (US Department of Defense, 1982; USSR Ministry of Defense, 1982) reach entirely different conclusions, each portraying an emerging margin of superiority for the other side.

Precise assessments of relative Soviet–American military strength may be impossible to make, but the trend over time is clear:

> The Soviet Union has been able substantially to erase the wide gap in strategic capabilities that existed at the end of World War II and during the two following decades. This was a period in which the United States lost, but the Soviet Union did not gain, an invulnerability to attack; it was a period in which each side's capability of inflicting damage on the other spiraled upward, leaving stagnant means of defense; and it was a period in which any major innovation of either country inspired the other to match or exceed the originator. [Larson, 1978: 184]

Rough parity seems to be the most plausible overall estimate of relative superpower military strength today, especially if one adheres to the view that in the nuclear age there is a threshold above which 'more' or 'less' loses its significance. Both superpowers have acquired second-strike capability, but neither has achieved a degree of invulnerability granting first-strike capability.

The relationship between the stupendous military might of the superpowers and global influence is not entirely evident (cf. Jönsson, 1979b). Several observers maintain that nuclear weapons have destroyed the previous direct correlation between military capabilities and political power (see e.g., Nash, 1975: 23). 'The paradox of contemporary military strength is that a gargantuan increase in power has eroded its relationship to policy,' says Henry Kissinger (1969: 59, 60), adding that nuclear capability 'no longer translates automatically into influence.' These lines, incidentally, have been quoted with approval by his Soviet colleague Georgi Arbatov (1970).

By invalidating the traditional continuity between threats and the overt use of the weapons on which the threats rest, nuclear weapons have elicited widespread and strong expectations of their non-use. Such expectations go a long way toward explaining observable limitations in the superpowers' exercise of power. It is, in other words, not the credibility of the nuclear *capability* that is reduced, but of the *intention* to use this capability. Hence the limitations of the seemingly boundless power base.

> Once it became clear that neither of the two rivals wanted to use (or could easily use) precisely that supply of power that made it one of the 'superpowers,' once it became clear that, being in a bottle, the two scorpions had lost some of their sting, other beasts decided they had their chance. [Hoffmann, 1968: 35]

In short, it is abundantly clear that the 'absolute' weapon does not confer upon either superpower any absolute power. Let us, therefore, next look behind the military facade and compare the geographic, demographic and economic capabilities of the two superpowers.

Geography

Territorial size, location, and borders are geographical factors which generally enter calculations of national capabilities.

Size. In terms of territorial size the Soviet Union is by far the largest country in the world. It occupies 8.6 million square miles, sprawls across large portions of two continents, and is more than twice the size of the United States.

The vastness of the Soviet Union may, however, be both an asset and a liability. On the one hand, great size allows for military maneuverability. Using a defense-in-depth strategy, Russia has been able to thwart the large-scale invasion attempts by Napoleon and Hitler. On the other hand, vast size poses difficult transportation problems. While two-thirds of the Soviet population and industry are to be found in European Russia, four-fifths of its energy resources are in Siberia (cf. Schwartz, 1975: 7).

Location. The Soviet preponderance in size is largely offset by its disadvantageous geographical location, its 'high latitude position.'

Virtually all of its territory lies north of the 45° parallel, and only the southern part of the Ukraine, the Caucasian and the Central Asian area are in the same latitude zones as the northern part of the United States (cf. Figure 6).

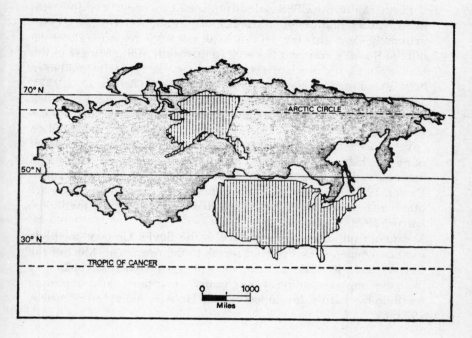

Source: Parker, 1972: 40

Fig. 6 Latitudinal position of the Soviet Union relative to the United States

The different global positions of the United States and the Soviet Union entail divergent climatic conditions. Generally speaking, the severe Russian climate contrasts strongly with the humid, temperate climate of the United States. The Soviet Union might derive some military benefits from this. 'General Frost' has, for example, joined 'General Distance' to blunt the invasions of both Napoleon and Hitler (Schwartz, 1975: 8). However, for the most part the climatic differences work to the disadvantage of the Soviet Union. Only about one-fourth of the Soviet Union's vast territory is arable or cultivated and much of the rest is permafrost, whereas the United States has nearly half of its territory in arable land or cultivated pasture. This factor thus scales the USSR down in size so that it roughly matches the United States (cf. Cline, 1975: 18).

Furthermore, the USSR is disadvantaged by its poorer endowment in the natural conditions of warmth, moisture and soil which makes for extremely short growing periods in all but a few regions. 'The great bulk of Russia's cropland lies well to the north of the latitude of the United States, and much of it is of such poor quality that it would have been abandoned long ago by American farmers' (Parker, 1972: 157). There is no area in the USSR comparable to the American corn belt where sun, moisture and soils combine to yield consistently high returns (Larson, 1978: 17). Thus, in the words of one geographer, 'given equal technology and capital inputs the Soviet Union can never hope to achieve . . . an average level of productivity from its cropland resource approaching that of the United States' (N.C. Fields, quoted in Parker, 1972: 149). Mining, transportation, housing and industry are other areas which are adversely affected by the climatic disparity (cf. Larson, 1978: 17–18).

Another important consequence of the Soviet Union's northerly location concerns its restricted access to the open seas. Most of the Soviet coast is ice-locked during the winter, which helps explain why 'with the longest coastline of any country, a maritime, naval, or trading tradition has hardly developed' (David Hooson, quoted in Schwartz, 1975: 8).

Borders. Bordering on two major oceans, the United States has common land frontiers with only two other states, which have neither threatened America militarily nor rivaled it in politico-economic power. The Soviet Union, by contrast, has common land frontiers with twelve states. Within five hundred miles of their territories lie four more countries in the case of America, eighteen more in the case of the Soviet Union (cf. Parker, 1972: 42). In terms of natural barriers, the Soviet Union is relatively inaccessible from the north, south and east, but its long western border with the rest of Europe lies unprotected. The United States, while traditionally enjoying protection from its remoteness, is more accessible; its borders with Canada and Mexico are easily passable. Yet, while the exposed western frontier has been a constant source of Soviet vulnerability and a major invasion route of foreign armies, easy access has facilitated the development of commercial and cultural ties betwen the United

States and Canada. Although the significance of natural barriers has been diminished by recent developments in transportation and weapons technology, the need for secure and defensible frontiers in the west continues to occupy a prominent position among the worries of Soviet leaders (cf. Schwartz, 1975: 8–9). In the words of Colin Gray (1981: 14), 'it is the geopolitical inheritance of the USSR to believe that "boundaries are fighting places." '

All in all, it is difficult not to agree with Paul Dukes' (1970: 20) conclusion with regard to geographical factors:

> If, as is often alleged, the twentieth-century struggle is indeed between godless Communism and Christian democracy, there can be no doubt that the Almighty weighted the scales in favour of his principal adherents and against his chief adversaries when he arranged the basic geographical conditions of the U.S.A. and the U.S.S.R.

Demography

In terms of population size, the United States (232 million) and the Soviet Union (262 million) are dwarfed by India (684 million) and China (1.1 billion). Like territorial size, however, great numbers may be a mixed blessing. In assessing the strengths and weaknesses of a population base, one must take into account the entire demographic mix, including not only the size but also the growth, age and sex composition, geographical distribution, homogeneity, and education of the population.

Population growth. There are obvious historical differences between the population of the United States and that of Russia.

> Russian expansion involved much more incorporation of existing ethnic groups and much less settlement of free land. Moreover, because of the unimportance of immigration in Russian history, even the settlement of the more or less empty lands coming under Russian rule took the form principally of an eastward movement of population from the western part of the Russian Empire rather than of an influx of settlers from outside the country. In contrast, immigration was decisive in American expansion of both territory and population. [Larson, 1978: 20]

Thus, by the end of the nineteenth century the American population was growing more rapidly than the Russian. Owing to catastrophic population losses in this century — World War I, the revolution and civil war, famine, epidemics, collectivization, purges, and finally World War II — the Soviet population has not described a normal growth curve; according to one estimate (Feshbach: 1978:56), the Soviet population is today about one-half the size it would have been under normal conditions. In World War II alone the Soviet Union suffered some twenty million casualties.

The population of the United States, in contrast, has grown at a more even and normal rate. American losses in World War II numbered less than 300,000, and American casualties in the Korean and Vietnamese wars have had no significant impact on population size. The effect of American wartime losses is much less than that of car accidents which have caused well over a million deaths in the United States since 1945. Hence, whereas in 1940 the population of the USSR was 47 percent greater than that of the United States, in 1970 it was only 18 percent greater (cf. Parker, 1972: 205). Existing and projected demographic trends entail manpower supply problems for the USSR which are expected to continue throughout the remainder of this century (cf. Feshbach, 1978: 56).

Age and sex composition. The age composition of the American population corresponds more closely to the ideal 'population pyramid' than does the ill-balanced Soviet profile resulting from the demographic catastrophes mentioned above, which affected not only the age groups in which they took place but also, through reduced birth rates, coming generations with 15–45 year intervals (Parker, 1972: 208).

The fact that the male population bore the brunt of the large wartime Soviet demographic losses has resulted in a pronounced sex imbalance. At the time of the 1959 census, males accounted for only 45 percent of the Soviet population. By 1970, the share had risen to 46.1 percent, and the figure for the 1979 census is 46.6 percent. This indicates a decelerating 'recovery' rate during the last decade. The Soviet sex ratio is expected to be below 'normal' into the next century (Feshbach, 1978: 56). The distribution between the sexes in the United States, by contrast, roughly follows the normal — in 1979 males accounted for 48.7 percent of the United States population (UN, 1979a).

Geographical distribution. The main difference between the superpowers concerns the distribution between urban and rural areas. While the flight from the countryside into cities continues in both superpowers, the Soviet rural population is still remarkably large for a modern industrial economy. In 1970 44 percent of the Soviet population lived in rural areas, as compared with the corresponding American figure of 26.5 percent (Schwartz, 1975: 14). And still in 1980 rural residents constituted 37 percent of the Soviet population (Hedlund, 1983: 13).

In comparison with the United States, the Soviet Union is still in mid-urbanization. The mass movement of people from the farm to the city, which has virtually been completed in the United States, still goes on in the Soviet Union and will continue into the twenty-first century. [Hough, 1980: 19]

Homogeneity. Neither superpower is ethnically homogeneous. Both are dominated by European peoples, but both have large minorities of non-European peoples. The federal structure of government in the USSR is composed of territorial units delimited according to major ethnic concentrations, whereas ethnic diversity has played no role in American federalism. This means that the 'nationality problem' assumes special significance in the Soviet Union (cf. below, p. 98). Another specific trait of the Soviet Union is the marked decline in the birth rate among the Slavic population, coupled with sharply increasing birth rates in the Central Asian and Transcaucasian republics. In 1959, the Great Russians formed 54.6 percent of the total population, in 1970 53.4 percent, and in 1979 52.4 percent (Feshbach, 1982: 35). The annual growth rate of the Great Russian population was only 0.70 percent in the 1970–9 inter-censal period, as compared to 2.47 for the population of Muslim origin (Feshbach, 1982: 29). In 1979 the youngest age cohorts — 0 to 9 years — accounted for only 14–16 percent of the population in the Slavic and Baltic republics, as compared to 29–30 percent of the population in Tadzhikistan, Turkmenistan, and Uzbekistan. The trend is furthermore toward increased differentials, and it has been estimated that 'by the year 2000, the youngest cohorts of the six Muslim republics will total some 85 percent of the total for cohorts in the same 0 to 9 years of age in the RSFSR' (Feshbach, 1982: 33).

These differentials in population growth entail labor shortages in the traditional regions of industrial concentration and economic growth, whereas the main labor increments are in the less industrialized regions (cf. d'Encausse, 1979: 33). This imbalance is aggravated by the fact that 'Soviet Muslims have shown little propensity to migrate out of their native republics, little enough out of Central Asia' (Rywkin, 1979: 3). The unbalanced population growth will also have a major impact on the nationality structure of future draftees for the armed forces.

> In the year 2000 the 'less trustworthy' border populations will comprise almost three-quarters as much as the Russian Republic's potential military personnel, compared with somewhat over one-third in 1970. The military will need to train non-Slavic, primarily rural cohorts in the Russian language and to introduce them to the technology of modern armed forces. [Feshbach, 1978: 59]

There is no American counterpart to these specific Soviet problems of ethnic imbalance. Although the black, Hispanic and Asian ethnic groups display markedly higher rates of growth than the rest of the American population, they still constitute no more than 11, 6, and 1.5 percent respectively of the total population (cf. Newsweek, 1983: 20).

Education. Demographic capability assessments involve not only quantitative but also qualitative elements. In our age of advanced technology, it is no longer so much a matter of how many 'hands' are available for employment and conscription as how many trained brains. Consequently, the level of education must be included in an assessment of human resources.

At the time of the Russian revolution, less than 30 percent of the Russian population were literate, as opposed to over 90 percent in the United States. Heavy Soviet investment in education after 1917, including literacy programs for adults, narrowed this gap, and by 1945 the USSR had also reached a 90-plus percentage rate of literacy (Larson, 1978: 22). While their educational systems differ, both superpowers today spend similar amounts on education and the number of students enrolled at different levels is impressive.

Measured in terms of the proportion of the entire population given access to, and graduating from, higher-level educational institutions, the United States leads the Soviet Union by a rough 2:1 ratio (cf. Brzezinski, 1976: 27). The 'brain drain,' from which America benefits, further accentuates the American advantage in the educational field.

In sum, the Soviet Union, despite its numerical edge, seems to be in a more disadvantageous position than the United States as far as human capabilities are concerned. Specifically, the uneven population growth, the ill-balanced age and sex structure, and the imbalanced growth of nationalities present critical problems for the Soviet supply of labor and of draftees for the armed forces and, ultimately, for economic efficiency and growth.

Economic Capabilities

Both superpowers are richly endowed with natural resources. The mineral wealth of the United States is less abundant and lacks the universality of the Soviet resources. On the other hand, the unfavorable natural environment of the USSR imposes serious disadvantages. Moreover, in the economic, as in the demographic, sphere, the relatively continuous and even development of the United States contrasts with the dramatic irregularities and recurring catastrophes which characterize Soviet economic history.

On the eve of World War I the United States had already become the world's greatest industrial power, whereas Russian industrial output, constituting one-eighth of the American output, rated below that of Britain, France and Germany (Larson, 1978: 24). The Soviet Union suffered immense destruction during both World War I and the revolution, so that when the first five-year plan was launched in 1928, the Soviet economy had just barely recovered to its pre-war levels. Through enormous efforts, involving costly and harsh methods, great progress was achieved, while at the same time the United States was sliding into the Great Depression. Yet the USSR was, in 1941, economically and militarily weaker than its German attackers, and the economic damages suffered as a result of the war were staggering. Stalin's reconstruction program, however, largely succeeded in rehabilitating the productive capacity of basic Soviet industry, and today the Soviet economy is the second largest in the world (cf. Schwartz, 1975: 20–4).

Yet the gap between American and Soviet economic capabilities is considerable. In 1950 the Soviet GNP amounted to only 34 percent of the United States GNP. Rising to some 47 percent by the late 1960s (Schwartz, 1975: 25), the Soviet GNP in 1979 was 45.5 percent of the United States value (UN, 1979b). Given the larger Soviet population, the USSR lags even further behind in terms of GNP per capita, where it ranks below not only several Western countries but also some of its East European allies, such as East Germany and Czechoslovakia (and the leading United States position is rivaled by small West European states, such as Switzerland and Sweden, and oil-rich countries, such as Kuwait) (cf. Cline, 1975: 148–51).

GNP figures, however, give only a rough sense of overall economic capabilities. The discrepancies between America and the Soviet economy are, for instance, much less pronounced in the industrial sector where the USSR, as a result of its deliberate policy favoring heavy industry, in some instances (such as iron ore and steel production) leads the United States. On the other hand, in the agricultural and consumer sectors the Soviet Union lags far behind.

In 1976 Soviet consumption per capita was estimated at roughly 35 percent of the American level (Bergson, 1981: 33). Agriculture continues to be the Achilles heel of the Soviet economy. In the Soviet Union a larger land area is cultivated than in the United States, yet it produces about one-sixth less total output value (Millar, 1977: 9). Only after World War II did the proportion of agricultural workers in the total labor force of the Soviet Union drop below one-half, a stage reached in the United States by the 1870s (Larson, 1978: 37). While today less than 4 percent of the American labor force employed in agriculture produce a food supply well above domestic needs, Soviet farmers, constituting some 20 percent of the total labor force, fulfill their planned objectives only erratically. And since Soviet agriculture accounts for over one-fifth of the GNP, a disproportionately large figure for an industrialized economy, poor performance in the agricultural sector tends to seriously affect the entire economy (cf. Schwartz, 1975: 27, 31; Hedlund, 1983: 6–12).

The adverse natural conditions of Soviet agriculture have already been mentioned. Yet the disparity in agricultural performance points to another crucial difference in the American and Soviet economies: that of labor productivity. In order to produce its much smaller GNP the USSR has had to employ about the same number of workers in the industrial sector as the United States, and seven times as many in farming (Larson, 1978: 37). According to official Soviet statistics, the output per worker in Soviet industry was 40–50 percent of that of their American counterpart in 1963 (Schroeder, 1970: 21). And Murray Feshbach (1978: 62) estimates the current labor productivity of Soviet basic workers at about 70–75 percent of the American level, while the productivity of the numerous auxiliary workers (85 for every basic worker in the USSR, as compared with 38 per 100 in the United States) is at a level of only 20–25 percent.

This 'productivity gap' is largely the result of a technological lag. With the exception of a few defense-oriented priority sectors, the level of Soviet technology is far behind that of the United States. Nowhere is this as evident as in the production and utilization of computers. The inability to sell Soviet products in foreign markets also testifies to the technological backwardness of the Soviet civilian economy (cf. Schwartz, 1975: 31). While profit-seeking competition in the United States provides strong incentives for technological advance, Soviet firms have more disincentives than incentives to innovate. The introduction of new equipment and methods delays fulfilment of the plan, and new proposals must go through a labyrinthine process of bureaucratic approvals. Soviet research breakthroughs are either never developed, developed only for military purposes, or developed only after considerable delay (cf. Parker, 1972: 136–9; Schwartz, 1975: 32; Brzezinski, 1976: 157; Smith, 1976: 232–5).

To be sure, a parallel may be found in the economic slowdown experienced by both superpowers in recent years. The decline of the dollar, 'stagflation,' energy crises and unemployment have become well-publicized aspects of the American economy. There is no dearth of alarmist voices. Interestingly enough, these do not include Soviet *amerikanisty* who have shown considerable reluctance to see profound implications in the American economic difficulties and continue to view American economic strength as essentially durable (see Schwartz, 1978: 8–17).

Concurrently, the Soviet Union has entered a period of decelerating economic growth or even stagnation. There is considerable agreement among Western analysts that the recent decline in the rate of growth will inevitably continue through the 1980s. Hence:

> In the 1980s the Soviet Union will not be able to appear to be an economic super-power even if the state of affairs in the West were not to improve. On the contrary, the development gap between the USSR and the main Western powers will stabilize, leaving the USSR at an intermediate level. [Sokoloff, 1979: 34]

The Soviet economic decline has in recent years extended to the external sphere, where a rapidly growing trade deficit and hard-currency debt to the West are aggravated by the mounting debt burdens of its East European allies (cf. e.g., Höhmann, 1982).

In brief, despite its undeniable achievements, the Soviet economy has been, and continues to be, second to the United States in most respects. The only Soviet advantage seems to be in terms of raw materials and energy resources where the USSR is virtually self-sufficient (though oil production is an uncertain prospect), whereas the United States is dependent on imports of several vital items. On the other hand, the major Soviet weaknesses appear to lie in the fields of agriculture and technology. The vulnerability following from these shortcomings is suggested by the increasing Soviet reliance on imports of grain and advanced technology from the West.

Aggregate Capabilities

How are we, then, to make an aggregate assessment of American and Soviet capabilities? The same problem arises as in assessing the interrelationship and relative potency of different independent variables explaining foreign policy in general. Is the relationship between different capabilities 'additive' or 'multiplicative'? And how are we, for instance, to weigh economic capabilities *vis-à-vis* military capabilities? The common approach of adding up the different capability components according to some kind of measurement and weighting formula seems as dubious as studying explanatory variables separately and then adding them together.

Yet, just as in the explanation of foreign policy generally, reliance on a 'non-additive' model entails methodological problems. If we cannot just add individual capability components, how are we to grasp the complex interplay between different components? One step in that direction is to employ correlation analysis (in order to determine which capability indicators are strongly correlated with each other) and cluster analysis (in order to detect patterns of mutually correlated indicators). One quantitative cross-polity study along these lines (Petrén, 1976) indicates that most capability indicators correlate strongly with each other, that a 'conventional cluster' of economic and military capability indicators can be identified, and that the one indicator correlating most strongly with other indicators in recent years (and thus suitable as a shorthand capability index) is energy consumption.

Whichever method is employed, virtually all analysts agree that the United States and the Soviet Union rank above all other states. Moreover, there is broad consensus as to the overall American lead *vis-à-vis* the USSR. Though ranking higher than all other states, the Soviet Union is second to the United States in all capabilities except military ones. According to one quantitative estimate (Petrén, 1976: 49), the United States accounts for about one-third of the total 'conventional' capabilities of the world, whereas the Soviet share amounts to some 15 percent. Other states trail behind with shares of 5 percent or less of the world total.

The same overall pattern emerges if we use energy consumption as a shorthand index of aggregate capabilities. The United States lead over the USSR is considerable (roughly a 2:1 ratio), but not as great as the gap between the superpowers, on the one hand, and other states, on the other (Petrén, 1976: 91).

Socio-economic Systems

The US–Soviet gap in overall capabilities, I shall argue, is compounded by differences in social and economic systems. To say that the American and Soviet socio-economic systems are different follows the conventional wisdom. The two superpowers are commonly regarded as the chief exponents of antithetical economic systems. The United States is a market economy, governed by the free operation of the laws of supply and demand, where economic decisions are made by individual producers and consumers. The Soviet Union, in contrast, is an administered or command economy in which administrative bodies make decisions for the whole economy. Social systems are frequently defined and classified in terms of economic relationships. And the distinction between the 'socialist' Soviet society and 'capitalist' American society is propounded by Marxists and non-Marxists alike.

To be sure, there are analyses suggesting the convergence of the American and Soviet economic systems. Chinese propaganda contends that such convergence has, in fact, already occurred, insofar as the Soviet Union has gone capitalist. A number of Western analysts, on the other hand, argue that recent changes in the two economic systems suggest a future convergence in a novel system which is neither capitalist nor socialist, in the same way that two streams merge and lose their previous identity in the new river. In the Soviet Union some market mechanisms have been infused through economic reforms in the past decade. Concurrently, planning and state intervention have assumed greater importance in the American economy.

There are also theories predicting the ultimate convergence of the American and Soviet social systems. These are based on the argument that modern industrial practices require and dictate the emergence of common cultures and values and similar forms of social organization. The resulting society is labeled 'post-industrial' (Bell, 1973) or 'technetronic' (Brzezinski, 1976). In these conceptualizations, the changed significance of science and technology in industrial development rather than the ownership of the means of production is seen as the main determinant, and the resulting mass consumption society is characterized, *inter alia*, by the centrality of the professional and theoretical class.

While recognizing the universal significance of the 'scientific-technological revolution,' the Soviets vigorously deny the ensuing convergence of capitalist and socialist society. Soviet theorists strongly affirm that it is the social system in which the achievements of the scientific-technological revolution are *used*, not those in which they are *generated*, which will shape the purposes served and the social effects: the net effect is progressive and constructive under socialism, exploitative and degenerative under capitalism (cf. Gouré *et al.*, 1973; Laird, 1975; Laird and Hoffmann, 1980).

I shall not delve deeper into the debate over convergence theories which seldom addresses the question of the possible foreign policy impact of trends in the American and Soviet socio-economic systems. Instead I propose two fundamental aspects of relevance to foreign policy where the United States and the Soviet Union diverge. One concerns the international ramifications of the economy and society; the other the autonomy of the economic and social systems.

International ramifications. Theories of *imperialism* ascribe to leading capitalist powers a penchant for aggressive expansionism. While the European colonial powers served as the prototype of the classic imperialism theories, the United States has been singled out as the prime symbol of modern imperialism. Marxist-inspired theories of imperialism are characterized by economic determinism. In Lenin's classic formulation, imperialism is inexorably linked with capitalism; it is, in fact, the highest stage of capitalism. Similarly, a number of contemporary radical analysts contend that America's foreign policy is essentially a response to the structural needs of American capitalism. While Lenin and other early theorists focused upon the need to find new markets for surplus goods and overseas outlets for investment capital, as the motive force of aggressive expansionism, modern theorists have pointed to the need to import scarce raw materials as a supplementary — or alternative — factor determining American foreign policy. In the neo-Marxist perspective, American foreign investment and trade, American enterprises abroad, and the dependence on raw materials sources abroad for modern technology, all contribute to the need for the United States to control its external environment. The imperatives of control guide American foreign policy. The American policies of intervention, military alliances, foreign bases, military and development aid as well as the United States assumption of world banking leadership and the domination of the dollar as a world currency (at least until the 1970s) follow from this striving for control (cf. e.g., Magdoff, 1969; Kolko, 1969; Fann and Hodges, 1971).

The critics of explanations of American foreign policy in terms of imperialism argue along the following lines (cf. e.g., Tucker, 1971; Aron, 1974): First, the United States, like the Soviet Union, appears to be all but self-sufficient. The ratio of its foreign trade to its gross national product is only between 4 and 5 percent, a very low figure by international standards. And while American investment abroad is indeed impressive in its sheer magnitude as well as its dramatic rate of growth, its significance for the domestic economy, in terms relative to this economy, is more modest. Moreover, the bulk of American foreign assets and investments is to be found in industrialized Western countries where investment does not necessarily result in control. Finally, America's dependence on foreign raw materials sources should not be overestimated. In the case of most raw materials, American imports are merely a question of convenience, since the United States either possesses them — in which case scarcity means scarcity of high-yield deposits — or has the technology to provide substitution, whether vertical (one raw material for another) or horizontal (a synthetic substance for a raw material). The United States, in other words, is better off in this respect than most other industrialized countries, save the Soviet Union. The Japanese and the Europeans, for example, are much more dependent on foreign raw materials sources.

It is also worth noting that Soviet analysts do not consider the problem of raw material shortages a terribly serious one for American economic development (cf. Schwartz, 1978: 14). Contemporary Soviet Americanists have also modified the orthodox Marxist tenet of a direct causal link between 'monopoly capital' and an aggressive, militaristic foreign policy (Schwartz, 1978: 19–23).

No elaborated theory linking non-capitalist economic systems with foreign policy behavior has been developed and subjected to such thorough and critical discussion as the theories of imperialism. The obvious corollary of the Marxist conceptualization of imperialism — that socialism entails peaceful foreign policy behavior — has, of course, been dwelt on by the Soviet Union. Yet it has not appeared entirely convincing in view of the historical record. Soviet propaganda has justified temporary aberrations from the peaceful path by the continued existence of predatory capitalism, arguing that only in a system of socialist states are genuinely peaceful relations possible. Its critics, on the other hand, have pointed to the vehemence of the Sino-Soviet split in refutation of such claims. It is also significant that Marxist critics of Soviet foreign policy have found it necessary, first, to re-evaluate the Soviet economic system and to demonstrate its basically capitalist nature (state monopoly capitalism) in order, then, to analyze Soviet foreign policy in terms of imperialism (social imperialism). This has been the line followed by China as well as Maoist-inspired analysts in the West.

Even if we deny any deterministic relation between a capitalist economic system and aggressive expansionism, on the one hand, and between a socialist economic system and peaceful foreign policy, on the other, there still remain significant dissimilarities between the American and the Soviet economies in their differing international orientations and ramifications.

The disparities in American and Soviet economic strength after World War II had world-wide repercussions.

America's role in the first postwar decade depended greatly on the fact that the U.S. was the single large, undamaged storehouse upon which the rest of the world could draw, or hope to draw, for postwar reconstruction and development. Consequently, Washington was in a position to use its economic assets to promote its foreign policy objectives. These included the stabilization of the capitalist order and the prevention of anticapitalist shifts, the creation of alliances linking non-Communist countries with the United States under U.S. leadership, and the concomitant spread of American influence through both the industrially developed and underdeveloped countries. In contrast, the Soviet Union was weaker economically at the end of the war than at the beginning in absolute terms (if not relative to other war-damaged countries), and especially in comparison to the United States. Specifically, the USSR was in no position to use economic assistance as a means of consolidating its position in states coming under Soviet influence, still less to use economic reprisals against adversaries. Russia was itself in need of aid. [Larson, 1978: 59–60]

The establishment of Soviet influence in Eastern Europe was not eased by any economic aid comparable to the US Marshall Plan. On the contrary, it involved involuntary 'aid' flows from Eastern Europe to the USSR. Furthermore, the Soviet Union was the first post-war victim of the American capability to apply economic sanctions. Lacking resources for economic warfare, the USSR, by contrast, has not applied economic sanctions outside the socialist camp.

Though no longer as glaring as in the immediate post-war period, the differences in international ramifications of the American and Soviet economies persist. While foreign trade and investment constitute important parts of the American economy, the Soviet economic system is characterized by greater autarky. In absolute terms, the annual United States trade turnover is more than three times that of the USSR; and American trade represents about 12 percent of total world trade, as compared to the Soviet figure of roughly 4 percent. The area composition of Soviet trade is, moreover, considerably less diversified than that of the United States. More than half of total Soviet trade is with other socialist states. Economic relations are, of course, not limited to bilateral interstate transactions. As a market economy, the United States participates far more than the USSR in multilateral economic relations and plays a predominant role in private transnational relations from which the planned economies are absent. In the realm of foreign investment, the differences are especially glaring between the virtual lack of Soviet activity and the staggering scale of American enterprises abroad, which would in the aggregate comprises one of the largest economic entities in the world, with a gross product greater than that of all countries except the United States itself, the Soviet Union, Japan, West Germany, France, and Britain (Woodruff, 1975: 81).

These dissimilarities have obvious foreign policy implications. The foreign economic activity of the United States creates a broad variety of interests and commitments which American foreign policy-makers have to take into account and are often called upon to protect. It also contributes to perceptions of vital American stakes in the internal developments and events of other countries. For the Soviet Union, the corresponding 'pull' factors resulting from foreign economic activity are negligible.

Just as the American economy has global ramifications, so American society, more than any other, maintains linkages with the entire globe. The American way of life is massively disseminated by means of movies, television, magazines, and a wide variety of

American products. American society, Brzezinski (1976: 34–5) concludes, has emerged as 'the first global society in history' and has become 'increasingly difficult to delineate in terms of its outer cultural and economic boundaries.'

Soviet society, by contrast, is far more secluded. In comparison with American society, it maintains far less contacts with, and has a negligible impact on, the outside world. To mention just one small but not insignificant example, some 5 million American tourists went abroad in 1970, and Americans accounted for 30 percent of the total amount spent on international travel (see Woodruff, 1975: 65). The number of Soviet citizens who are allowed to go abroad, though difficult to ascertain, amounts to no more than a few hundred thousand per year, most of whom make short visits to other socialist countries (Matthews, 1978: 51). Moreover, Soviet society is no longer a source of inspiration or model for the rest of the world. The Soviet Union has by and large lost its prestige as the first socialist society or as the center of Marxism-Leninism (cf. Aron, 1979: 3).

In short, American global presence contrasts with Soviet seclusion. These global linkages give the United States greater access — but also render it more accessible — to influence relations with other countries. Through its global web of economic and cultural ties the United States has far more 'strings to pull,' and the internationalized 'American way of life' ensures greater responsiveness to United States demands abroad. By the same token, these multiple global ties make the United States more sensitive and responsive to outside pressures than the more insulated Soviet Union.

Autonomy. The degree of political control is another important criterion by which the American and Soviet economies and societies can be differentiated. The cornerstones of American economic policy have traditionally been free enterprise, free competition, and free world trade; whereas the pillars on which Soviet economic policy has been built are a priority system for resource allocation favoring heavy industry, a command system of planning and management, and foreign trade autarky. Similarly, while American society is characterized by limited and dispersed control and a large sphere of private morality, monopoly of control and a restricted sphere of private morality are associated with Soviet society.

The historical roots of Soviet 'totalitarianism' and American 'pluralism' are frequently cited. The governmental absolutism of tsarist rule is seen as the forerunner of present-day Soviet controls, in the same way that contemporary American society was shaped by early immigrants as an antithesis to the oppression that they had escaped. Americans and Russians, therefore, differ in their attitudes toward power and authority; whereas inbred mistrust of authority is an American tradition, 'six centuries of authoritarian rule from Ivan the Great and Ivan the Terrible forward had made Russians monarchists in their bones long before Lenin and Stalin came along' (Smith, 1976: 250).

Opportunities for the articulation of support and demands from society at large are incomparably greater in the American system, founded on free expression and the free flow of communication, in comparison with the Soviet system of controlled and compartmentalized communication and a limited range of free expression. In the field of foreign policy this entails, first, differences in terms of information about the international environment. The foreign reporting of the controlled Soviet media is scanty and fragmentary, and Soviet citizens in general do not have access to alternative sources of information, such as foreign travel and foreign mass media. Moreover, in addition to being less informed about the outside world, Soviet citizens also have fewer opportunities to articulate their opinions and exert pressure on foreign policy-makers. To mention one obvious example, no counterpart to the activities and the weight of the American anti-war movement in the 1970s could conceivably exist in the Soviet Union.

Nor does multi-ethnicity have the same direct and tangible impact on foreign policy in the USSR as it does in the United States. Since the beginning of the twentieth century, ethnic groups, which couple loyalty to America with bonds of affection for their country of origin, have tried to influence American foreign policy by lobbying.

So far had the process advanced by the mid-1970s — with Jews and Greeks exercising well-proven clout, blacks bringing increasing influence to bear on American policy toward Africa, and Hispanics (including many illegals) looming as the next prospective major ethnic political force — that by 1975 it could be plausibly argued, as it was by Nathan Glazer and Daniel P. Moynihan, that the immigration process could be considered 'the single most important determinant of American foreign policy.' Foreign policy, they wrote, 'responds to other things as well, but probably first of all to the primal facts of ethnicity.' [Mathias, 1982: 32]

Although there is some evidence of growing attention among regional Soviet leaders to foreign policy matters in recent years (Hauslohner, 1981) and of dissenting standpoints by Ukrainian, Belorussian and Baltic party bureaucrats over the invasion of Czechoslovakia in 1968 (Valenta, 1979), the 'nationality problem' does not have an equally immediate impact on Soviet foreign policy. However, suppressed nationalism in the USSR represents a volcano which may well erupt in the future. In the longer run, then, nationalism in the Soviet Union probably constitutes a graver societal stress than the open and legitimate lobbying by ethnic groups in the United States.

In sum, the United States and the Soviet Union differ markedly concerning the extent of control over society by the polity. The incomparably greater political control over society in the USSR endows Soviet foreign policy with an outward appearance of consensus and coherence, while American foreign policy often appears more volatile, equivocal, and incoherent due to the lack of control over a diversified society. This difference is commonly thought to favor the Soviet Union. In the estimate of one observer (Cline, 1975: 125), 'the fact that the USSR has a coherent strategy and a tightly controlled population multiplies the brute power it projects into the international arena.'

Such assertions about a unilinear relation between a controlled society and international influence seem too simplified, however. One could well argue that American foreign policy derives a certain degree of moral strength and legitimacy from the government's greater interaction with, and responsiveness to, society.

At any rate, the possible advantages in terms of international influence that the Soviet government may enjoy as a result of its control over society are offset by the disadvantages accruing from the seclusion and scant international links of the Soviet socio-economic system.

The International System

The differentials in potential power identified in the preceding discussion of non-military capabilities and socio-economic systems are amplified by certain trends in the international system as a whole. It should be noted at the outset that international systemic factors are rarely adduced in explanations of superpower foreign policy. The reason for this is fairly obvious. The superpowers are generally seen as shaping the international system rather than as being influenced by it. The existence of another superpower is considered to be the only restriction on a superpower's freedom of action and superpower relations are regarded as one of the principal factors determining the state of the international system (cf. Goldmann, 1978: 94). Robert Keohane (1969: 295–6), for example, conceives of an international hierarchy headed by two 'system-determining' states — the United States and the Soviet Union — and with a majority of 'system-ineffectual' states. On the other hand, there are those who contend that superpowers may be more affected than other states by changes in the international system.

> Major and violent changes in an international system are unavoidably directed against the incumbent of major power in the system, just as revolutionary changes in a society cannot but affect the standing of the social elite. [Liska, 1967: 20]

Recent years have witnessed heated discussions among international relations scholars about the changing international system. Has the 'anarchic' international system of the 'realist' school been replaced by a system characterized by 'complex interdependence'? Some argue that global changes have been so profound as to warrant a 'paradigm shift'; others have wondered whether it is really the world that has been transformed or the perceptions and attention of scholars that have changed to include new areas of international relations which had been previously overlooked. This debate has generated several stimulating and provoking ideas and insights as well as a considerable amount of confusion. In any event, it has brought into focus certain trends and tendencies in the post-war international system (which are not entirely created by the superpowers) to which we now turn our attention.

There are, first of all, some prominent developments which have had symmetrical implications for the two superpowers. The post-war international system has developed into a truly global one, which for the superpowers entails the risk of becoming victims of the 'malady of too many pies.'

> The argument is frequently made that the enormous nuclear power possessed by both the United States and the Soviet Union limits their effectiveness with respect to weaker states because their strength cannot usefully be translated into achieveable gains. Even

had nuclear weapons never been devised, however, both the United States and the Soviet Union would still be limited at present by the variety of their activities. The complexity of the present international hierarchy has combined with bipolarity at the top to create a situation where both superpowers are required to act in a wide variety of areas simultaneously, and this breadth of activity is inhibiting. [Spiegel, 1972: 233]

Whereas the superpowers have to disperse their attention over a huge number of games and players and cannot always keep their internal bureaucratic coalitions together, weaker states may benefit from 'the asymmetry of attention' and their greater cohesion and concentration (cf. Nye, 1974: 992; Hoffmann, 1978: 128).

Another troublesome development for both superpowers has been the gradual erosion of the markedly bipolar structure of the late 1940s and early 1950s. The 'Cold War coalitions' have been gradually disintegrating, at the same time as a growing number of nonaligned states have chosen to remain outside the superpower orbits.

The foundation of the bipolar coalition structure has been undermined, as the threat from the opponent has been perceived on both sides to be less acute. This development has given rise to non-military issues, primarily economic ones, as major subjects of bargaining within the coalitions which, in turn, reinforces the erosion of the coalitions. Moreover, the coalitions have gradually lost their earlier 'feudal' character, where interaction between the two blocs was mainly between the leading powers, lesser members rarely dealing bilaterally with members of the opposing camp (cf. Galtung, 1966). Now East-West contacts at different levels are expanding and have acquired legitimacy (see e.g., Brown, 1974: 7–119; Laux, 1981).

The other major modification of the tight bipolarity of the immediate post-war era has followed from the growing assertivenes on the part of peripheral states which, having consciously attempted not to enter the magnetic fields of the superpowers, are now beginning to challenge their dominant position. Ronald Steel (1977: 30) puts it well:

While America and Russia have been consumed by the struggle to restrain each other from attack and to spread their rival ideologies, the once-intimidated spectators have been straying off into the wings and setting up their own sideshows.

The attenuation of the East-West polarization has facilitated the emergence of North-South issues and polarization between rich 'have' countries and poor 'have-not' countries. It is not simply a question of the early bipolarity being superseded by new polarizations or diffusion, but rather of different structures being superimposed on — and partly intertwined with — each other.

> The new lines of interdependence by no means obliterate the cold war coalitions; rather they intersect or supplement the established patterns, sometimes contradicting, sometimes reinforcing them. [Brown, 1974: 109]

While it is thus possible to discern trends in the post-war international system which appear to corrode the leverage of both superpowers, there are at the same time evolutions which have asymmetrical impacts. First, the era following World War II has seen not only a dramatic increase in the number of states but also the rise of new types of actors and new interaction networks. International organizations have expanded at an exponential rate in terms of the number of persons engaged and nations represented, the types of questions dealt with, and the number of acronyms appropriated. In addition, a number of subnational and transnational actors have challenged the exclusive position of the state in the international system.

Second, the utility of military force as instrument of state interaction seems to have diminished. Klaus Knorr's (1966: 16) early hunch has since been echoed by many:

> Indeed, we strongly suspect that, during the past two decades, some means of international influence other than military power have — relative to the exertion of military strength — appreciated in value.

A third, related development is the expansion of issues on the international agenda. There is no longer a self-evident hierarchy of issues, headed by questions of military security. A number of issues which cannot readily be solved or affected by means of military force have moved to the top of the global agenda, in particular, economic ones.

As a result, the question has been raised as to whether it is any longer meaningful to speak of a single international system (cf. Goldmann, 1978; Lampert *et al.*, 1978). A more appropriate conceptualization might be in terms of 'multiple issue-based systems,' with each system featuring a unique case of actors dealing with a discrete set of issues, yet with linkages between systems either because of overlap among participant actors or because of the interdependence of the issues upon which they focus (Lampert *et al.*, 1978). In lieu of the classic 'billiard-ball' model in which international interaction is seen to be governed by the relative size and power of solid, impermeable units, this perspective evokes the imagery of 'a mass of cobwebs superimposed on one another, strands converging at some points more than others, and being concentrated between some points more than between others' (Burton, 1972: 43).

William Griffith (1975), for example, has described the emerging global pattern in terms of interlocking tripolar structures, with one political–military triangle, consisting of the United States, the Soviet Union, and China; and one economic triangle, made up by the United States, Western Europe, and Japan.

These three trends — the diversification of actors, the diminished utility of military force, and the changing international agenda — seem to have increased the potential influence of the United States relative to the Soviet Union. For instance, while the United States is a member of 1,366 international organizations, the corresponding Soviet figure is only 600. The headquarters of 350 international organizations are located in the United States, but only 26 in the Soviet Union (Yearbook of International Organizations, 1981). Furthermore, a majority of the important multinational corporations are American-based. It might be argued that communist parties and national liberation fronts around the world provide a Soviet counterpart to the MNCs; and thus that both superpowers are linked to transnational networks. However, Soviet links with communist parties and national liberation movements are tenuous. And it is obvious that the United States maintains more links on different levels with the emerging diversified international system than does the Soviet Union. Whereas the United States appears in most issue-based international 'cobwebs,' the Soviet Union is excluded from several crucial ones, especially in the economic sphere. In Griffith's (1975: 1) terms, the United States alone is a member of both the political–military and the economic great-power triangles.

As a result of being linked one way or another to a greater variety of international actors, issues and interactions, the United States seems to have greater potential for influence relationships than does the USSR. This, of course, may work two ways. On the one hand, the United

States is potentially more influential. On the other hand, by virtue of its global presence, the United States offers 'maximum hostage surface' to others (Hoffmann, 1978: 215). In other words, it is potentially more sensitive and vulnerable to outside pressure: sensitive in the sense of being liable to suffer costly effects imposed from outside, and vulnerable in the sense of being unable to offset these costs by altering policies in an effort to change the situation (cf. Keohane and Nye, 1977: 12–13). In Stanley Hoffmann's (1978: 127–8) words, 'the United States may be at the top of almost every hierarchy of economic power, but here, as in the strategic realm, it is a Gulliver tied, not a master with free hands.'

While the American global involvement in interdependence games posits the United States as influencer as well as influencee, the Soviet abstention from these games may entail lesser exposure to risk but also implies a serious limitation of influence opportunities. 'Even Moscow's military cornucopia, and its skillful political exploitation of quarries of radicalism, are no substitutes for the influence derived from interdependence' (Hoffmann, 1978: 130).

The reduced usefulness of military force affects in particular the Soviet Union, whose superpower status rests to such a great extent precisely on its military capability. No longer a source of ideological inspiration and with neither its economy, standard of living, nor 'way of life' appearing particularly impressive to the outside world, the USSR owes its superpower status to its military strength (cf. Aron, 1979: 3). The military is the only truly successful sector of Soviet society, and the conspicuous and internationally recognized military might also contribute to the internal legitimation of the Soviet regime (cf. Bertelman, 1983: 47). Contrary to the United States, which has a wide array of strings to pull internationally, the USSR relies heavily on military instruments for influence. The growing irrelevance of military might to the playing of international games and the solution of outstanding global issues means that the Soviet Union increasingly finds itself in the position of a gambler who, after trying hard for many years, finally gets the perfect poker hand — only to discover that the other players have turned to playing bridge.

Even if we adopt a less holistic perspective on the international system and turn to a consideration of the shifts in the 'great power system,' the differences between the two superpowers prevail. The United States has enjoyed relaxed tension with other major powers over the past decade — the normalization of its relations with China in the 1970s being the most dramatic shift in the 'great power system.'

The Soviet Union has thus become the only superpower to experience acute tension with another major power, engaging much of its energy, time and resources in the entangling Sino-Soviet conflict. For instance, one-fourth of all conventional Soviet troops are deployed east of Irkutsk, and the 45 divisions along the Chinese border outnumber the 31 stationed in Eastern Europe (Bertelman, 1983: 16).

An even more dramatic illustration of the Soviet Union's inferior position in the 'great power system' is the stark fact that all non-Soviet nuclear weapons in the world are today targeted on the Soviet Union. It is also significant that the term 'encirclement,' so prevalent in the heyday of the Cold War, is reappearing in Soviet commentaries (now without the prefix 'capitalist') after having been in abeyance ever since the Soviets began to derive greater self-confidence from their nuclear-missile capabilities (see Dallin, 1980a).

On balance, then, the Soviet Union, by standing alone in the 'great power system' at the same time as it remains on the whole absent from — and reluctant to enter — the games of economic interdependence, seems to be more negatively affected by recent changes in the international system than the United States by forgoing important influence potentials.

Potential Influence: Summary

The preceding survey of capabilities, socio-economic systems, and the international system suggest a 'causal chain' pointing in the direction of significant US–Soviet differences when it comes to potential influence. If one takes a hard look at the material foundation of the Soviet Union's superpower status, one must conclude that it is a superpower only in a *military* sense. Whereas the American economy and society have global reach, the Soviet economy is far less internationalized and Soviet society extremely secluded. Furthermore, the inferior Soviet economic strength is compounded by its unfavorable geographic conditions and adverse demographic trends. Developments in the international system tend to reinforce these differences. As the games of economic interdependence assume greater significance in world politics, Soviet inferiority *vis-à-vis* the United States becomes accentuated. As pointed out by Robert Legvold (1977: 58),

In an interdependent world, self-sufficiency is inefficiency, increasingly so in the Soviet Union, and the Soviet leadership knows it.

How much of a world power is a nation without much power in the world economy?

It should be noted that the foreign policy implications of the US–Soviet differences in potential power are not immediately apparent. With respect to the Soviet Union, Raymond Aron (1979: 7) poses the question thus:

We all know Machiavelli's maxim: the disarmed prophet perishes. What of the prophets who have lost their prophecy and retain their arms?

If, as Philip Windsor (1979: 8) has argued, the 'dialectics of weakness' is the framework in which to consider Soviet foreign policy, this need not imply abated globalism. The conclusion emerging from the preceding analysis of sources of superpower foreign policy is rather this: While equally prepared for the superpower role perceptually and institutionally, the two superpowers appear to differ in their potential for global leverage.

PART II: AMERICAN AND SOVIET FOREIGN POLICY BEHAVIOR

4 Aid Relations with the Third World

Introduction

Before embarking on a scrutiny of superpower behavior in three cases — aid relations with the Third World, crisis management in the Middle East, and nuclear nonproliferation — let us take our bearings. The preceding analysis of possible determinants of superpower behavior has provided us with certain working hypotheses related to our research questions. With respect to the first question — do the two superpowers behave similarly in foreign affairs? — we have hypothesized that possible similarities can be accounted for by the superpower role and a 'causal chain' of historical 'lessons', ideological beliefs, and decision-making structure. As for the second question — are the two superpowers equally powerful? — the potential global influence of the United States is hypothesized to be considerably greater than that of the Soviet Union. The third question — has a superpower 'condominium' been established? — concerns whether the US–Soviet similarities have been transformed into collaboration and whether the power bases of the two superpowers have been utilized for joint exercise of power. In search of answers to these issues, let us turn, first, to an examination of American and Soviet aid relations with the Third World.

The decolonization process triggered by the end of World War II produced an expanding number of independent 'developing' or 'less developed' states (LDCs). Though widely different in terms of resources, population, history, culture, and political systems, these countries shared the common goal of *development*, of 'catching up' with the developed countries. The Bandung Conference of 1955 constituted the first effort at creating Third World identity and cohesiveness.

The Chinese revolution of 1949 and the Korean War of 1950–3 heralded a transfer of the superpower confrontation from the European center stage to peripheral Third World arenas. While merely a 'pawn' in early US–Soviet clashes, the Third World was soon to attract more intense attention on the part of the superpowers. As the demands of the increasingly conscious and cohesive Third World countries grew more and more insistent and vociferous and, concomitantly, the emerging nuclear stalemate barred direct super-power confrontation, American and Soviet attitudes to the Third World changed from benign neglect to hopeful interest.

To both superpowers, the Third World promised to turn into the principal battleground of their global struggle. By moving the battle-ground to the fluid Third World the superpowers hoped to avoid the risk of nuclear confrontation; and as the battleground shifted, so did the struggle itself. It now became not so much a political and military combat as an ideological and economic one — a campaign to convert allies and prove the superiority of one's development model.

Both combatants came heavily armed with historical 'lessons' drawn from their own past. The United States and the Soviet Union were both free of the stigma of colonialism, and both tried to capitalize on their non-colonial record and their professed anti-imperialist ideals in their efforts to establish authority among Third World countries. Both superpowers envisaged an evolution from backward toward more developed economies, and both saw industrialization as the key to such development. This 'common industrial ideology' emphasized technological and scientific achievements (cf. Horowitz, 1966: 63).

However, divergent attitudes to development flowed from their respective histories of nation-building. The United States with its 'remarkable achievement of converting society from agriculture to industry with minimal friction' by means of 'technological compen-sation for problems of the transition period' (Horowitz, 1966: 99) tended to be optimistic about the prospects for social change in the Third World and to believe that significant changes could result from marginal investments. The Soviets, on the other hand, tempered by their revolutionary experience, tended to be less sanguine and to view social change as a brutal and costly process involving massive assaults on the existing order (cf. Pye, 1960).

Development Aid

Foreign aid is not an entirely new phenomenon in the history of international politics. Subsidies and bribes have been established means of influencing foreign princes throughout the ages. Yet large-scale aid for the economic development of foreign countries is essentially an American innovation. World War II left vast areas of the world devastated. The economies of these regions could not recover without outside help, which only the United States could provide.

The enunciation of the Truman Doctrine in 1947 involved a massive program of foreign aid to Greece and Turkey, which set a precedent for the entire range of foreign aid programs which soon followed. Foreign aid became firmly based in the Cold War frame of reference. Aid could easily be justified as preventive action designed to avoid Greek-type insurgencies which might require even more costly military intervention (cf. Schurmann, 1974: 96). A few months after the proclamation of the Truman Doctrine the Marshall Plan was launched. The communist threat provided an important element in the acceptance within the United States of this large-scale effort to revive Europe (cf. Schurmann, 1974: 97).

Already in 1949, while the Marshall Plan was still in the beginning stages, President Truman declared as 'Point Four' in his inaugural address America's intention to extend technical assistance to the less-developed countries. 'In retrospect', writes Jacob Kaplan (1967: 42), 'the program appears as magnificent in concept as it was naive in detail.' In the 1950s it became increasingly clear that not only 'know-how' but also considerable funds were needed and requested by the developing countries. While the Point Four program was the first explicit American acknowledgment of a responsibility to help less-developed countries, the commitment to Europe's economic recovery, the build-up of NATO, and the Korean War precluded any extensive American development aid program until 1953.

The death of Stalin in 1953 also heralded Soviet interest in development aid. That year a small technical assistance agreement with Afghanistan was signed, and the Soviet Union gave up its previous refusal to contribute to the UN Technical Assistance Program. Khrushchev's and Bulganin's much-publicized goodwill tour of the Asian capitals in 1955 marked the beginning of a rapidly expanding Soviet aid program.

The evolution of American and Soviet economic aid commitments to the Third World is described in figure 7.[1]

A few general observations can be made on the basis of this overall picture. First, the magnitude of American aid commitments is incomparably greater than that of the Soviet program. This divergence is, of course, attributable mainly to the different economic strengths of the two superpowers. Yet even measured in percentage of GNP, the difference between American and Soviet aid commitments is considerable. In the 1970s average annual American aid amounted to less than 0.3 percent of her GNP, compared to about 0.03 percent for the Soviet Union (OECD, 1981: 164, 174). Thus it remains true that 'by

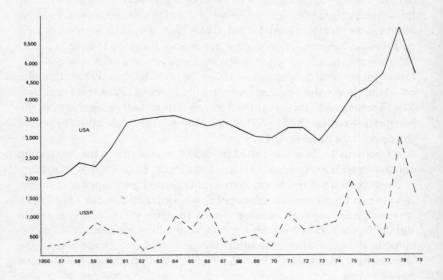

Fig. 7. US and Soviet aid extensions, 1956–79 (in $ million)
(Sources: OECD, 1968, 1974, 1978 for the United States; Holbik, 1968: 76; CIA, 1977, 1980 for the Soviet Union)

any measure the sum total of Soviet economic assistance is a fraction of American economic aid' (Walters, 1970: 92). Whereas the United States throughout the post-war period has remained the leading individual aid donor in absolute terms, the Soviet Union has trailed such countries as France, Germany, Japan, Canada, Britain and the Netherlands (cf. Horvath, 1970: 617; CIA, 1977: 11; OECD, 1978: 191). In 1977, for example, Soviet net aid, making up only one percent of all development assistance, was surpassed by eleven countries, including such small countries as Denmark, Norway and Belgium (Kanet, 1981: 337).

Second, since the early 1960s American, as well as Soviet aid flows, have stagnated (the rising American curve in the 1970s is attributable to inflation and the devaluation of the dollar). For instance, American aid measured as a percentage of GNP has never since surpassed the 1961 record of 0.65 — the 1980 figure was 0.27 (cf. OECD, 1981: 174; OECD, 1968: 266).

A discussion of the reasons behind this overall trend requires a more detailed examination of the superpowers' experience of foreign aid. This involves an inquiry into American and Soviet objectives and the influence derived from economic assistance.

Aid Objectives

The possible criteria employed by states when extending and allocating economic assistance to LDCs may be subsumed under two broad categories: those pertaining to the needs of the recipient, and those pertaining to the foreign policy interests of the donor (cf. McKinley and Little 1977 and 1979). The former aim at distributing aid among the poor countries in proportion to their needs, the latter at furthering donor interests by means of foreign aid.

The objectives guiding the aid programs of the superpowers, like those of other aid donors, are complex and ambiguous. Humanitarian objectives are frequently referred to in official statements issued to justify and explain aid efforts. Even if they should not be discounted altogether, humanitarian incentives have never been the overriding concern of the superpowers. Edward Mason's (1964: 27) observation on American attitudes to aid pertains equally to the Soviet Union. Recognizing that humanitarianism as a fundamental motivation has certainly played an important role for individuals engaged in aid efforts in the Third World, he concludes that 'the foreign aid program is formulated and promoted in an administrative and political setting that is not very amenable to humanitarian considerations.'

To simplify somewhat, if recipient need were the main concern of the donors, we would expect the poorest countries to be the chief beneficiaries of aid. In different quantitative studies, Robert McKinlay and Richard Little (1977, 1979) as well as Eugene Wittkopf (1975) have failed to find any significant correlation between the distribution of American aid and recipient need measured in terms of GDP per capita or other variables (such as per capita calory consumption and number of doctors per 100,000 population). No corresponding analyses of Soviet aid exist to my knowledge, but there is strong reason to believe the results would not differ significantly. For instance, of the 31 least-developed countries (LLDCs) in terms of per capita income, literacy rate and share of manufactures in national output,[2] only 18 have received any aid from the USSR — the United States, by comparison, extended economic assistance to 23 of the LLDCs in the fiscal year 1977 (US AID, 1978: iv). The aid extended to the LLDCs represents 17.5 percent of total Soviet aid in the 1954–76 period. If we exclude Afghanistan, which has received the lion's share of Soviet aid to the LLDCs but which can be assumed to have received aid for other than humanitarian reasons (cf. below), the figure drops to 7 percent. It should also be noted that 6 of the 18 LLDCs receiving Soviet aid have been given only symbolic total sums of $5 million or less during the entire 1954–76 period (cf. CIA, 1977: 11-13).

Aid may, however, also be seen as an instrument of foreign policy. The donors, in other words, allocate economic assistance in pursuance of their own interests. Such less than altruistic objectives have in particular been ascribed to the two superpowers (cf. e.g., Kanet, 1973: 453; Walters, 1970: 46). Donors may have a varied range of foreign policy interests in extending aid. The donor interests most frequently cited in the literature on American and Soviet economic assistance include: (1) pre-empting the influence of the other superpower while enhancing their own influence; (2) inducing internal development in accordance with their own model; and (3) seeking economic benefits.

(1) Cold War objectives. American and Soviet aid policies have been characterized as 'a succession of improvisations conditioned by the Cold War' (Holbik, 1968: 28). While this general impression seems to be widespread, we need to take a closer look at some of the cited indicators of Cold War objectives.

The geographical distribution of aid recipients is one such indicator. In a statistical study, Eugene Wittkopf (1975) found support for a 'containment' interpretation of American aid policy, insofar as proximity to the communist world appears to be a major determinant of American economic assistance. It is significant that the law regulating American foreign assistance between 1951 and 1961 was labeled the 'Mutual Security Act.' In the 1954–7 period three-fourths of all American aid to LDCs was directed to only twelve countries, all military allies (Kaplan, 1967: 49). And Robert Walters (1970: 79) has noted that as of 1968 '12 less developed countries which are contiguous to the Communist bloc countries have received one-half of total US economic aid to the third world.'

It takes no statistical analysis, however, to discover that proximity to the Western world is no determining factor of Soviet economic assistance. Instead, the Soviet Union has concentrated its aid efforts in much the same regions as the United States (cf. Table 6).

Countries in the Middle East and Asia — the main Third World arenas of the Cold War — have received more than 70 percent of total American and Soviet aid. It therefore seems reasonable to interpret the aid policies of the superpowers in terms of security interests, in terms of seeking allies

Table 6: US and Soviet aid extensions to the Third World, by region

	USA (1946–78) %	USSR (1954–79) %
Middle East	20.0	43.2
South Asia	21.0	27.3
East Asia	32.4	1.4
Latin America	18.2	5.3
Africa	8.5	22.6

Sources: US AID, 1978; CIA, 1980

and pre-empting the influence of the adversary in the superpower tug-of-war. The low share of Soviet assistance to countries in Latin America (excepting Cuba) is also worth noting. This reflects the traditionally low Soviet profile in the American 'sphere of influence.' While the Soviets have cautiously sought to take advantage of unrest and anti-Americanism in Latin America, they have not had the capacity to create these conditions themselves (cf. Smith, 1971). And Soviet economic commitments in Latin America, though increasing over the years, are still very modest compared with the efforts in the Middle East and Asia.

The extent to which changes in superpower relations have affected aid policies may be another indicator of Cold War objectives on the part of the United States and the Soviet Union. If the two superpowers engage in development assistance chiefly in order to enhance their own and to pre-empt their rival's global influence, one would expect the interest in aid to vary with US–Soviet tensions. Aid would be considered more important in periods of high tension than in periods of *détente*, when the sense of threat from the other superpower is less acute and the LDCs lose some of their significance as chess pieces in the superpower game. And, at least in a macro-perspective, we can observe this correlation. The leveling-off of American and Soviet development aid beginning in the early 1960s coincides roughly in time with the incipient relaxation of tension between the superpowers in the wake of the Cuban missile crisis. Although it is extremely difficult to disentangle complex causes and effects, their coincidence seems significant.

Both superpowers were becoming disillusioned, realizing that denial of the other superpower's influence did not necessarily entail enhancement of their own influence. No dramatic Cold War realignments had taken place in the Third World as a result of the 'aid competition.'

Pre-emptive aid policies gave way to tolerance of mutual aid presence, and even limited co-operation, in many LDCs (cf. Walters, 1970: 243).

As foreign aid became 'decoupled' from the Cold War, it became increasingly difficult to mobilize domestic political support for large assistance efforts. In the years following the Korean War, the American administration could successfully justify aid commitments in terms of containment (cf. Kaplan, 1967: 44-5). But since foreign aid is a 'political orphan,' lacking the permanent support of beneficiary interest groups (cf. Holbik, 1968: 45; Kaplan, 1967: 163-4), the toning down of the anti-communist justification entailed eroding support for the aid program. For instance, Willard Thorp (1971: 8) notes that 'since 1965, the proposals for foreign aid put forward by the President have met with more and more difficulty in Congress.' David Blake and Robert Walters (1976: 130) point to the fact that Congressional cuts of administration requests for aid appropriations averaged 31 percent in the 1968–72 period, as compared with 18 percent in the 1963–7 period.

Although the internal Soviet debate on foreign aid is by no means as public and acrimonious as in the United States, signs of disagreements and eroding support of the Soviet aid effort began to accumulate by the mid-1960s (cf. Walters, 1970: 220-3). New themes were injected into official Soviet discourse which prevail to this day. The USSR is said to best carry out its 'internationalist duty' by ensuring its own domestic economic development, while the LDCs must assume the prime responsibility for their own problems; and it is admitted that foreign aid is an economic burden to the USSR (cf. Schwartz, 1973: 218-20). Also in the mid-1960s, Soviet Third World specialists became engaged in a relatively outspoken debate which reflected growing disenchantment and also questioned some of the rationales for Soviet aid (cf. Valkenier, 1970b).

In sum, there are signs indicating that 'the emergence of a limited superpower *détente* removed a major incentive for the United States and the USSR to compete with each other in offering aid to states throughout the Third World' (Blake and Walters, 1976: 129).

This is also the way in which the evolution of superpower aid policies is commonly interpreted in the Third World. To many developing countries, East–West *détente* and the gradual improvement of superpower relations originally appeared to be a precondition for their own success. *Détente* was expected to contribute to world peace and an international climate in which concern for East–West issues would give way to North–South issues, and superpower co-operation in tackling the problems of underdevelopment and poverty would be facilitated. The frustration of these expectations caused great disappointment. The relaxation of American–Soviet tension seemed to cause not increased attention to the problems of the LDCs, as expected, but instead, growing indifference to the Third World, not only on the part of the superpowers but also among the rest of the developed world (cf. Gupta, 1969, 1971). From the Third World's viewpoint, the 'painful reality is that the period of improvement of great power relations has also been a period of sharp decline in the developed world's concern for the economic development of these countries and a general adverse movement in the economic relationship between the Third World and the rest of the world' (Gupta, 1971: 122).

(2)   Influencing the internal development of recipients. Along with the Cold War objectives of seeking allies in the global superpower struggle, the United States and the Soviet Union have also posited themselves as models or examples to the Third World and have tried to encourage development in accordance with this model within recipient countries.

As noted above, the common denominator of the American and Soviet development models is their heavy stress on industrialization. This is reflected in considerable overlapping in the nature of their assistance. The bulk of American and Soviet aid has gone to the industrial sector, 'with both the United States and the USSR giving substantial aid to the infrastructure of the recipients' economies — transportation, communication, irrigation, and electric power' (Walters, 1970: 148). Yet there are also obvious differences in operational emphasis flowing from divergent development models. Thus, while 'the United States has always attempted to maximize the contribution of its aid to the private sector of the recipient and to the promotion of American private foreign investment in the less developed countries' (Walters, 1970: 132), 'virtually all Soviet aid efforts are directed toward the enhancement of the state sector' (Walters, 1970: 142). Some 75 percent of all Soviet aid is estimated to have been designated for the construction of an industrial base in the state sector of recipient countries (Kanet, 1981: 337).

(3)   Economic benefits. Third World countries are rich in natural resources, several of which are essential for industrialized countries, and at the same time represent large potential markets. Donors are

therefore likely to supply aid in order to promote economic relationships with the LDCs and to safeguard the supply of vital commodities.

As Cold War objectives lost their urgency in the wake of superpower *détente*, economic self-interest came to the fore in the Soviet aid program. Since the mid-1960s there has been an increasing emphasis on a 'stable and mutually advantageous division of labor' in Soviet–LDC aid relationships. It is explicitly stated that one aim of Soviet relations with the LDCs is to strengthen its own economic basis and reduce the West's economic superiority. As expressed by Premier Kosygin at the twenty-fourth party congress in 1971.

> Our cooperation with these countries [the LDCs], based on the principles of equality and respect for mutual interests, is acquiring the nature of a stable division of labor, counterposed to the system of imperialist exploitation in the sphere of international economic relations. At the same time, through the expansion of trade with the developing countries the Soviet Union will receive the opportunity to satisfy the requirements of its own national economy more fully. [CDSP, 1971: 10]

This shift of emphasis, which thus coincided in time with the disenchantment, waning optimism, and internal differences of opinion noted above, entailed strict co-ordination of aid and trade, aid in the form of commercial credits, and Soviet insistence on a quid pro quo for their assistance (e.g. in the form of loan repayment in valuable commodities such as oil, gas or iron ore) as well as greater attention to questions of economic feasibility involving thorough scrutiny of potential projects and joint planning (cf. e.g. Valkenier, 1970a). Thus, the Soviets recently granted Morocco a large credit in return for repayment in phosphates, and had earlier provided assistance to Afghanistan, Iran and Iraq in return for petrocarbons (cf. Kanet, 1981: 338). In addition, the fact that virtually all Soviet aid consists of exports of machinery and equipment assures markets for Soviet industrial production which is otherwise not very competitive on the international market (Kanet, 1981: 338-9).

No corresponding clear-cut shift of emphasis can be discerned in the American aid program. Economic benefits have always loomed large in American discussions of foreign aid. In 1964 David Bell (quoted in Holbik, 1968: 19), then head of AID (Agency for International Development), stated that 'the fundamental purposes of our aid program have been the same since the end of World War II, and in addition to humanitarian and security considerations cited the importance 'to our own economic progress that there be greater production and greater purchasing power in the less developed countries leading to a larger trade and a better opportunity for American overseas investment.' And Henry Kissinger in 1976 reaffirmed the view that 'our own prosperity is closely linked to raw materials, the markets, and the aspirations of the developing countries' (quoted in US Congress, 1977: 42).

One could also point to operational features of both the American and the Soviet aid programs which indicate concern with economic benefits. As for the terms of aid, a relatively large share of American assistance has traditionally been in the form of non-repayable grants. Even if there has been a gradual shift from grants to loans during the 1960s (in 1962 65 percent, in 1968 45 percent of American aid commitments were grants), partly as a result of congressional pressure, grants still account for more than half of the American aid commitments (cf. Thorp, 1971: 96-7; OECD, 1981: 180-1).

Unlike the United States, the Soviet Union has always extended its aid on a predominantly credit basis. Approximately 95 percent of the Soviet aid program is currently estimated to be in the form of loans (US Congress, 1977: 61; Donaldson, 1981: 375). In the same way that the traditional American preference for grants dates back to the Marshall Plan, the Soviet preference for loans has its precedence in the aid to the socialist countries in Europe (Walters, 1970: 150, 160).

On the other hand, American aid contains more visible 'strings' than Soviet aid. American aid is generally tied to purchases in the United States. The proportion of aid funds spent in the United States increased markedly in the 1960s, from some 40 percent in 1959 to over 90 percent in 1968 (cf. Walters, 1970: 157; Holbik, 1968: 60-1). Only in the 1970s have some steps been taken toward untying American economic assistance.

The 'strings' of Soviet aid are less visible, but nevertheless exist. Most Soviet aid is tied to the purchase of Soviet equipment (cf. Walters, 1970: 166; US Congress, 1977: 62; Donaldson, 1981: 375). In addition, the common Soviet practice of making loans repayable in traditional exports makes for annual negotiations to determine the nature and prices of goods to be delivered in which the USSR can reap economic benefits (Walters, 1970: 166). In recent years the Soviet Union has exacted harder terms than before for economic aid and has more often than before demanded loan repayment in hard currency in an obvious effort to reduce its own hard-currency deficit (cf. CIA, 1977: 1; US Congress, 1977: 62).

In sum, there are indications of economic self-interest in the aid programs of both superpowers. In the Soviet case these have become increasingly apparent as the Cold War objectives have lost some of their urgency.

Influence Derived from Aid

The American aid program would seem to provide a comparatively better basis for influence in the Third World than that of the USSR. It is substantially larger. Moreover, the United States is far more capable of satisfying Third World economic demands, offers more advanced technology, and benefits from an established Third World–Western infrastructure of trade mechanisms (US Congress, 1977: 170). While there is a flow of private American capital to the LDCs exceeding the value of official development aid, official aid and trade are the only economic means available to the USSR. And whereas the American aid program from its inception had a global character, the Soviet assistance efforts have been — and are to an increasing degree — geographically concentrated to regions proximate to its own territory.

There is thus no Soviet counterpart to the American aid 'encircle-ment' of the USSR. Inferior economic capabilities forced the Soviet Union primarily to pre-empt and countervail American attempts at influence in regions close to its own borders. The USSR had to acquiesce in a 'strategy of denial,' the principal objective of which was 'to transform regions that formerly constituted secure power bases for the West into contested areas' (Lowenthal, 1977: 257-8). Moreover, when the Soviet Union eventually acquired 'global reach' capacity, the tendency to concentrate on the 'national liberation zone' (a crescent extending from North Africa through the Middle East and South Asia to South-East Asia) (cf. US Congress, 1977: 55) was reinforced by the Sino-Soviet rivalry. The 'national liberation zone' is also proximate and important from the Chinese point of view. The Soviet Union thus has the additional objective of denying Chinese influence in these areas and has become engaged in a new 'aid competition' with its communist rival.

Soviet leaders have themselves drawn attention to their economic limitations by clearly inferring that increased aid to the Third World represents a zero-sum equation in which Soviet citizens are the losers. In 1964 Khrushchev admitted that 'when the Soviet Union helps the young developing countries, giving them a portion of the wealth amassed by its own labour, then it is limiting its own possibilities for a certain period of time' quoted in Yellon, 1970: 251). And Soviet Foreign Minister Gromyko in 1976 described bluntly the constraints placed on the Soviet aid program:

> It is natural, however, that the Soviet Union's potential for rendering economic assistance is not infinite. Of course, the Soviet state cannot fail to be concerned for the wellbeing of its own people. The Soviet Union . . . allocates funds to render the developing countries economic and technical assistance on the basis of its own capabilities. [quoted in US Congress, 1977: 132]

Yet the success of foreign aid in terms of influence is not necessarily commensurate with the size of the program and the donor's economic strength. Several advantages of the incomparably smaller Soviet aid program have been noted. It is far better co-ordinated and directed than the American program which suffers from administrative fragmentation and a lack of co-ordination between aid and trade policies. It is characterized by concentration in terms of projects and recipients to a greater extent than the fragmented American program. The Soviet Union has also at times derived psychological benefits from being the second aid donor without the stigma of prior involvement, although this advantage has naturally decreased in importance over time (cf. Walters, 1970: 240-1).

An overall assessment, however, suggests that neither superpower has been particularly successful in furthering its own foreign policy goals. Though differing in primary aims, the American and Soviet aid programs show certain similarities when compared as foreign policy instruments, as noted above. Both superpowers offer aid in pursuit of 'milieu goals,' that is, they attempt to change the international environment in order to achieve their own interests (cf. Walters, 1970: 46-7). The American and Soviet influence attempts are two-pronged: on the one hand, the superpowers seek allies in their global struggle; on the other hand, they posit themselves as models and try to incite development in accordance with this model.

No decisive realignments have taken place in the Third World as a result of superpower foreign aid. Robert Walters' (1970: 242) conclusion that there have been 'no cases where aid has changed the allegiance of a less developed country in the Third World' remains valid. Instead, the LDCs have consciously sought to remain outside the

East–West conflict and have thereby been able to extract aid funds by playing the superpowers off against each other as long as Cold War objectives prevailed. The aid relations with their respective allies have also increasingly suggested to both superpowers that recruiting allies does not necessarily imply greater influence. In the Soviet case,

> Their experience with Cuba brought home to them just how expensive — and thankless — the support of an underdeveloped ally can be. So long as the client state remains noncommunist, the Soviets have considerable leeway in determining the levels of assistance to be provided. Once it becomes a full-fledged member of the socialist camp, however, Moscow's commitments to defend it and see that its economy stays above water are almost inevitably forced upward. [Smith, 1971: 1127]

Similarly, Robert Keohane (1971) has dwelt upon the considerable influence of small Third World allies of the United States. Leaders in Saigon, Seoul and Bangkok have frequently been able to take advantage of America's crusading spirit and anti-communism in extracting aid commitments.

Moreover, one can point to 'few cases where even a dominant aid presence has assured a rapport between recipient and donor on major issues of foreign policy' (Walters, 1970: 242). Evidence of gratitude or allegiance in return for development aid have been hard to discern, whereas examples of the opposite are readily found.

> Over the years, all major aid donors have witnessed votes against their position on crucial issues before the United Nations, as well as public displays of hostility (such as attacks on embassies or other facilities) within the less-developed countries, to which much of their economic aid has flowed. This holds true for Communist aid donors as well as Western states. The Soviet Union has seen anti-Soviet rallies held in stadia constructed with Soviet aid. During the Cuban missile crisis in 1962, Guinea refused to permit Soviet aircraft bound for Cuba to land for refueling at the Conakry airport, which had been constructed with Soviet aid. [Blake and Walters, 1976: 131]

Nor have the superpowers been able to mold the LDCs in their own image. Neither liberal democracies nor socialist one-party states have flourished in the wake of American and Soviet foreign aid. And, as we have seen, both superpowers have lost the initial confidence in their ability to steer development in the direction of their respective models.

Why, then, have the superpowers been relatively unsuccessful in converting their development assistance into influence? One reason is, of course, that their aid programs have not been of such a magnitude as to create dependency relationships, in terms of either asset dependency — expressed as the ratio between aid and the recipient's GNP — or source dependency — the ratio between aid from the superpower and total aid received (cf. McKinlay and Little, 1977: 66-7).

The chief reason for the lack of influence derived from the American and Soviet aid programs appears, however, to be the existence of the rival aid-giving superpower. In the early years the recipients were able to play the two superpowers off against each other, and each superpower was more concerned with pre-empting the influence of its rival than maximizing its own influence. Even after Cold War objectives have lost some of their urgency, either superpower has been reluctant to withdraw from aid relations or press its demands too hard lest the rival superpower should capitalize on the ensuing resentment. Thus, the superpowers tend to neutralize each other's influence potential.

Arms Transfers

Since the 1950s, arms transfers to Third World countries have become one prominent strand in the multiple web of relationships between rich and poor countries. Most wars which have taken place over the past decades have been fought in the poorer parts of the world, and the weapons used in these wars have come almost entirely from rich, industrialized countries (SIPRI, 1975: 7). The United States and the Soviet Union have been the dominant suppliers of major weapons to the Third World, together accounting for about two-thirds of total arms deliveries (SIPRI, 1975: 16-17).

As in the case of economic aid, the United States was first on the scene. Programs of military aid were begun in the Philippines in 1946, in Greece and Turkey in 1947, and in China in 1948. The earliest American efforts were directed primarily toward Western Europe, and in the early 1950s military assistance was provided outside Europe largely to build up a Western collective security system and erect a chain of military alliances along the periphery of the USSR and China.

When the Soviet Union joined the arms transfer race in the mid-1950s and pre-emption of Soviet influence became an added incentive, the geographical scope of American military assistance was expanded. Arms were delivered not only to 'allies' but also to 'friends.' In the 1960s there was an increased emphasis on the internal 'threat' to developing countries, and American military assistance was increasingly designed to train local forces to combat guerrilla activities (for accounts of the origin and evolution of American military assistance see SIPRI, 1975: 49-76; Farley *et al.*, 1978: 20-6; Lewis, 1980: 188-91).

Until 1955 the Soviet Union supplied arms only to other socialist countries. The earliest transfers of Soviet arms to Third World countries were carried out with other East European countries, especially Czechoslovakia, as intermediaries. Initially the overriding Soviet concern was to weaken the military alliances which the West was forming around the USSR's borders. After 1960, the number of countries receiving Soviet arms deliveries increased, as Moscow generally appeared willing to supply arms to countries turning away from Western arms agreements. And since the late 1960s the Soviet Union has proved willing to supply weapons more generally, as part of its apparent readiness to compete for influence on a worldwide basis (for accounts of the origin and evolution of Soviet military assistance, see SIPRI, 1975: 77-122; Joshua and Gibert, 1969).

If statistical data on development assistance are shaky, this applies *a fortiori* to arms transfers. The validity, reliability, and comparability of existing data sources have been called into question (cf. Laurance and Sherwin, 1978; Leiss, 1978; Sherwin and Laurance, 1979; Fei, 1980). Arms transfers are most commonly measured in terms of dollar value, either the actual price paid as in the ACDA (U.S. Arms Control and Disarmament Agency) data, or a dollar valuation of actual production cost as in the SIPRI (Stockholm International Peace Research Institute) data. Since superpower arms transfers to the Third World involve a substantial element of grants and subsidies, the latter technique reflects the economic value of the delivered weapons more truly. An alternative — preferable but far more complex — measurement would be in terms of *military* utility (cf. Leiss, 1978). Reliability tests of data from the two main sources, ACDA and SIPRI, yield less than perfect correlations (see Laurance and Sherwin, 1978: 97-100). This stems from the fact that ACDA and SIPRI use divergent methods of measurement and data presentation. SIPRI and ACDA data both include annual exports by major suppliers; ACDA in addition provides bilateral donor-recipient data for aggregated five-year periods. Neither source contains annual data on a donor-recipient basis. Whereas ACDA figures cover all types of weapons, SIPRI figures cover major weapons: ships, aircraft, tanks, and missiles. Finally, SIPRI relies on open, ACDA on classified sources.

The subsequent analysis will be based predominantly on SIPRI data. Again, as in the case of development aid, my main concern is the trend over time in superpower transfers to the Third World. And in terms of overall American and Soviet trends, the data sources do not diverge significantly. The evolution of American and Soviet arms transfers to the Third World is described in Figure 8.

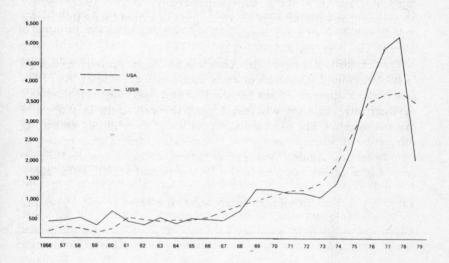

Fig. 8 US and Soviet arms transfers to the Third World, 1956–79 ($ million, at constant 1975 prices)
(*Sources:* SIPRI, 1977, 1982)

While the United States, as we have seen, has greatly outstripped the Soviet Union in the amount of development assistance, Soviet military aid approximates — and in certain years surpasses — that of the United States. Unlike development aid, arms transfers from the superpowers have not tended to stagnate in recent decades. On the contrary, arms transfers have escalated both in quantitative and qualitative terms. Up to the early 1960s, the superpowers withheld their more sophisticated weapons from LDC clients, and deliveries consisted mainly of obsolete or obsolescent equipment. But in recent years countries in Third World conflict regions have been receiving the most advanced arms produced by the United States and the Soviet Union, sometimes before these weapons are fully assimilated by the supplier's own forces (cf. SIPRI, 1975: 16; Kemp *et al.*, 1978: 394).

The dominant position of the superpowers is more pronounced in the field of arms transfers than in development aid. In the 1962–81 period the total value of arms transfers to the Third World from the United States was more than twice the size, and from the USSR slightly less than twice the size, of the combined total of Britain and France, the third and fourth ranking arms suppliers (cf. SIPRI, 1982: 192-3). Moreover, the superpowers have to a greater extent than other major suppliers delivered weapons as grants or at subsidized prices and low interest rates (cf. SIPRI, 1975: 12).

The similarities between the American and Soviet programs extend to the regional distribution of arms transfers (cf. Table 7). As in the case of development aid, the Middle East and Asia constitute the focus of superpower interest, whereas Africa has received the least amount of arms supplies. The predominant position of the Middle East among recipients of superpower arms transfers has been accentuated in recent years, accounting for 62 percent of total United States, and 57 percent of total Soviet, supplies in the 1970–6 period (SIPRI, 1978: 226).

Table 7:   US and Soviet arms transfers to the Third World, by region, 1950–72

	USA %	USSR %
Far East	43.3	28.5
Indian subcontinent	4.3	17.9
Middle East	39.3*	44.5
Africa	2.7	4.4
Latin America	10.5	4.8

* Including arms transfers to Greece and Turkey (17.7 percent of total arms transfers).

Source: SIPRI, 1975: 52-3, 82-3.

Objectives of Arms Transfers

Arms transfers, unlike development aid, cannot readily be explained or justified in terms of humanitarian objectives. To the non-altruistic donor interests cited in the previous discussion of development aid, at least two more objectives need to be added when it comes to the arms transfer policies of the two superpowers: military objectives and crisis management.

(1) Cold War objectives. As in the case of development aid, the pre-emption of the other superpower's influence while enhancing their own was a dominant concern guiding the American and Soviet arms supply programs from their inception. In the early 1950s, when the United States alone was active in arms transfers abroad, these were seen as the natural means of attaining the foreign policy goal of rebuilding American allies' capacities to defend themselves against communism. By the mid-1950s, when the United States began to fear competition from the Soviet Union in the area of arms transactions, a pre-emptive element was added, and the 'if we don't, someone else will' argument for arms transfers gained currency. One of the main considerations became to ensure that a potential recipient did not acquire weapons from the Soviet Union (cf. Cahn, 1979: 121; SIPRI, 1975: 66). Similarly, the immediate Soviet concern when entering the arms transfers race was to pre-empt the influence of the United States. The Cold War competition entailed a steadily widening circle of recipients of arms supplies from both superpowers. Whereas early American military aid was reserved for her allies and the USSR originally supplied arms only to countries which were not on good terms with the West, both superpowers gradually proved willing to undermine the influence of the rival superpower by providing potential recipients with an alternative source of supply and in the process came to be less restrictive in their choice of recipients. Although some countries — most prominently India and Iran — thus received arms from both superpowers, the most common pattern became that of one local rival receiving military aid from Moscow and the other from Washington (cf. Gibert, 1970: 1125-30). Since the outbreak of Sino-Soviet rivalry, Moscow has pursued the additional objective of pre-empting Chinese influence in its arms transfer policy.

(2) Military objectives. Since the mid-1960s, arms transfer relationships

have increasingly been perceived by both superpowers as chips to be cashed in gradually for strategic access. The United States and the Soviet Union have become engaged in a global competition for basing rights, naval facilities, and overflight privileges as a quid pro quo for arms transfers.

The two superpowers started from different points of departure. During the first decade of the Cold War the Soviet Union was almost totally lacking in overseas facilities, whereas the United States and its allies were provided with a very extensive global basing network. The initial Soviet arms transfers in the mid- and late-1950s did not immediately translate into overseas basing facilities for the USSR. Only in the mid-1960s, when the Soviet naval expansion and efforts to close the strategic nuclear gap were initiated in the wake of the humiliation suffered in the Cuban missile crisis, did the Soviet Union show a keen interest in overseas facilities. The USSR has since built a global basing system mostly through arms client relationships, while the United States has experienced basing problems as a result of the vastly increased economic and political costs demanded by formerly willing clients (cf. Harkavy, 1979, 1980).

(3) Crisis management. One rationale for American and Soviet arms transfers is to lessen the likelihood of superpower involvement in local conflicts around the world. By keeping its client sufficiently well armed and trained, the superpower patron can avoid committing its own forces to the area. An explicit formulation of this objective is found in the so-called Nixon Doctrine of the early 1970s which called for a lower American profile in the security affairs of the LDCs while opening the prospect of greater freedom to sell or give arms to offset the decline of direct American military presence.

An additional crisis management incentive is to ensure — through the types and quantities of weapons supplied and by controlling the supply of spare parts, ammunition, etc. — that if war breaks out, it is limited in intensity and duration (cf. Snider, 1976: 7-8). Such considerations have, above all, guided American and Soviet arms transfer policies in the Middle East (cf. Chapter 5 for a more extensive treatment of American and Soviet crisis management techniques in the Middle East).

(4) Influencing the internal development of recipients. The aim of encouraging desired internal developments in recipient countries, prominent in superpower development aid, figures in arms transfers

as well, though to a much lesser extent. Such considerations were of negligible significance in the early arms transfer programs when Cold War objectives prevailed. Soviet military aid was, for example, provided to regimes which openly persecuted local communists, such as Syria and Egypt. In recent years, however, there has been growing emphasis among both superpowers on actively cultivating relations with the military establishment, which is either the actual or potential *locus* of power in many recipient LDCs, through technical advisers and the training of client states' military personnel. The importance of training and establishing informal contacts with 'tomorrow's political leaders' is given prominence (cf. SIPRI, 1975: 55, 70; Pajak, 1979: 156).

In the same way that one long-range goal of Soviet military aid has clearly been to strengthen the 'progressive' orientation of the army in Third World countries (cf. Saivetz, 1980: 147), the American military assistance program aims at long-term effects in the direction of democratic government (cf. Lefever, 1980: 291)' SIPRI, 1975: 69-70). The attempts by the Carter administration to make arms supplies conditional on the recipient's adherence to human rights represent a rare example of the open and direct use of arms transfers to influence the internal development in recipient countries.

(5) Economic benefits. While commercial motives play a dominant role in the arms transfer policies of several medium-range donor countries, they are of only secondary importance to the superpowers. Neither the American nor the Soviet defense industry depends on arms exports; only a small fraction of the total defense production is exported. Moreover, the actual earnings from arms supplies have not been high, as the main American and Soviet recipients have been supplied with arms either as military assistance or at discount prices and on favorable credit terms (cf. SIPRI, 1975: 49, 78-9).

This general picture has changed somewhat in recent years, however. There has been a marked shift in American arms transfer policy from grants to sales. The proportion of total American arms exports that was sold rather than given away increased from an average of 14 percent in the 1950–64 period to 91 percent in 1974 (Kaldor, 1979: 215). Particularly in the case of American weapons sales to Persian Gulf states following the 1973–4 oil price hikes, the economic motivations were evident (cf. Pierre, 1982: 24).

At the same time, Soviet credit terms have become noticeably harder. Prices for Soviet weapons are approximating those of the

West, repayment schedules are more strictly observed, and the Soviet Union is increasingly demanding that repayment be made in hard currencies. Thus, among the largest recipients in recent years have been those countries able to pay in cash, such as Libya, Iraq, and Algeria (Pierre, 1982: 75).

The economic recession in Western industrialized countries, the oil crisis and the problems of certain defense industries, especially aerospace companies which are becoming increasingly dependent on exports, have contributed to the new stress on short-term economic benefits in American arms transfer policy. The recent entrance of commerical considerations into Soviet arms supplies is apparently related to the growing Soviet debt burden. The production of arms is one area where the Soviet Union has a comparative advantage, and a relatively large share of total exports — some 8–10 percent — consists of armaments. Hence, the sales of arms for hard currency is one obvious solution to Soviet debt problems (cf. Kaldor, 1979; US Congress, 1977: 71; Pierre, 1982: 78-9). For instance, Soviet arms sales in 1977 were estimated to generate some $1.5 billion in hard currency (Kanet, 1981: 347; Pajak, 1981: 387).

In summary, we find in the arms transfer programs of the two superpowers the same evolution from predominant Cold War objectives toward more complex and manifold motivations as we found in development aid. Unlike development aid, however, the lessened urgency of Cold War objectives has not entailed a decline in superpower arms transfers. This leads us to a consideration of the conceivable influence derived from these arms transfers.

Influence Derived from Arms Transfers

As we have seen, the superpowers expect similar effects from arms transfer relationships as from development aid, only the desire to extend their own influence while pre-empting that of the other superpower is even more overt and explicit. Existing studies indicate that the superpower influence assumed to flow from arms transfers can hardly be substantiated empirically. There is obviously no one-to-one correlation between arms transfers and influence. In order to assess the effectiveness of arms transfers as an instrument of political leverage, a number of contextual factors have to be considered. Context, rather than level of arms supplies, determines outcomes.

First, the potential influence accruing from arms transactions is not unidirectional. The supply of weapons creates ties between the supplier and the recipient, but it is not self-evident who will influence whom. Leverage, more often than not, is a 'two-way street.' By bringing about a wider diffusion of military power from north to south, the superpowers reinforce the emergence of a more multipolar world, in which their freedom of maneuver will be increasingly narrowed. The instability of Third World regimes generates problems of control over weapons systems and raises the specter of re-transfers, seizure, theft, or accessibility; high-technology weapons could easily fall into the hands of hostile actors, including the other superpower. The logistics and assimilation of large-scale, high-technology transfers usually require direct, 'in-country' supplier participation which creates significant administrative and operational difficulties and often engenders feelings of hostility among the host population at large. Soviet-Egyptian and US–Iranian arms supply relationships offer recent and graphic examples of these political costs (cf. Kemp *et al.*, 1978: 396-407).

Assessments of the *relative* influence the superpowers might derive from arms transfers usually focus on (a) the supplier-recipient relationship; (b) the types of weapons transferred, and (c) the temporal aspects of influence attempts.

Supplier-recipient relationship. Anne Hessing Cahn (1979: 111) has constructed a heuristic matrix, relating arms transfers and supplier influence, which covers several relevant — and more or less interrelated — variables associated with the supplier-recipient relationship in a given arms transaction (cf. Table 8).

Being the sole source of arms would seem to create such dependencies that the supplier's attempts at influence are likely to succeed. For instance, most basing arrangements have occurred where the recipient receives all or most of its arms from one supplier whereas, conversely, multiple-source acquisition of arms has usually occurred where no superpower has significant strategic access (cf. Harkavy, 1979: 182; Harkavy, 1980: 147). Yet, a sole-source relationship may at the same time enhance the leverage of the recipient. 'If the supplier is so conspicuously committed to the recipient that it fears disengagement, it may become the captive of a recalcitrant recipient' (Cahn, 1979: 108). The superpowers' global confrontation and crusading spirit present their clients with bargaining strength. As Robert Keohane (1971: 163) has put it, 'leaders who believe in domino theories not only have to talk to the "dominoes," they have to listen to them and believe them as well.' The US–South Vietnamese and, perhaps to a lesser degree, Soviet–Cuban relationships are cases in point.

Table 8:   Influence derived from arms transfers

Supplier's influence is maximised when the recipient:	*Recipient's influence is maximised when the recipient:*
has no alternate sources of supply	has multiple sources of supply, especially cross-bloc
cannot pay for the arms	has the ability to pay
is a 'pariah' state within the inter-national community	has multiple diplomatic and cultural relations within the international community
has no indigenous weapons-production capability	has an indigenous weapons-production capability
does not occupy a strategic geographic position	occupies a strategic geographic position
has a small storage capacity for spare parts	has ample storage capacity for spare parts
perceives a real threat to its national survival	does not perceive a real threat to its national survival
does not possess scarce un-substitutable raw materials	possesses scarce unsubstitutable raw materials
requires supplier personnel for weapons maintenance and training	has sufficient technically trained indigenous personnel
perceives that receiving arms from supplier is particularly prestigious	perceives that the seller's prestige is 'on the line'
has such a strong ideological orientation that switching suppliers is precluded	is ideologically unhindered in switching suppliers

The leverage of a dependent client increases whenever it controls a 'strategic asset,' such as geostrategic location, bases and port facilities, or important resources (cf. e.g., Kemp *et al.*, 1978: 396). For instance, David Ronfeldt (1978) has argued that in the 1970s the Cuban and Iranian 'superclients' had considerable bargaining leverage *vis-à-vis* their respective superpower by virtue of their geopolitical location on the borders of the other superpower in combination with their intense nationalism, strong personal leadership and activist security concep-tions. Conversely, the ability of a superpower to cash in on dependencies created by arms transfers is greater when the recipients are politically, ideologically, and economically dependent on the supplying superpower for support; politically. in the sense that they cannot obtain the necessary political support against adversaries from another supplier; ideologically, in the sense that their ideological orientation precludes them from switching suppliers; economically, in that those who lack sufficient cash have to depend on various forms of financial aid from the supplier in order to acquire the arms they desire (cf. Snider, 1976: 32-3).

If a recipient country may thus gain a certain amount of influence even when it is dependent on one of the superpowers as its sole source of supply, the potential for recipient leverage increases when there are multiple sources of supply. This opens the possibility of playing off one superpower against the other, especially for nonaligned recipients. However, the 'blackmail' pattern does not appear to be as common in arms transfers as in development aid. Recipient countries have tended to rely on one or the other superpower rather than on both (cf. Gibert, 1970: 1125-6; Semmel, 1982: 284). There are, however, certain prominent exceptions to this rule.

Iran was long adept at playing off one superpower supplier against the other. In the period 1965–74, Iran received $574 million in arms transfers from the Soviet Union (a figure comparable to that of North Korea) and $1,178 million from the United States (ACDA, 1975: 74). India and Pakistan are other examples of countries which have over the years benefited from the superpower rivalry by securing arms supplies from both sources (cf. Gibert, 1970: 1127, 1129). In both these cases, the Chinese threat has been a facilitating condition. Up to 1970 South and South-east Asia formed the only region where mutually-supplied countries outnumbered sole-source countries (Gibert, 1970: 1129).

In recent years recipient countries have increasingly diversified their sources of supply. The typical pattern then 'seems to involve securing hardware within a major weapons class primarily from one supplier but choosing different suppliers across weapon classes' (Mihalka, 1980: 50). Yet mutual superpower supply is still rather rare. In 1974–80 no leading Third World recipient was a leading arms customer of both the United States and the USSR (Semmel, 1982: 284). Latin America and Africa remain largely outside the arena of US–Soviet competition, the United States competing primarily with other Western countries in Latin America and the Soviet Union competing with the former colonial powers in Africa. While the clients of each bloc tend to be arrayed against each other in Asia and the Middle East, a number of Arab countries have recently moved to acquire mutual superpower supply of military equipment in obvious efforts to challenge the effectiveness of arms relationships as political levers (cf. Mihalka, 1980: 61-3).

Type of weapons. The performance characteristics of the supplied weapons have an obvious bearing on the potential leverage derived from arms transfers. The transfer of sophisticated, high-technology weapon systems in general enhances potential supplier leverage by making it increasingly difficult for recipients to switch from one main arms supplier to another. Whereas arms transferred in previous decades tended to be unsophisticated, relatively simple to maintain without major 'in-country' supplier assistance, and fairly easy to replace with equivalent weapons from alternate sources, the transfer of advanced weapon systems tends to render supplier-recipient relationships more permanent and less 'breakable.' Switching to another main supplier becomes a matter of almost prohibitively long time periods and involves retraining of personnel, reindoctrination of staff officers, and redeployment of weapons. Moreover, the higher attrition rates of modern warfare increase dependency upon resupply (cf. Kemp *et al.*, 1978: 394-5; Ra'anan, 1978: 136-7).

A country manufacturing a particular weapons system for which there is no equivalent system in terms of performance characteristics in other manufacturers' arsenals derives more leverage than it would otherwise possess. Take combat aircraft, for instance. First, these weapon systems are produced by relatively few suppliers and therefore seem to offer the suppliers more leverage than, say, light and medium tanks, assault guns, and other weapons which are manufactured by a greater number of suppliers. Second, there are noteworthy asymmetries between Soviet and American weapon system designs, intensified by differing strategic doctrines and military tactics. Soviet strategic doctrine emphasizes single-purpose air defense systems, whereas American doctrine relies on highly sophisticated multi-purpose systems. The United States has therefore produced some of the most sought-after combat aircraft in the world to which no equivalent can be found (cf. Snider, 1976: 23-8).

Temporal aspects. Influence deriving from arms transfers may occur at different points in time — before the outbreak of hostilities, during a crisis, at the end of a conflict, or as a reward for actions previously undertaken — and success depends in large measure on the timing of attempts at influence. The history of superpower crisis management efforts (cf. below, Chapter 5) strongly suggests that the manipulation of arms transfers is relatively ineffective at preventing the outbreak of hostilities but more effective at halting armed conflicts once they have been initiated. The need to replenish weapons, ammunitions, and spare parts consumed in the fighting creates dependencies on the main supplier. Even during hostilities leverage can be derived from the carrot or stick of *future* rather than present arms deliveries (cf. Cahn, 1979: 114-15; Snider, 1976: 19-20).

Transactions based on credit, which stretch over several years, provide multiple leverage points, whereas cash deliveries or grants are 'one-shot' affairs. Weapon systems which require continuing supplier maintenance or spare parts deliveries also offer long-term access points (Cahn, 1979: 115). Similarly, once the delivered arms have become integrated into the recipient's force structure, the supplier loses control and potential leverage. Therefore, the time to extract maximum influence for the supplier seems to be before the arms have been delivered or while the recipient still requires supplier assistance in absorbing it (Snider, 1976: 35-7).

In summary, then, arms transfers naturally create supplier-recipient interdependence. As the foregoing discussion indicates, the amount and direction of influence derived from such relationships are difficult to measure and sufficiently variable to defy easy generalizations. It is obvious, however, that arms transfers are far from reliable means to acquire long-term superpower influence in the Third World. Rarely have arms deliveries created endurable friendship between a superpower and a recipient LDC. In fact, supplier patterns have become increasingly volatile, and recent years have witnessed several bloc changes in arms supply (see Mihalka, 1980: 73). Like the Soviet Union in Indonesia, Ghana and Egypt, the United States has suffered conspicuous setbacks in areas where it has given military assistance — for example in Libya, Ethiopia and Iran.

Existing studies suggest that arms transfers have not enabled the superpowers to control the domestic or foreign policies of recipient countries. Nor have they been able to reconcile their own objectives with those of the recipients. Once they have extended military assistance, it becomes 'at best a precedent and an argument for continued aid, and at worst a resource at the disposition of the recipient for domestic or external use regardless of the stated purpose for which given' (Lewis, 1980: 196). In the relatively few cases where the recipients have behaved in accordance with superpower objectives, arms transfers have largely helped the recipients do what they have already wanted or found to be in their own interest (cf. Lewis, 1980: 196; Lefever, 1980: 280-1). Moreover, to the extent that arms transfers have been translated into apparent superpower leverage, 'that impact only worked in tandem with variables beyond direct supplier control, namely, the arms transfers to the recipients' adversaries and/or the amount of conflict in which the recipients are involved' (Snider, 1976: 50). Finally, the scope of superpower influence is limited, as many issue-areas seem to lie beyond manipulation via arms supply relationships: 'On balance, it appears that decisions on military questions or policy concerning war and peace are the categories most likely to be influenced by an arms supplier if he chooses to make the attempt' (Quandt, 1978: 129).

The trend over time also seems to be toward decreasing super-power leverage derived from arms transfers. A growing number of suppliers have entered the arms trade market, resulting in sharpened competition and eroding superpower dominance. Furthermore, recipient countries in the Third World have increasingly come to diversify their sources of supply and, in several instances, established defense industries of their own (cf. Moodie, 1980).

Despite the lack of evidence indicating a strong and positive relationship between arms transfers and influence, the strongly rooted belief among the decision-makers of both superpowers seems to be that such is the case (cf. Cahn, 1979: 106). As we have seen, American and Soviet arms supplies, unlike development aid, have not declined in recent decades. To the superpowers, arms transfers to the Third World have apparently entailed more tangible quid pro quos than development aid. Specifically, arms supply relationships have been instrumental in establishing and maintaining global military presence. This has been especially important for the USSR, the 'junior' superpower with fewer international connections, in its quest for superpower status.

> Despite periodic setbacks or coolness in one client country or another, the overall impact of the arms aid program appears to lie on the positive side of the Soviet foreign policy ledger. While local Communists have not appreciably advanced their causes in the developing countries, the Soviet presence and influence in these areas have grown rapidly in the past two and a half decades to a level perhaps only dreamed of by Stalin. Moscow likely has concluded that, although the policies of aid recipients frequently

have failed to parallel those of its own and though periodic polemics with some recipient states recur, the program has enhanced the Soviet Union's overall international position. (Pajak, 1981: 397)

Superpower Aid: Conclusions

Let us return now to the questions posed initially. Have the two superpowers behaved similarly in their aid relations with the Third World? Have they been equally influential *vis-à-vis* aid recipients? Have aid relations with the Third World been characterized by superpower 'condominium'? And are the observed similarities and dissimilarities attributable to the 'causal chains' suggested in Part I?

(1) There are obvious similarities in American and Soviet behavior toward the Third World. Both seem to have lost their initial confidence and optimism concerning the development potentials of the Third World. This has been reflected in a parallel stagnation of American and Soviet aid allocations since the mid-1960s, at the same time as arms transfers have assumed increasing significance. Furthermore, the regional distribution of the superpowers' development aid and arms transfers displays marked similarities, both Washington and Moscow assigning priority to the Middle East and Asia, the main Third World arenas of the Cold War. Behind these parallels one may discern similar foreign policy objectives.

These overall similarities should not obscure certain important differences. One concerns the size of the economic assistance programs, Soviet aid expenditures being but a fraction of American ones throughout the post-war period. This difference does not apply to arms transfers, where the efforts of the two superpowers have been equal in size. A second dissimilarity concerns the terms of aid. Whereas a large share of American economic and military assistance has traditionally been in the form of grants, the Soviet Union has extended its aid on a predominantly credit basis. This difference is, however, narrowing down, as both superpowers in recent years have tended to harden the terms of their assistance and pay more attention to economic self-interest.

The similarities thus seem to outweigh the dissimilarities. This is apparently also the predominant view among Third World countries. In different international forums the LDCs have made it clear that they consider Soviet Third World policies little different from those of the United States and the industrialized West (see e.g., Donaldson, 1981; Schechter, 1981).

The preceding analysis also suggests that underlying these similarities may be the hypothesized interplay of historical, ideological, and bureaucratic factors mediated through superpower role conceptions. In the early American and Soviet interest in the Third World we find a blend of historical 'lessons' and ideological beliefs. Analogies with their own past and with their early post-war policies elsewhere (especially in Europe) loomed large in the original aid policies of both superpowers. Moreover, each superpower saw the significance of the Third World and its own mission in the context of the global East–West struggle — as one aspect of the fight against the rival 'ism.' In short the 'enemy image/globalism' current dominated policy-making in Washington as well as Moscow.

As the foreign aid polices failed to produce tangible benefits in the global superpower competition, particularist concerns gradually came to the fore. In the United States, voices were increasingly heard which linked America's success in the Third World with its response to similar challenges at home (such as poverty and race relations). Similarly, in the USSR the view that the 'chief internationalist duty' of the Soviet people was to strengthen the Soviet economy and serve as an irresistible model to the Third World held sway. Developing countries were told to look to the example of other backward regions which had made the transition from feudalism to socialism, such as Soviet Central Asia and Mongolia.

Furthermore, in both superpowers the original enemy image of the adversary was modified and the mutual presence in the Third World was tolerated. Abated globalism in combination with modified images of the adversary entailed stagnation in the aid flows from both superpowers as well as hardened aid conditions.

If other currents found expression in American and Soviet aid policies, they never supplanted the original 'enemy image/globalism' current. Rather, the increased emphasis on arms transfers testifies to the continued strength of globalism and enemy images in both superpowers. Competition with the other superpower has also precluded drastic reorientations of aid policies in the face of obvious failures. In short, to withdraw from the foreign aid race would be to shrink from the superpower role.

While important for both superpowers, the Third World assumes special significance for the 'junior' superpower with less developed international ties as an avenue to global status. I have argued above that the Soviet Union has tended to look to the United States as 'role referent' in its quest for recognized superpower status. This seems to apply to aid relations with the Third World as well. Not only did the Soviet Union follow the American lead in extending aid and transferring arms to the LDCs; one important motivation for Soviet aid was also 'to present the image of the USSR as a first-rate power rivaling the United States economically, technologically, politically, and militarily' (Walters, 1970: 32). The Third World continues to be central to Soviet superpower status, as pointed out by several observers.

The USSR is a world power, and as such it sees itself pursuing a global range of interests. To concede an absence of direct Soviet interests in any part of the world would be an admission of diminished status. . . . Beneath the elaborate superstructure of ideological motivation and great power interests, Soviet policy in the Third World may, after all, be just an exercise in role-playing. [Pick, 1981: 10-11]

Thus for the Soviets the Third World has political value, mainly because it presents political opportunity and because it is the instrumentality for expanding and globalizing Soviet influence and power. The Third World enables the Soviet Union to magnify its great power role on the world scene as regional interests of the individual LDC's merge with Soviet global interests. The Third World connection sustains the Soviet compulsion to maintain both its prestige and its status as a great world power. [US Congress, 1977: 49]

(2)   The preceding analysis has emphasized the limitations of superpower influence in the Third World as a result of development aid and arms transfers. Neither superpower has been able to control the internal development of LDCs or recruit dependable allies through their aid programs. In the same way that the Soviet entry in the mid-1950s offset American influence in the Third World, so the emergence of China from isolation offset Soviet influence. For countries preferring to avoid a Western orientation, an alternative now exists to reliance on the Soviet Union. In addition to the old tactics of playing the superpowers off against one another, the LDCs have the possibility of exploiting the communist rivalry. A somewhat larger degree of influence and more tangible benefits may have accrued from superpower arms transfers, but these have largely been limited to military-security issue-areas. Moreover, the trend over time seems to

be toward decreasing rather than increasing superpower control, as the LDCs have made conscious attempts to reduce their dependence on the superpowers.

These common trends notwithstanding, there are important differences between the United States and the Soviet Union. Specifically, the inferior strength and autarkical character of the Soviet economy constitute serious handicaps in Moscow's aid relations with the LDCs. Soviet presence in the Third World has always been less extensive than that of the United States, and the tendency to concentrate aid efforts on the 'national liberation zone' close to its own borders has in recent decades been reinforced by the Sino-Soviet rivalry.

The relative Soviet inferiority has become ever more apparent in recent years. One study (Defense Monitor, 1980: 6) concludes that 'Soviet inability to hold the allegiance and support of important Third World countries over the long term has been the major weakness of the Soviet Union in attempting to expand its influence.' For quite some time the USSR could make political capital out of anti-Western sentiments in the Third World, out of its declaratory support of LDC claims, and out of being the second aid donor without the stigma of prior involvement. Now that the LDCs charge the Soviet Union with 'equal responsibility' and defy Moscow to match its verbal support with concrete measures, few effective Soviet 'bargaining chips' remain and 'the Soviet Union's days as a Southern cheerleader without responsibilities would appear to be numbered' (Hansen, 1979: 6). It is becoming obvious that the Soviet Union's relative isolation from international economic and monetary transactions limits its ability to influence the issues considered most important by the LDCs today. The Soviets' political ambitions in the Third World, increasingly boosted by their military instrumentalities, are in serious danger of being undermined by Moscow's limited international economic capabilities (cf. Donaldson, 1981: 359, 378; Valkenier, 1981: 259).

In summary, superpower aid relations with the Third World are turning into a subject of mutual frustration and disillusionment. Concomitantly, the contrast is becoming increasingly apparent between the multifaceted American economic ties with the LDCs, of which foreign aid is but one — and not necessarily the most important — aspect, and the limited Soviet ability and will to use the aid instrument to wield influence in the Third World.

(3)   Development aid to the Third World is definitely no realm of exclusive or predominant superpower control. The combined American

and Soviet share of the total net aid flow in 1980 was only some 30 percent (OECD, 1981). Even in the case of arms transfers, where superpower dominance has long prevailed, the Big Two are losing ground. Whereas the United States and the Soviet Union in 1967 together accounted for 82.6 percent of world arms transfers (according to ACDA figures), their share had by 1976 dropped to 67.2 percent (Cahn, 1980: 174).

Moreover, superpower aid efforts have been characterized by rivalry rather than co-operation and aid relations have been strictly bilateral. To be sure, in the wake of frustrated foreign policy goals intensified US– Soviet collaboration has been the subject of internal discussions in both superpowers. Thus, some Soviet Third World specialists have recently suggested the desirability of including the West in trilateral arrangements and joint ventures in the Third World (see Valkenier, 1979: 23, 26). Similarly, during the warmest days of *détente*, several Americans assumed that the two superpowers could co-operate in aiding the LDCs (cf. Desfosses, 1981: 384). These ideas have, however, not yet been translated into official policy in either of the superpowers. In sum, therefore, it is impossible to speak of any superpower condominium in the area of aid relations with the Third World.

Notes

1. Foreign aid statistics are problematic generally. In their officially released figures, governments tend to compute aid differently. There is no one source which compiles American and Soviet aid statistics on a compatible basis. I have chosen OECD figures in the United States' case and CIA figures in the Soviet case as the least unreliable ones. The fact that my primary interest lies in identifying trends over time rather than comparing absolute figures tends to attenuate the reliability problem somewhat.
2. A first list of the least-developed countries, made by the UN in 1971, identified 25 countries (cf. UN, 1971: 232-5). Later additions to the list have brought the number of LLDCs up to 31 (cf. OECD, 1981: 88).

5 Crisis Management in the Middle East

Introduction

The relationship between the two superpowers has often been described in paradoxical terms. Raymond Aron (1967: 536-72) sees the United States and the Soviet Union as 'enemy partners' (frères-ennemis), and Coral Bell (1971a, b) has used the phrase 'adverse partnership' to characterize the contemporary superpower relationship.

Crisis management is of the essence in such a relationship. Bell (1971a: 31-7), for instance, considers crisis management the most important among different conventions of the US–Soviet 'adverse partnership.' The hovering threat of mutual nuclear devastation compels the superpowers to keep their rivalries and clashes within certain limits which, in turn, calls for a modicum of co-operation. Confrontations between the United States and the Soviet Union thus resemble fighting in a canoe. A blow hard enough to hurt may easily overturn the canoe (cf. Schelling, 1966: 123).

The United States and the USSR are, however, seldom alone in the canoe. In the post-war era most crises engaging the Big Two have originated and been enacted in more or less remote areas. Hence, superpower crisis management typically implies not only controlling the rivalry between themselves but also bringing pressure to bear on the local conflict parties (cf. Holbraad, 1979: 100).

The Middle East holds a prominent position in the post-war history of US–Soviet crisis management. The perennial Arab–Israeli conflict has repeatedly erupted in acute crises and open hostilities involving the superpowers. The purpose of this chapter is to scrutinize the record of superpower crisis management in the Middle East in view of our overriding questions: Have the United States and the Soviet Union displayed similar behavior? Have they proved to be equally powerful? And have they established a sort of condominium? In order to carry out such an analysis the conceptualization of 'crisis' and 'crisis management' must first be considered.

Crisis and Crisis Management

International crises, offering 'a microcosm of ongoing changes in international politics' (Young, 1968: 93), have attracted considerable attention among researchers. While there is broad agreement concerning the importance of studying international crises, no generally accepted definition of the term *crisis* exists.

A basic distinction might be made between *situational* and *procedural* definitions of crisis. Charles Hermann (1969, 1972b) is probably the most influential exponent of the former approach.In his classification of foreign policy situations according to degree of threat, decision time, and decision-maker awareness, crisis situations are characterized by high threat, short decision time, and surprise. Another common conception is that of crisis as an intermediate ideal type of state interaction between normal interaction and war (cf. e.g., Adomeit, 1973: 3-4).

Other scholars, whose principal focus has been on the dynamics of decision-making and interaction in international crises, have suggested definitions in terms of process. To view crisis as an inherently dynamic phenomenon rather than a static situation is in accordance with the original Greek meaning of the word as a turning point. Moreover, such a conceptualization serves our purpose of analyzing the kind of interaction sequences among superpowers and their clients called crisis management. In this alternative conception, a crisis is understood as a process of interaction representing a marked discontinuity in the regular flow of interaction and involving perceptions of a dangerously high probability that large-scale violence might break out (cf. e.g., Young, 1968: 9-14; Snyder and Diesing, 1977: 6).

Glenn Snyder and Paul Diesing (1977: 11-15) have attempted to delineate the sequence of crisis interaction. The first act of severe coercion is labeled the *challenge*. Although stimulated or motivated by a *precipitant* (such as the flow of Soviet armaments into Cuba in 1962), the challenge (e.g. the American demand that the missiles be withdrawn) initiates the crisis by posing a distinct possibility of war. In order for a crisis to occur, the challenge must be *resisted* by the challenged party. The conjunction of challenge and resistance produces *confrontation*. The confrontation phase may result either in war in which case the crisis is over and the parties move into a different type of interaction — or in capitulation or compromise — in which case the confrontation is followed by a *resolution* phase. This conceptualization is summarized in Figure 9 in which the solid horizontal lines represent the intensity of conflict behavior.

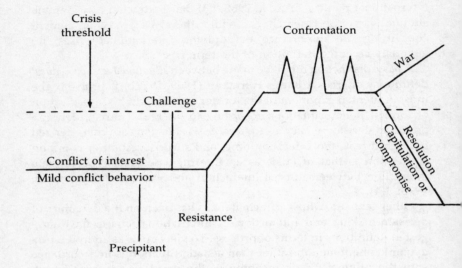

Fig. 9. Crisis phases (Snyder and Diesing, 1977: 15).

The notion that whatever occurs might result in the outbreak of war conforms to ordinary usage of the term crisis, and manipulating the risk of war and the fear of escalation is at the core of *crisis management*. The psychological and less tangible aspects of crisis management have become accentuated in this age of two nuclear superpowers. Nuclear technology has entailed an enormous widening of the gap between the values at stake in a conflict and the cost of war. War avoidance has come to be equivalent to disaster avoidance. The objective balance of military capabilities has furthermore become much less relevant to assessments of comparative resolve in crisis than in pre-nuclear times. Hence the manipulation of force short of war is becoming a substitute index of resolve.

Crises and crisis management may, in fact, be regarded as surrogates for war in contemporary superpower relations.

In any system, there must be some mechanism for change and for resisting change. Historically the ultimate mechanism has been war, but since war is no longer a plausible option between the nuclear powers, they have turned to threats of force and the demonstrative use of force short of war as a means of getting their way. [Snyder and Diesing, 1977: 456]

Superpower crisis management can therefore be regarded as 'a competition in risk taking, characterized not so much by tests of force as by tests of nerve' (Schelling, 1966: 94). The primary instruments of crisis management are *signals*, that is threats or offers communicated to the adversary (cf. Bell, 1971a: 35-7; 1971b: 73-5). Signaling may be incomplete or indirect. Communication in crises is, in fact, often tacit, involving nonverbal acts with adversaries watching and interpreting each other's behavior, 'each aware that his own actions are being interpreted and anticipated, each acting with a view to the expectations that he creates' (Schelling, 1963: 21). In other words, superpower crisis management can be seen as a bargaining process of a semi-tacit nature.

The existence of nuclear weapons, while urging greater prudence and constraint in crisis maneuvering on the part of the superpowers, has at the same time entailed a tacit raising of the 'provocation threshold,' thus increasing the range of available coercive moves to include a broad array of physical acts which might earlier have precipitated war.

Prior to the nuclear age, there were not many options available between verbal diplomacy and actual war. Options were pretty much limited to an occasional naval demonstration and the mobilization of land and naval forces. Since 1945, however, the crisis 'escalation ladder' has been lengthened; an arena of 'force short of war' has developed wherein states may use a variety of physical maneuvers to demonstrate resolve. [Snyder and Diesing, 1977: 453]

Signals, whether verbal or nonverbal, must be *communicated* and *made credible*. To be effective, they must first of all be perceived by the adversary. It will be ineffective if the adversary is somehow unavailable for the signal. Conversely, a signal may be perceived regardless of whether it has actually been sent or not. The behavior of the opponent may, for example, be anticipated or simply misunderstood. If the signal is perceived, the key problem of credibility remains. This problem, while common to all bargaining processes, assumes special significance in crises.

In a fundamental sense, crises increase the importance of strategic bargaining by sharply emphasizing the roles of political will and credibly communicated resolve. Because crises are relatively short, coercive, dangerous, and characterized by uncertainty, the importance of superior will and resolve tends to rise significantly in comparison with that of possessing superior capabilities in any physical sense. [Young, 1968: 175]

In crises such as those in the Middle East the communication and credibility problems are aggravated by the existence of multiple audiences and actors. Signals have to be communicated and made credible not only to the main adversary but also to the local conflict parties, domestic audiences, allies and third parties.

Strategies and Tactics in Crisis Management

As suggested above, crises involving the superpowers represent bargaining situations, that is situations characterized by the coincidence of co-operative and conflictual elements as well as interdependent decisions (cf. Jönsson, 1979a: 8-9). This implies that two basic strategies are available to the superpowers: *coercion* and *accommodation*. The goal of coercive strategies is to win. The constraint is to do this without war or excessive risk of war. In other words, the goals of the parties are in conflict and the constraint represents a common interest. On the other hand, the goal of accommodative strategies is to reach a settlement defusing the issue as a potential source of future crises. The constraint is to accomplish this with minimum concessions by one's own side. Here, the goal reflects the common interest whereas the constraint represents the conflicting interests. Whichever principal strategy a superpower chooses to adopt, some mixture of coercive and accommodative tactics is usually employed in its implementation. The complex interaction between the two sets of goals and constraints means that each superpower wishes to coerce prudently or accommodate cheaply or, more likely, to find the optimal blend of both (cf. Snyder and Diesing, 1977: 207-8; Williams, 1976: 52-5).

Conditions of crisis are apt to produce a combination of pressures to engage in clear-cut demonstrations of resolve and to undertake risky actions for bargaining purposes on the one hand, and to act prudentially in response to perceived increases in the dangers of destructive outcomes on the other hand. [Young, 1968: 1977]

Accommodation includes not only promises, concessions, and other co-operative moves *vis-à-vis* the other superpower but also moves to restrain local crisis parties. Similarly, coercion implies threatening the chief adversary as well as 'unleashing' and supporting local clients.

The strategic choice between accommodation and coercion entails a number of tactical options. Or, put differently, 'subsumed within the overall tension between coercion-to-win and avoidance-of-war are several subdilemmas' (Snyder and Diesing, 1977: 211). Two sets of options — or dilemmas — have received particular attention in the literature on crisis management. One concerns the art of commitment, the other the manipulation of shared risk (cf. Schelling, 1966: 35-125; Snyder and Diesing, 1977: 211-51). The first set of tactical choices, commit vs. preserve options, relates to the danger of miscalculation; the second set, manipulate vs. minimize risk, relates to the danger that the parties lose control of events.

Commit vs. Preserve Options. Thomas Schelling (1963: 22) has depicted the art of commitment as the 'power to bind oneself.' A commitment, incurred to demonstrate resolve, is a move that induces the other actor to choose in one's favor. It underscores one's current position by making it more difficult to yield from it. Hence it is intended to constrain the adversary's choice by affecting his expectations of one's own behavior (cf. Schelling, 1963: 122, 160).

To incur a commitment entails a loss of flexibility. It runs the risk of 'establishing an immovable position that goes beyond the ability of the other to concede, and thereby provoke the likelihood of stalemate or breakdown' (Schelling, 1963: 28). A commitment, especially a provocative one, often triggers a counter-commitment by the adversary. A dangerous escalation in commitments might ensue.

The obvious alternative if one wishes to remain free to react flexibly to the adversary's moves is to preserve a maximum range of options. Then, however, flexibility is bought at the expense of demonstrated resolve and coercive potency. The actor runs the risk that the adversary regards such flexibility and accommodation as signs of weakness and perceives chances of winning by remaining firm or hardening his commitments.

In short, the dilemma is this: commitment maximizes the chances of winning but flirts with disaster; option preservation maximizes the chances of avoiding war or extreme levels of destruction but risks being bested in the crisis contest of wills. A large part of the crisis management problem is to resolve this dilemma optimally. [Snyder and Diesing, 1977: 212]

In will be recalled that signals in crisis management may consist of verbal as well as physical moves. The commit vs. preserve options dilemma appears in either case. In formulating verbal signals, the main choice is between clarity and ambiguity. When it comes to physical moves, the dilemma appears as the choice of whether to begin high or low on the escalation ladder.

Maximum clarity of verbal commitments and forceful acts which preclude retreat tend to produce maximum credibility but entail serious losses of prestige and bargaining reputation if they fail their aims and the actor has to back down. Conversely, ambiguity and 'starting low' preserve options and minimize costs and risk in case of failure, while sacrificing credibility and hence coercive potency (cf. Snyder and Diesing, 1977: 211-34).

Manipulate vs. Minimize Risk. Crises 'tend to generate perceptions among decision-makers that their ability to exercise a conscious influence on the course of events is declining' (Young, 1968: 96). The risk of inadvertent war through loss of control is shared by the main crisis parties, and it may emanate from local actors or subordinates getting out of control or from events acquiring a momentum of their own.

One conceivable tactic is to raise the level of shared risk in the hope that the adversary then prefers to back down. 'Pressure is exerted on the adversary not by threatening deliberate violence but by raising the danger that war will occur through autonomous processes beyond the control of either party' (Snyder and Diesing, 1977: 234). 'Brinkmanship' is a label often assigned to such tactics of manipulating the shared risk of war.

An 'asymmetrical distribution of fears' (Young, 1968: 21) seems to be a prerequisite for effective 'brinkmanship.' An actor appearing to worry less about the risks associated with a crisis acquires advantages by being able to adopt more intransigent postures than its adversary.

The opposite tactic is to minimize the shared risk of war, to keep clear of the brink and deliberately avoid being drawn into the abyss. This is the obvious alternative when the prerequisite of an 'asymmetrical distribution of fears' is lacking.

Intramural and Adversary Crises

As far as superpower crisis management is concerned, a distinction can be made between 'intramural' and 'adversary' crises (Bell, 1971b: 7-9). Intramural crises take place within the walls of an alliance or a sphere of influence, adversary crises engage both superpowers directly or indirectly. Notwithstanding important intramural aspects of crises in the Middle East, these have principally been adversary crises from the superpowers' point of view. Yet a discussion of superpower crisis management would be incomplete without at least a brief digression into American and Soviet conduct in intramural crises.

There appears to be tacit agreement among the superpowers on certain 'rules of the game' concerning their behavior in intramural crises. First, there is a tacit understanding on mutual spheres of influence: each superpower accepts, and agrees to abstain from interfering or exercising influence within, regions dominated and penetrated by the other (cf. Kaufman, 1976: 9-11; Doran, 1976: 11-12).

> Although both superpowers try to stimulate centrifugal forces among each other's allies, neither wishes to see the emergence of new centers of military power — least of all nuclear power — that might endanger its own management of power. To this extent each has an interest in the other's preponderance within its coalition. [Osgood and Tucker, 1967: 171]

The superpowers' spheres of influence have therefore increasingly turned into 'Al Capone alliances' (Keohane, 1971: 180): remaining a faithful ally protects the small state not primarily against external threats but rather against the superpower itself.

With respect to superpower conduct in intramural crises, the behavior and, in particular, the verbal strategy of the United States and the Soviet Union reveal a number of implicit 'rules of the game:' (1) A member nation of a regional community cannot escape the 'jurisdiction' of the community; (2) The community (under the aegis of the superpower) may formulate norms of behavior for its members; (3) Whether or not a member lives up to these norms is determined by the other members of the community; (4) If the other members (in particular, the superpower) decide that a member is not complying with the norms, they have the right to use force to change the behavior of the recalcitrant member. This is not considered as aggression but rather as collective self-defense; (5) The expansion of an alien ideology is viewed as foreign subversion, an incident of aggression against which the regional community may take collective self-defense measures; (6) Invasion by the other members of the community may be undertaken if demanded by 'loyal' leaders of a member state even if they are not formally in government. These implicit norms — or shared mutual expectations about future conduct — have evolved through the 'echo phenomenon' of American and Soviet verbal justifications of their interventions in Latin America (Guatemala 1954, Dominican Republic 1965) and Eastern Europe (Hungary 1956, Czechoslovakia 1968), respectively (Franck and Weisband, 1972: cf. Scott, 1970).

As a corollary of the norms of non-intervention in each other's sphere of influence and unchallenged intervention within one's own sphere of influence, the superpowers seem to have reached a tacit understanding to pursue their keenest rivalry in the 'grey zones' of the world (cf. Holbraad, 1979: 110). The Middle East has over the years' been a principal arena of conflict and competition between the Big Two. The occasional eruptions of armed violence in the region — which, from the viewpoint of the regional actors, have been full-scale wars — have to the United States and the USSR represented 'adversary crises of local balance' (Bell, 1971b: 8), insofar as they have dangerously increased the probability of superpower clashes. Against the background of the foregoing general discussion, let us now turn to a review of American and Soviet attempts at crisis management in the Middle East in 1956, 1967 and 1973.

The Suez Crisis, 1956

The Suez crisis of 1956 represented the first US–Soviet involvement in, and attempt to influence the development of, a regional conflict in the Middle East. These early superpower efforts at crisis management were interpreted by many observers at the time as a first indication of nascent US–Soviet collusion and condominium (cf. Holbraad, 1979: 20). Such images of the crisis have lingered. For instance, Oran Young (1968: 55) excludes the Suez crisis from his study of coercive crisis bargaining on the grounds that it was 'characterized by effective, though tacit, Soviet–American coordination to guarantee the stability of the international system.'

To be sure, the Suez crisis established the United States and the Soviet Union as *the* external crisis managers in the Middle East, at the expense of Britain and France. But as an exercise in crisis management, let alone *joint* crisis management, it leaves much to be desired. Specifically, the signaling of the superpowers was, as we shall see, characterized more by ineptitude than by sophistication. The two superpowers were still novices at crisis management, and their collusion in the resolution of the crisis was accidental rather than premeditated.

The precipitant of the Suez crisis was President Nasser's nationalization of the Suez Canal Company on July 26, 1956, one week after the American government withdrew its earlier offer of a $56 million loan to help finance the building of the Aswan Dam. Britain and France reacted strongly against the seizure of 'an international waterway' and against the violation of the 1888 Convention, according to which 'the Suez Maritime Canal shall always be free and open, in time of war as in time of peace, to every vessel of commerce or of war without distinction of flag' (Stoessinger, 1977: 83). For Britain and France it was not only a matter of safeguarding the economic rights of their shareholders in the Suez Canal Company or of protecting a vital economic artery. To both, as well as to Egypt, the Suez Canal had a non-material, symbolic significance. While for Egypt it became a symbol of surging nationalism, to Britain it symbolized her status as an empire and a world power and to the French — the principle designers, directors and operators of the Canal — it was a tangible monument to *la France civilisatrice*.

In the weeks following Nasser's action Britain and France sounded out the American reaction and sought for a joint Western response. The Soviet Union had, through the 1955 arms deal and intensified diplomatic contacts, become involved in the fate of Egypt. The stage was thus set for an encounter of the superpowers.

Pre-Crisis Signaling

The three-month period between Nasser's seizure of the Suez Canal and the Israeli and Anglo–French invasion of Egypt in late October saw abortive attempts to steer clear of an open confrontation. A conference of the maritime nations interested in the status and operation of the Suez Canal was convened in London on August 16. The London conference achieved nothing except an eighteen-nation proposal — initiated by the United States and not supported by the USSR — for an international 'non-political' body to administer the Suez Canal. This proposal was submitted to, and promptly rejected by, Nasser. A second London conference was convened on September 19.

Attended by the eighteen 'majority' states, the conference considered a Users' Association plan suggested by US Secretary of State John Foster Dulles. A 'voluntary' Association was in fact established, though it did not affect the further course of events but was reduced to a temporary side show of 'diplomatic pantomime' (Johnson, 1957: 78-9). On September 22, the day after the conclusion of the London conference, Britain and France in defiance of the United States made an appeal to a deadlocked UN Security Council.

Differences in outlook between the cautious superpowers and their more militant clients entailed highly ambiguous American signaling and Soviet passivity in the initial stage of the conflict. After inviting France and the United States to tripartite consultations in London, British Prime Minister Anthony Eden on July 27 sent a telegram to President Eisenhower urging the United States to join in decisive counter-measures against Egypt. Pointing out that 'we are unlikely to attain our objectives by economic pressures alone,' Eden declared Britain's readiness 'in the last resort, to use force to bring Nasser to his senses' (Eden, 1960: 428). American signaling *vis-à-vis* its allies created the impression in London and Paris that the United States might support, or at least condone, British–French military actions. At the tripartite talks in London, Secretary Dulles told the British and French Foreign Ministers that 'force was the last method to be tried, but the United States did not exclude the use of force if all other methods failed'; a similar message was conveyed in a letter from Eisenhower to Eden (Eden, 1960: 436-7; Finer, 1964: 90-1). Yet upon his return, Dulles, in reply to the question 'what would happen if the London conference failed?,' stated: 'We have given no commitments at any time as to what the United States would do in that unhappy contingency' (Documents on International Affairs, 1956: 155).

In presenting the idea of a Users' Association, the Americans again engaged in ambiguous signaling *vis-à-vis* its allies. Asked about the American reaction to the eventual resort to force by Britain and France, President Eisenhower in a press conference of September 11 answered cryptically that 'if after all peaceful means are exhausted, there is some kind of aggression on the part of Egypt against a peaceful use of the Canal, you might say that we would recognize that Britain and France had no other recourse than to continue to use it even if they had to be more forceful than merely sailing through it' (Documents on International Affairs, 1956: 203). Two days later, Dulles, in reply to a similar question, stated that 'force, if justifiable at all, is only justifiable as a last resort' (Documents on International Affairs, 1956: 212).

A joint US–British–French formulation, used by Dulles in his press conference and by Eden in his speech before the House of Commons, held that Egyptian interference with the operations of the Users' Association would be a breach of the 1888 Convention, in which event the parties concerned would be 'free to take steps to assure their rights through the United Nations or through other action appropriate to the circumstances' (Documents on International Affairs, 1956: 214; cf. Eden, 1960: 482). Both Dulles and Eden were asked to explain the meaning of these words; they both declined to do so, since the agreed purpose was to leave the course of future action deliberately vague so as to maximize pressure on Egypt (Eden, 1960: 484). Yet Dulles, on his part, emphasized that the United States did not intend to 'shoot its way through' if met by force and that 'each nation has to decide for itself what action it will take to defend, and, if possible, realize its rights which it believes it has as a matter of treaty' (Documents on International Affairs, 1956: 215, 217). Eden's retrospective comment on Dulles's statements is noteworthy:

> It would be hard to imagine a statement more likely to cause the maximum allied disunity and disarray. . . . The words were an advertisement to Nasser that he could reject the project with impunity. We had never been told that a statement of this kind was to accompany the announcement of the Users' Club. Had we known that they were to be used as an accompaniment to the American announcement, we would never have endorsed it. [Eden, 1960: 483-4]

Moreover, the United States appeared to vacillate on the other type of leverage envisaged under the Users' Association plan — economic sanctions — as well. Dulles had recommended that the users make a concerted rerouting of their ships if Egypt failed to co-operate, thereby making a 'dry ditch' of the Suez Canal (cf. Finer, 1964: 235). Now Eisenhower in his press conference said: 'A program of economic sanctions has never been placed before me as of this moment, never' (Documents on International Affairs, 1956: 203). And Dulles assured that 'it is not our purpose to try to bring about a concerted boycotting of the Canal' but 'each country would have to decide for itself what it wanted its vessels to do' (Documents on International Affairs, 1956: 212). Not only did this equivocation erode the credibility of the threats in Cairo, but above all it undermined Britain's and France's confidence in the United States.

Though less far-reaching, there were differences between the Soviet Union and its client, Egypt, as well. While objecting to the calling of the London conference without prior consultations with the USSR or other signatories to the 1888 Convention and to the biased selection of participants, the Soviet Union agreed to attend the conference. Nasser, in contrast, flatly refused to participate. He considered it a deliberate insult that he was not consulted beforehand and objected to London as the site of the meeting. And whereas Nasser at that time favored UN discussion of the crisis, the Soviet Union did not support the idea (Smolansky, 1965: 583). It is also noteworthy that, contrary to widespread expectations in the West, the Soviet Union did not step in after the American refusal to finance the Aswan Dam but in various ways demonstrated its lack of enthusiasm for the project (Laqueur, 1959: 232). Nor was Moscow informed of Nasser's move to nationalize the Suez Canal in advance (Micunovic, 1980: 100-1, 104).

The Soviet Union by and large remained a bystander during the initial stage of the conflict. While not participating in the abortive second London conference, it continued to uphold the Egyptian cause, dispatched a number of Soviet and East European pilots to help fill the gap after the departure of most Suez Canal pilots (Smolansky, 1965: 585; d'Encausse, 1975: 74), and apparently stepped up arms shipments to Egypt (Laqueur, 1959: 236). The USSR expressed its alarm at the build-up of British and French forces in the eastern Mediterranean and repeatedly warned that any military action would entail 'serious international complications' (Smolansky, 1965: 584-6).

The ambiguous American signaling apparently instilled Soviet fears of a concerted Western action. One Soviet government statement argued that the United States was supporting the British and French military preparations while ostensibly advocating a peaceful settlement (Documents on International Affairs, 1956: 226). Even at the time of the Security' Council deliberations in mid-October, Soviet press commentaries dismissed allegations about the 'growing rift' between the United States and its allies and maintained that there were 'no significant differences' between their positions. Egypt, on the other hand, was careful not to identify the United States with the British and French actions (Smolansky, 1965: 586-7).

On October 29 Israeli forces invaded the Sinai peninsula and advanced rapidly both toward the Straits of Tiran and toward the Suez Canal. On October 30 France and Britain issued an ultimatum to Israel and Egypt pledging Anglo–French armed intervention unless 'all warlike action' was stopped within twelve hours. Following Egypt's rejection of the terms, British and French air assaults on Egypt began on October 31. From the viewpoint of the two superpowers this course of events represented a challenge which, if resisted by Egypt's supporter, the Soviet Union, would transgress the crisis threshold and increase the likelihood of a superpower clash.

Crisis Management

The Israeli and Anglo–French invasions of Egypt placed both superpowers on the horns of a dilemma. The United States could either support the Anglo–French action, thereby risking a superpower confrontation and alienating Third World opinion, or condemn it, which would give a gratuitous victory to the USSR, jeopardize NATO, and strengthen the Soviet presence in the Middle East (cf. Aron, 1967: 474-5). For the Soviet Union the option was between endangering its national security in a possible clash with the Western powers, or abandoning President Nasser to his fate, which would entail a serious loss of prestige and influence in the Arab world and throughout the Third World (cf. Smolansky, 1965: 587). An aggravating factor for the Soviet Union was the simultaneous upheaval in Hungary.

The American reaction was swift and determined. President Eisenhower immediately let it be known through his press secretary that he had obtained 'his first knowledge' of the Anglo–French ultimatum 'through press reports' (Documents on International Affairs, 1956: 263), and at the UN the United States, to the consternation of Britain and France, sponsored a resolution which called upon Israel to withdraw its forces 'behind the established armistice lines' and upon all UN members to 'refrain from the use of force or threat of force' (Documents on International Affairs, 1956: 264).

The American initiative was 'warmly welcomed' and given an affirmative vote by the Soviet UN representative (Finer, 1964: 368). After French and British vetoes in the Security Council, the United States and the Soviet Union agreed to evoke the Uniting for Peace procedure. A resolution proposed by the United States, the gist of which was similar to those which had been vetoed by France and Britain in the Security Council, received Soviet support and was adopted by the General Assembly. It was a unique manifestation of superpower consensus in the United Nations.

In comparison with the surprisingly decisive and uncompromising American reaction, the Soviet Union showed considerable caution and restraint at this stage. The concurrent Soviet armed intervention in Hungary undoubtedly contributed to this caution. No threats of Soviet actions on behalf of the assaulted Egyptians, no commitments to the active defense of Cairo were issued. Moreover, immediately after the Israeli invasion and the Anglo–French bombardment of Egypt both Soviet technicians and advisers and recently delivered IL-28 jet bombers were withdrawn from Egypt (Smolansky, 1965: 603; Glassman, 1975: 19-20). Moscow's passivity was not lost on the Arab leaders at the time (cf. Glassman, 1975: 15; Hottinger, 1975: 109-10, 112; Smolansky, 1965: 597).

Only on November 5, one week after the outbreak of hostilities and on the same day that Britain and France landed invasion forces in Port Said, did the Soviet Union seize the initiative. Soviet Premier Bulganin sent messages to the leaders of France, Britain, Israel, and the United States. Concomitantly, Soviet Foreign Minister Shepilov addressed a letter to the UN Security Council. These communications contained conditional commitments of varying severity and explicitness, spelling out the possible consequences of the failure of Anglo–French and Israeli forces to cease fire in Egypt and withdraw their troops. There was an inverse relationship between the severity and the explicitness of these warnings and threats. In order of decreasing severity and increasing explicitness, four conditional commitments may be distinguished (cf. Speier, 1957: 318): (1) a warning of global war as a result of the Suez crisis; (2) implicit threats of Soviet strategic rocket strikes on Britain and France; (3) a threat of unilateral Soviet intervention in the Middle East; (4) an 'offer' of joint Soviet–American intervention under UN auspices.

(1) The vague warning that the fighting in Egypt might 'spread to other countries and develop into a third world war' appeared in all of Bulganin's messages except the one to Israeli Prime Minister Ben-Gurion which merely stated that the Israeli government, by 'acting as an instrument of outside imperialist forces,' had put 'in jeopardy the very existence of Israel as a state' (Documents on International Affairs, 1956: 291-2).

(2) Not being regarded as the principal actor, Israel was also exempted from the specific threats of Soviet rocket strikes which were issued in the letters to Eden and Mollet. These contained many parallel passages, but also an interesting graduation of threats which might reveal 'the Soviets' estimate as to who among the recipients had strong and who weak nerves' (Ulam, 1971: 258). To both Eden and Mollet the threat of rocket strikes was made in the non-committal form of a

conditional question. In his letter to Mollet, Bulganin merely asked rhetorically: 'In what situation would France find herself were she attacked by other states that have formidable means of destruction?' (Documents on International Affairs, 1956: 290). The threat was, however, made more specific in the communication to Eden. Britain was reminded that she might be attacked by 'stronger states, possessing all types of modern destructive weapons' including 'rocket weapons' (Documents on International Affairs, 1956: 289).

The inherent credibility of the implicit Soviet threats was low. The USSR in 1956 possessed limited capabilities to engage in a strategic rocket attack. There was confidence in the West of overwhelming strategic superiority over the Soviet Union, and of American readiness to retaliate if the USSR were to attack Britain and France (Glassman, 1975: 16). Moreover, the vague character of the threats, the lack of any time stipulation within which Britain and France were to comply with the Soviet demands, the lack of any accompanying preparedness moves, and the simultaneous proposals for UN — or American–Soviet — intervention in the Middle East combined to reduce the credibility of the threats.

(3) The threat of unilateral Soviet intervention in the Middle East, too, was 'so cautiously phrased, and the proposed action so carefully justified, that the appearance of a threat was technically avoided' (Speier, 1957: 320). Shepilov's note to the Security Council proposed UN, alternatively Soviet–American, intervention in the event that Britain, France, and Israel failed to cease fire and withdraw. Shepilov also added: 'The Soviet government, on its part, declares its readiness to make its contribution to curbing the aggressors, to defending the victims of aggression and restoring peace, by dispatching to Egypt the necessary air and naval forces' (Documents on International Affairs, 1956: 287). In a similar vein, Bulganin in his letters to Eden and Mollet expressed the determination of the Soviet Union to 'crush the aggressors by the use of force' (Documents on International Affairs, 1956: 289, 291). The wording created the impression that the proposal for UN, or joint Soviet–American, intervention might have been made in order to derive from its rejection a justification for unilateral Soviet intervention in the Middle East (cf. Speier, 1957: 322).

(4) The idea of joint superpower military action to defend Egypt, which was hinted at in Shepilov's note, was spelled out in quite explicit terms in Bulganin's message to Eisenhower:

The Soviet Union and the United States of America are both permanent members of the Security Council and great powers possessing all modern types of weapons, including atomic and hydrogen weapons. We bear a special responsibility for stopping the war and restoring peace and tranquility in the area of the Near and Middle East. We are convinced that if the governments of the U.S.S.R. and the United States firmly declare their determination to ensure peace, and come out against aggression, then aggression will be ended and there will be no war. [Documents on International Affairs, 1956: 293]

Bulganin's message, which affirmed Soviet readiness to enter into immediate negotiations with the United States concerning the implementation of joint US–Soviet action, caused great concern in Washington. A reply was drafted with unusual speed. Within a few hours the White House issued a statement categorically rejecting Bulganin's proposal for joint US–Soviet action as 'unthinkable.' A counterthreat was issued to the implied Soviet threat of unilateral intervention: If new forces were introduced in the Middle East without a UN mandate, the statement said, 'it would be the duty of all United Nations members, including the United States, to oppose any such effort' (Documents on International Affairs, 1956: 294). The threats to Britain and France and the warning that a third world war might develop were ignored in the statement, but Eisenhower is known to have made it clear to the Soviet leaders that the United States would retaliate in the event of a nuclear attack against its British and French allies (Smolansky, 1965: 599; Johnson, 1957: 124; Holbraad, 1979: 29).

The prompt verbal American response was underpinned by certain preparedness moves. The Continental Air Defense Command, the Sixth Fleet, and the Strategic Air Command were alerted. A naval force, including aircraft carriers, began to steam toward Europe (Speier, 1957: 325; Smolansky, 1965: 599). These moves were, however, not made public (Ulam, 1971: 259).

Concomitantly, the United States exerted strong diplomatic pressure on Britain, France and Israel to achieve a ceasefire. At the same time as the United States assured its European allies that the nuclear 'umbrella' still protected Western Europe, it was made clear to London and Paris that they could not count on American assistance if they found themselves engaged in fighting with Soviet volunteers in the Middle East, that is, if the Soviet Union decided to carry out its threat of unilateral intervention (Holbraad, 1979: 30). In messages to London, Paris, and Tel-Aviv, the United States government demanded a ceasefire as recommended in the US-sponsored General Assembly resolution of November 2. The United States declared that it intended to stick to the UN Charter and that the three countries, if they failed to comply, could not count on continued American support (cf. Holbraad, 1979: 31; Finer, 1964: 422, 429, 432).

On November 6, less than twenty-four hours after the Soviet dispatches, Britain, France and Israel agreed to a ceasefire. American pressures, a run on the pound, and internal opposition in combination with the Soviet threats compelled Eden to take the lead in calling off the military action in Suez. The UN General Assembly established an Emergency Force (UNEF) under the administration of Secretary-General Hammarskjöld to supervise the ceasefire and troop withdrawal. The crisis was moving into a resolution phase.

Summary

How, then, is one to assess the attempts by the United States and the Soviet Union to manage the crisis? As suggested at the outset, the parallel of American and Soviet crisis management efforts in 1956 demonstrated their ineptitude rather than sophistication, at signaling. First, neither superpower was able to control the course of events leading up to the acute crisis. The eventual outbreak of hostilities apparently took both by surprise.

Direct US–Soviet communication was rare throughout the crisis. The commitments incurred were ambiguous in wording and were not backed by preparedness moves or actions — the only exception being the American response to the Soviet diplomatic moves of November 5, in which case the preparedness moves were, however, not well advertised. Both superpowers were reluctant to manipulate risk. It could be argued that the November 5 Soviet combination of threats represented one such effort, but then it must be remembered that these threats came only after Moscow was assured of the American attitudes toward both the Hungarian and Suez crises (Smolansky, 1965: 591). In brief, whereas the Cold War conflict prevented even tacit co-operation in crisis management, mutual fear of a major East–West confrontation barred a more active manipulation of risk and stronger commitments. The fact that the strategic doctrines of both superpowers at the time of the Suez crisis were couched in terms of 'massive retaliation' obviously narrowed the range of available instruments for crisis management. The United States and the Soviet

Union alike were unprepared, intellectually as well as materially, for the limited employment of force. Fear of escalation prevailed, and the 'provocation threshold' was still lower than that to which we have since become accustomed.

The Suez crisis also revealed power asymmetries between the United States and the Soviet Union: 'throughout the Suez crisis Soviet freedom of action was profoundly limited by the position of the United States which, in the last analysis, was the only great power able to influence the outcome of the conflict' (Smolansky, 1965: 591). In the wake of the crisis the Soviet Union argued that its 'determined' stand was the decisive factor in halting armed aggression against Egypt (Smolansky, 1965: 594-5). However, most observers agree that the pressure that the United States brought to bear on Britain, France and Israel was decisive in resolving the crisis, whereas the Soviet Union 'entered to push down what was already toppling' (Finer, 1964: 417). The Soviet Union 'spoke loudly, but carried a small stick.' The tardy and rather empty Soviet threats probably had a certain impact in Washington. But the United States in 1956 not only enjoyed military superiority *vis-à-vis* the USSR but was also the only superpower with leverage over the 'aggressors.'

The parallel action of the United States and the Soviet Union at the decisive stage of the Suez crisis can hardly be labeled a superpower concert or condominium. The Soviet bid for condominium was categorically rejected by the United States. The seriousness of the Soviet proposal is debatable. The idea of US–Soviet co-operation in the Middle East and subsequent division into American and Soviet spheres of influence may well have been very attractive to Moscow, but the probability of its success was quite low. Yet it constituted a useful diplomatic device by which the Soviets could improve their position without taking any appreciable risks. The predictable American refusal to participate could be construed as an indirect approval of the Anglo–French–Israeli military adventure. This theme was, in fact, prominent in Soviet post-crisis propaganda (see Smolansky, 1965: 594).

The long-term 'intramural' aspects of superpower crisis managment in 1956 were perhaps the most important ones. Both the United States and the Soviet Union demonstrated beyond doubt that there were only two superpowers in the world. Britain and France, which until recently had been the major external powers in the Middle East, were reduced to the rank of middle powers, regionally as well as globally, as a result of the Suez crisis.

It could also be argued that the regional actors, Israel and Egypt, emerged stronger and more confident from the Suez crisis: Israel, because of its demonstrated military skills, Egypt, because of its political triumph over Britain and France (Stoessinger, 1977: 91). To both superpowers the crisis brought home the need to control the regional actors at the same time as it gave a first indication of their less than complete ability to do so.

In brief, the Suez crisis, by establishing the United States and the Soviet Union as the principal extra-regional actors and strengthening the regional actors yet not solving the underlying regional conflict, set the stage for — as well as helping to complicate — future superpower efforts at crisis management in the region.

The Six-Day War, 1967

Between Suez 1956 and the Six-Day War in 1967 the conditions for superpower crisis management had changed in several significant ways. 'Massive retaliation' had given way to notions of 'flexible response' in both American and Soviet strategic thinking. As a result, the two superpowers were better equipped — doctrinally as well as materially — for limited employments of force below the nuclear threshold, and the fear of uncontrolled escalation was abated. In other words, the repertoire of instruments for crisis management had widened.

Furthermore, the superpowers had accumulated experiences of crisis bargaining and signaling. One seminal event was the Cuban missile crisis of 1962 when the Big Two came closer to the nuclear abyss than ever before. The crisis found the superpowers in a rare *direct* confrontation, and its resolution taught them important lessons concerning crisis management.

One important mutual lesson of the Cuban missile crisis was the paramount need to avoid a nuclear confrontation. Another lesson which was brought home to the Soviet Union in particular concerns the usefulness of naval forces for crisis management. They permit accessibility, freedom of action, and an open line of retreat from impending collision; capable of conspicuous presence and withdrawal, they offer readily perceived and understood signaling instruments; and they are not dependent on bases in the interior of other countries' territory. The American naval blockade proved effective in the Cuban missile crisis, and the operations of the American Sixth Fleet in Lebanon 1958 and elsewhere in the

Mediterranean had demonstrated the utility of naval forces in Middle East crises specifically. After 1962 an impressive Soviet naval buildup began in general, and in the Mediterranean in particular. Several reasons have been adduced by observers in the West. One contributing factor seems to have been that 'the Cuban crisis of October 1962 . . . persuaded the security planners in Moscow that a Soviet fleet continuously deployed in the Mediterranean would reinforce Soviet diplomacy' (Hurewitz, 1969: 14).

Within the Middle East, finally, the complexity of regional grievances and conflicts had become ever more apparent, at the same time as the involvement and commitments of the two superpowers came to be defined in dichotomous East–West terms. With respect to both moral and military support, Israel and Egypt stood out as the main clients of the United States, and the USSR, respectively. Soviet arms deliveries to Egypt expanded after the Suez crisis, and in 1962 the United States gave up its earlier policy of abstention from Middle Eastern weapons supply and began to deliver arms to Israel to offset the threatening Egyptian military superiority (Glassman, 1975: 31).

Such were the new conditions, as the superpowers in the early summer of 1967 again moved, or were led, toward confrontation in the Middle East.

Pre-Crisis Signaling

The origins of the Middle East crisis of 1967 are not easy to trace. An immediate precipitant was the combination of growing tension along the Israeli–Syrian border and a domestic crisis within Syria in the spring of 1967 (cf. e.g., Laqueur, 1969: 71-82). A coup in February 1966 had brought an extremely anti-Israeli left-wing faction of the Ba'ath party to power in Syria. The new regime soon received political support and extensive aid commitments from the USSR. As a result of frequent border clashes and Syrian-based al Fatah raids into Israel, which were openly supported by Syria, tension along the Israeli– Syrian border mounted steadily.

To forestall alleged Israeli plans to invade Syria, Egypt, on May 14 1967, mobilized its armed forces and ordered two divisions into Sinai. Two days later Egypt requested the withdrawal of the United Nations Emergency Force (UNEF) from the positions in Sinai which it had occupied since the Suez crisis. UN Secretary General U Thant complied on May 18. The next day UNEF ceased to exist, and Egyptian units occupied its positions along the Israeli border. On May 22 Nasser announced that Egyptian forces had reoccupied Sharm el-Sheikh and closed the Straits of Tiran to Israeli shipping, thereby completing the challenge that dramatically raised the likelihood of war in the Middle East.

During this buildup phase both American and Soviet signaling *vis-à-vis* their clients was ambiguous. Since its Arab clients held the initiative in the early phase of the crisis, the Soviet Union played a more important role than the United States, which remained relatively passive.

Between May 1966 and May 1967 the Soviet media frequently echoed news in the Syrian and Egyptian press about major Israeli troop concentrations on the Syrian border (Laqueur, 1969: 73-4). The same theme recurred in official Soviet statements (cf. Morison, 1970: 214-15; Glassman, 1975: 39). The frequent repetition of the same themes would seem to make such Soviet statements less ominous and credible in the eyes of most observers. Walter Laqueur (1969: 175) even contends that the Soviets themselves 'were not impressed by their own arguments and . . . did not expect a war.' Yet Soviet reports about Israeli troop concentrations in the spring of 1967 came to play a key role in the initiation of the Middle East crisis.

In early May the Syrian government was experiencing a new domestic crisis. To discredit internal opponents, the Ba'ath regime attempted to link the domestic disturbances to a co-ordinated imperialist plot spearheaded by Israel, and raised alarms about the imminent threat of an Israeli invasion (cf. Laqueur, 1969: 79-80; Horelick, 1972: 586). The Soviet Union, as so many times before, echoed the Syrian line but also, more significantly, conveyed to Egypt unsubstantiated reports about Israeli troop deployments on the Syrian border and an Israeli plan for a large-scale attack on Syria. Most observers agree that the Soviet Union did so in order to spur the Egyptians into military support of Syria. An Egyptian display of force *vis-à-vis* Israel under the provisions of the new Egyptian–Syrian defense pact would presumably fortify the unsteady Syrian government and deter Israeli intervention that might endanger the survival of the Damascus regime. The retreat of Israel in the face of Soviet-inspired Arab unity would no doubt have enhanced Soviet prestige (cf. Laqueur, 1969: 80, 230; Glassman, 1975: 39-40; Horelick, 1972: 583; Jabber and Kolkowicz, 1981: 424).

Soviet efforts to manipulate their Egyptian clients in support of their more vulnerable Syrian ally were not successful, however. The Egyptians apparently recognized that the reports of Israeli troop concentrations were false. Israel repeatedly invited the Soviet ambassador to visit the Syrian border region to see for himself whether troops were deployed there. On each occasion he refused. Reports from UN observers confirmed the absence of any military buildup along the border (Glassman, 1975: 40). And after the war it was reported that the Egyptian Chief of Staff, after a personal visit to Syria to investigate reports of Israeli troop concentrations, reported back that the Soviets 'must be having hallucinations' (Horelick, 1972: 587).

Yet the Egyptians decided to act. Why? Two — not totally incompatible — explanations have been offered. One holds that Nasser may have believed that even in the absence of troop concentrations the alleged Israeli attack on Syria was in the offing. It has been pointed out that the most likely scenario would have been an Israeli air and paratroop attack on Damascus for which no major troop buildup along the Syrian border would be required (cf. Horelick, 1972: 587; Whetten, 1981: 47). The other possibility is that Nasser interpreted the Soviet combination of misinformation and declarations of support as encouragement to pursue a more anti-Israeli policy which might at the same time revive his declining prestige in the Arab world (cf. Horelick, 1972: 587; Mangold, 1978: 117).

The available evidence indicates that the Soviet Union approved Nasser's initial move, the conspicuous dispatch of Egyptian troops into the Sinai beginning on May 14, but was increasingly concerned about his subsequent actions. To be sure, Nasser's demand for the withdrawal of UNEF was formally supported by Moscow. But Soviet diplomats at the UN let it be known that Moscow had not been consulted and was taken by surprise (Glassman, 1975: 40-1). The Egyptian decision to close the Straits of Tiran met with Soviet reticence. Nasser's acticns were on the whole given only cursory notice in the Soviet press. An obvious effort was made to play down and de-emphasize the crisis (Morison, 1970: 218-19; Laqueur, 1969: 177; Whetten, 1981: 49). And after the Six-Day War Soviet sources repeatedly insisted to Western observers that the Soviet Union was neither consulted nor informed about Nasser's May 18 and May 22 moves (Horelick, 1972: 588; Howe, 1971: 74), that Nasser in Moscow's view went too far and acted in defiance of Soviet warnings (Glassman, 1975: 43-44). The Soviet Union did, in fact, have good reason to be worried about the Tiran Straits blockade. First, it was in the Soviet interest to uphold international law governing international waterways, lest its own access to the Danish and Turkish straits be jeopardized. Second, the blockade challenged the validity of the commitments the United States had given to Israel in 1957 to guarantee free passage through the Straits of Tiran and consequently raised the specter of direct American involvement (Whetten, 1981: 49).

The main thrust of early American signaling was to warn Israel not to act unilaterally. On May 17 President Lyndon Johnson sent a cable to Israeli Prime Minister Levi Eshkol in which he stated: 'I am sure you will understand . . . that I cannot accept any responsibilities on behalf of the United States for situations which arise as the result of actions on which we are not consulted' (Johnson, 1971: 290). Israel, on its part, was probing the extent of American support. Thus, Eshkol's reply to Johnson's letter requested that the United States should reaffirm, and communicate to the Soviets, its commitment to Israel's security. On May 19 Johnson did write to Soviet Premier Kosygin, declaring American support of Israel as requested, but suggesting in addition a 'joint initiative of the two powers to prevent the dispute from drifting into war' (Quandt, 1977: 40-1).

On May 23, the day following the closing of the Straits, both the United States and the Soviet Union made public statements of policy which must have been received with less than enthusiasm among their respective clients. First, both superpowers assured their desire to preserve peace in the Middle East. President Johnson asserted that the United States 'strongly opposes aggression by anyone in the area, in any form, overt or clandestine' while earnestly supporting 'all efforts, in and outside the United Nations . . . to reduce tensions and to restore stability' (Howe, 1971: 53). The Soviet government, expressing its 'firm belief' that 'the peoples have no interest in a military conflict in the Middle East,' assured that 'the Soviet Union is doing and will continue to do everything in its power to prevent a violation of peace and security in the Near East and safeguard the legitimate right of the peoples' (Ro'i, 1974: 439).

Second, and more important, neither superpower made any strong, unequivocal commitment on behalf of its clients. 'The United States,' said President Johnson, 'is firmly committed to the support of the political independence and territorial integrity of *all* the nations of that area' (Howe, 1971: 53; emphasis added). And in a subsequent UN debate Ambassador Arthur Goldberg declared that the American attitude to the crisis was not one of 'partisanship' (Howe, 1971: 54). The Soviet Union was, on the face of it, more forthcoming *vis-à-vis* its Arab clients, but its promise of support was cloudy: 'should anyone try to unleash aggression in the Near East he would be met not only by the united strength of Arab countries but also by *strong opposition* to aggression from the Soviet Union and all peace-loving states' (Ro'i, 1974: 439; emphasis added). Did 'strong opposition' mean armed resistance or political opposition? The wording was no doubt deliberately vague to allow different interpretations, but two details in the Soviet government statement suggest that less than armed resistance was implied: (1) 'All peace-loving states' were envisaged as sharing the Soviet reaction; (2) Elsewhere in the statement states which had 'declared their determination to help Syria in the event of an attack by Israel' were enumerated — the list included only Arab states and not the Soviet Union (Ro'i, 1974: 438). Similar statements in the Soviet press around the same time made the same omission (Dawisha, 1979: 40).

As their hedging suggests, the United States and the Soviet Union were at this juncture concerned about the possibility of a direct superpower confrontation. Another indication is that direct US–Soviet interaction intensified. Via diplomatic channels, each superpower assured the other of its desire to preserve peace in the Middle East and avoid a direct superpower clash (cf. Laqueur, 1969: 162; Young, 1967: 56; Holbraad, 1979: 84).

Via diplomatic and informal exchanges (cf. Johnson, 1971: 291; Howe, 1971: 55-6; Whetten, 1981: 49), the superpowers seem to have reached a tacit agreement to restrain their respective clients. On May 26 Israeli Foreign Minister Abba Eban had a 'direct and frank' conversation with President Johnson in Washington. In a formulation that was to recur frequently in the days to follow, Johnson warned that 'Israel will only be alone if it decides to go alone.' The Israelis were told to show restraint for at least two weeks. The Israeli cabinet on May 28 decided with the narrowest possible majority to accede to the American request (cf. Johnson, 1971: 293-4; Quandt, 1977: 48-55; Holbraad, 1979: 82).

The Soviet Union, for its part, took parallel mesures to restrain Egypt. Through several channels, Moscow conveyed the message that Egypt could not count on Soviet military support if it attacked Israel (Glassman, 1975: 41; Dawisha, 1979: 41). Most dramatically, on May 27 the Soviet ambassador in Cairo awakened Nasser at three in the morning with a message from the Kremlin requesting him not to initiate hostilities. According to Israeli intelligence reports passed on by the Americans to Moscow, Egypt was planning an attack on May 27. Despite Nasser's denial of any such plans, the Soviet ambassador cautioned Nasser not to fire the first shot (Glassman, 1975: 42; Dawisha, 1979: 41).

In the event, however, the superpowers proved unable to control their clients. One conclusion both Israel and Egypt could draw from superpower signaling in the buildup phase was that neither the United States nor the USSR was about to intervene militarily. And whereas the superpowers communicated mutual unwillingness to 'unleash' their clients, the latter were all the time looking for hints of a 'green light' in the ambiguous signaling of their protectors (cf. e.g., Glassman, 1975: 41; Laqueur, 1969: 141). Egypt and Israel counted on the superpowers to deter each other from intervention while supporting, or at least condoning, their clients' unilateral moves.

The military buildup continued on both sides. The blockade of the Straits of Tiran was not lifted, nor were Egyptian troops withdrawn from the Israeli border. In addition, Jordan on May 30 unexpectedly signed a defense agreement with Egypt. Against this background, the newly-formed Israeli coalition government, with Moshe Dayan as Minister of Defense, decided in favor of 'preventive' war. On the morning of June 5 Israel launched its counterforce strike against Arab air bases with devastating success.

Crisis Management

With the outbreak of hostilities, the superpowers abandoned their earlier caution and 'under-involvement' (Whetten, 1981: 53), both becoming increasingly engaged. Whereas the ambiguity dissipated, the basic messages remained the same. The United States and the Soviet Union repeated and underscored their mutual readiness (1) to avoid a superpower confrontation, and (2) to restrain their clients.

The immediate reaction of both superpowers as war broke out was to get in touch with each other. At about 5.30 a.m. on June 5, Secretary of State Dean Rusk sent a message through normal channels indicating that the United States was 'astonished that fighting had commenced' and was 'ready to do everything we could to end the fighting and help restore the peace' (Howe, 1971: 90; Quandt, 1977: 61-2). In the first use of the hot line in the four years of its existence, Kosygin called Johnson at 8.00 a.m. He expressed Soviet concern over the fighting, called for US–Soviet co-operation in bringing about a ceasefire and expressed the hope that the United States would urge restraint on Israel. Johnson in his reply agreed that the two superpowers should stay out of the fighting and encourage a ceasefire (cf. Johnson, 1971: 298; Quandt, 1977: 62).

The mutual readiness to avoid a superpower confrontation, which was indicated in the initial hot line exchange between Moscow and

Washington, was signaled in several different ways throughout the acute phase of the crisis. Already on June 6, Kosygin and Johnson again communicated over the hot line. One of the subjects raised was the false Arab allegations that American aircraft had taken part in air attacks on Egypt. Reminding Kosygin that Soviet intelligence knew the location of American ships and planes, Johnson suggested that this information be passed on to Cairo (Johnson, 1971: 299). Moscow never gave currency to the Arab allegations, which could be seen as an attempt to draw the Soviet Union into the war, and reportedly informed its Arab clients that it knew the accusations to be false (Glassman, 1975: 54).

The hot line was used again on June 8 in connection with the erroneous Israeli attack on the American electronic intelligence-gathering ship *Liberty*. In order to avoid misunderstandings, Johnson informed Kosygin that American carrier aircraft were on their way to investigate the incident, pointing out that this was the sole purpose of the flights and requesting that the proper parties be informed. Kosygin replied that the information had been immediately conveyed to the Egyptians (Johnson, 1971: 301).

These verbal assurances of non-involvement were reinforced by American and Soviet actions, in particular naval movements. This was the first time Soviet and American warships operated in close proximity to each other during a major international crisis (Howe, 1971: 29) and hence an initial test of the signaling potentials of naval forces in superpower crisis management. In mid-May the main portion of the United States Sixth Fleet was in the western half of the Mediterranean. In response to developments in the Middle East, there was a move eastward, as could be expected. Yet this preparedness move was circumscribed in several important ways to signal the American intention to avoid military involvement. First, the main body of the Sixth Fleet stopped south of Crete, within striking distance but well clear of the actual fighting, where it remained after the outbreak of hostilities. Since Soviet naval forces shadowed the American ships, this signal was no doubt received and understood. Second, to create an impression of 'business as usual,' no scheduled port calls were interrupted or shortened. Third, the amphibious forces of the Sixth Fleet with nearly two thousand combat marines embarked stayed, as scheduled, in Naples until the third week in May, when they put into port in Malta. The visible retention of the marines in the central Mediterranean, a thousand miles, or three days away from Sinai, represented another readily understood signal of American non-involvement. The impact of this move was doubtless enhanced by its striking contrast to past American reactions to potential challenges throughout the globe, including the Middle East. In the Lebanon crisis of 1958, for instance, the United States tripled the number of marine battalions and substantially increased the number of ships in the area prior to the actual requirement to use them. Finally, the carrier *Intrepid*, which was on her way from the east coast of the United States to Vietnam via the Suez Canal in late May, rather than reinforce the fleet in the Mediterranean, completed her transit as scheduled. Moreover, instead of coming under the Sixth Fleet Commander when entering the Mediterranean, as would normally be the case, *Intrepid* remained directly under the Commander in Chief, Naval Forces, Europe, in London, and the request for Suez transit clearance went to Egypt, not from the Sixth Fleet but from London (cf. Wylie, 1969: 58-60; Howe, 1971: 69-71, 143-4, 147-8).

The Soviet Mediterranean fleet, in addition to supervising and reporting the movements of US ships, was used for signaling purposes as well. Movements of Soviet ships were equally circum-scribed throughout the crisis. Beginning on May 31 the Soviet Union transited ten additional ships to the Mediterranean from the Black Sea. The Turkish government was notified on May 22 of the impending transit of the Bosporus in accordance with the eight-day period of notice stipulated by convention. This could be seen as a response to American naval movements at that time and minimum fulfillment of Moscow's alleged promise to Nasser to match any American escalation. The types of ships sent into the Mediterranean were probably meant to signal Soviet desires to avoid a confrontation with the United States. The augmentation consisted mainly of vessels to sustain the existing taskforce and did not significantly alter the naval balance. No amphibious ships, submarines, or cruisers were added. Moreover, when hostilities broke out in the Middle East, Soviet vessels not engaged in shadowing remained in their anchorages near the eastern shores of Crete and Cyprus (Howe, 1971: 76-8, 117; Wells, 1979). In short, Soviet naval behavior seems 'to have been deliberately orchestrated to reassure the United States that the Mediterranean Squadron did not intend to take any part in the crisis' (Jabber and Kolkowicz, 1981: 438).

If the avoidance of a US–Soviet clash was one major theme of verbal and tacit superpower signaling during the Six-Day War, the need to restrain their respective clients was another leitmotif. This was expressed in mutual requests to the opposite superpower to exert influence on its client as well as unilateral moves to restrain their respective clients. The first exchange on the hot line contained a hint of concerted efforts to influence the protagonists. Yet the superpowers were not very successful in this regard. As before, they were torn between the need to demonstrate support of their clients and the need to bring an effective halt to hostilities which might eventually engage them in direct superpower confrontation. Since it was Israel which was winning the war, the burden of exercising a restraining influence fell primarily on the United States.

This was graphically demonstrated in the June 10 diplomatic confrontation between the superpowers as a result of Israeli advances in Syria after the adoption of a UN Security Council ceasefire resolution. On the morning of June 10 Kosygin sent a hot line message to Johnson in which he spoke of a 'very crucial moment' fraught with risks of a 'grave catastrophe' and threatened 'necessary action, including military,' unless Israel halted its military operations within the next few hours (Johnson, 1971: 302). Around the same time, some East European diplomats hinted at the UN that 'volunteers' might be dispatched to the Arabs (Glassman, 1975: 56).

Johnson in his reply stressed that the United States 'had been pressing Israel to make the ceasefire completely effective and had received assurances that this would be done' (Johnson, 1971: 303). Informing the Israelis of the Soviet threat, the United States insisted on a termination of hostilities and advised that the Soviet Union would probably react vigorously if Damascus itself were threatened (Whetten, 1981: 54; Glassman, 1975: 58). Concomitantly, the Sixth Fleet was ordered to move closer to the Syrian coast. In Johnson's own words (1971: 302):

> We all knew the Russians would get the message as soon as their monitors observed the change in the fleet's pattern. That message, which no translator would need to interpret to the Kremlin leadership, was that the United States was prepared to resist Soviet intrusion in the Middle East.

The fact that the Soviet threat of unilateral action, as in 1956, came at the end of a crisis when hostilities seemed to be about to cease creates the impression that 'the Soviet threat, like its 1956 precedent, may have been largely a gratuitous gesture to regain Arab political support' (Glassman, 1975: 58). Nor was the Soviet threat backed up by any preparedness moves. Soviet warships merely maintained their trailing positions, and Soviet airborne divisions were not put on a high state of alert (Whetten, 1981: 54). Moreover, against the background of Soviet military deficiencies and Israeli superiority in the area, the threat of Soviet military intervention was hardly credible (cf. Howe, 1971: 106; Glassman, 1975: 58). Although it was received with 'great concern and utmost gravity' (Johnson, 1971: 302) by American decision-makers, the effect of the Soviet threat was marginal; it added urgency to the earlier American attempts to make Israel accept a ceasefire and made the United States intensify its pressure on Israel. A ceasefire was, in fact, worked out and took effect on June 11.

Another noteworthy aspect of superpower efforts to restrain clients concerns arms transfers to the belligerents and applies primarily to the Soviet Union. First, the Soviet Union did not resupply the Arab belligerents during the course of hostilities — an important factor in view of the fact that Arab air forces were destroyed on the ground in the initial Israeli assault. This meant that many qualified Arab pilots remained available for combat if Soviet replacement aircraft had been provided (Glassman, 1975: 46, 53). In addition, Soviet arms transfers in the years prior to the crisis were designed to provide Egypt with a defensive rather than offensive capability (Glassman, 1975: 36-7, 62).

Summary

Against the background of the early experience of Suez 1956, what conclusions can be drawn concerning superpower crisis management in 1967? First, it became evident that the early expectation that US– Soviet collusion in the 1956 Suez crisis was the harbinger of superpower condominium did not materialize as the Arab–Israeli conflict again erupted in open hostilities. Neither superpower made any bids for condominium, comparable to the Soviet probing in 1956. Yet there was a novel element of superpower co-ordination in the 1967 crisis: the mutual adherence to, and reinforcement of, the norm proscribing a direct superpower clash.

The assumption of shared responsibility by the two superpowers for preserving international peace and stability reflected, in particular, increasing Soviet identification with the superpower role. Whereas in 1956 it had been a 'spoiler,' now it was placed in the position of a partial 'guarantor of the existing order' (Glassman, 1975: 61).

American and Soviet crisis management attempts in 1967, as in 1956, displayed considerable similarities. Compared to 1956, however, the parallels revealed vastly increased sophistication in signaling. As noted initially, the substitution of 'flexible response' thinking for the 'massive retaliation' doctrines had opened up a wider repertoire of signals below the nuclear threshold. At the same time, nuclear threats of the kind used by the Soviet Union a decade earlier were never issued in 1967. In contrast to 1956, signaling between the superpowers in 1967 was direct, employing a variety of channels including the hot line. Moreover, US–Soviet signaling was less ambiguous and better understood. Nor was it restricted to verbal messages alone. Both superpowers demonstrated their intentions and resolve through various forms of commitments. Specifically, the 1967 crisis saw the first mutual employment of naval movements as a principal signaling instrument, and the Soviet use of arms transfers represented an early suggestion of another useful means of crisis management.

Although the spectrum of instruments for signaling had widened to include military ones, both superpowers used them primarily to signal restraint rather than maximize shared risk, and neither incurred any irrevocable commitments.

If signaling between the superpowers improved significantly between 1956 and 1967, the same cannot be said of signaling to their respective clients. Especially in the initial phase of the 1967 crisis, American signaling to Israel and Soviet signaling to Egypt were characterized by dysfunctional ambiguity. The superpowers 'not only failed to restrain their clients but, by reacting too weakly to the unfolding situation, in effect actually encouraged them to move towards war' (Holbraad, 1979: 83).

What did the 1967 crisis reveal concerning the relative power of the superpowers? The picture in 1967 was more ambiguous than in 1956. In the short term, the United States appeared to be the strongest of the two superpowers. Its client had won the war. The United States had been proved to enjoy strategic superiority in the region — Soviet naval forces in the Mediterranean were inferior to the Sixth Fleet, and the USSR lacked large mobile units to put into immediate action in the Middle East. Apparently both American and Israeli decision-makers discounted any military danger from the Soviets (cf. Jabber and Kolkowicz, 1981: 429). Furthermore, American intervention during the war had been more decisive than Soviet action. It was American pressures on the victorious Israelis that had prevented a complete Arab collapse. The Soviet Union, in contrast, had backed a loser, whereas it had been on the winning side in 1956. Most of the military hardware it had shipped to the Arab states had been captured or destroyed during the war. Inevitably the Soviet Union suffered a loss of prestige, both as a result of the failure of Soviet arms, and its failure to live up to Arab expectations of support. As Bernard Lewis (1969: 646) aptly puts it, 'no one loves protectors, still less protectors who do not protect.' Finally one result of the Six-Day War was the closure of the Suez Canal which was a more vital waterway for the Soviet Union than for the United States. In particular, its closure negatively affected Soviet aid deliveries to North Vietnam (d'Encausse, 1975: 199).

Yet in the wake of the Six-Day War the view gradually gained ground that the Arab defeat paradoxically represented a long-term Soviet victory. The logic behind this is that a frustrated and needy loser generally offers far more foothold opportunities than a confident victor. And the Soviet Union, by rapidly resupplying arms to the Arabs and designating Soviet advisers and instructors to their forces, tied its defeated clients even closer to itself. At the same time, the American position *vis-à-vis* Israel was no stronger, and probably weaker, because Israel had shown that it could successfully defend its own interests in defiance of American advice.

The overall US–Soviet power equation emerging from the 1967 crisis may be less than clear, but one common denominator is the imperfect superpower control of their regional clients. The super-powers did not manage to prevent the outbreak of a war which neither apparently wanted. The events of the war took place very rapidly, letting the regional belligerents reach their own temporary level of accommodation before the superpowers were able to bring pressure to bear. In effect, as the crisis unfolded, the superpowers became increasingly dependent on their respective clients. 'They could not use the local powers in the global rivalry without being used by them for their ends' (Holbraad, 1979: 95). It could be argued that the superpowers' success in keeping themselves and each other out of the hostilities was bought at the expense of effective control over their clients.

The Yom Kippur War, 1973

The Six-Day War did not result in any settlement of the Arab–Israeli conflict, and the regional protagonists soon engaged in a 'dialogue by fire.' In fact, the 1967–73 period may be characterized as a long prelude to the Yom Kippur War. Four sets of developments in the 1967–73 period were of direct relevance to superpower crisis management as Arab–Israeli tension was again mounting toward open hostilities in the fall of 1973: (1) the continuous direct participation of both superpowers — albeit to differing degrees and with differing intensity — in the quest for a peaceful Middle East settlement; (2) the consolidation of both superpowers as indispensable arms suppliers to the regional protagonists; (3) the crisis management efforts in Jordan 1970 which taught important lessons, especially to the Americans; and (4) the signing of the 1972 and 1973 agreements heralding a superpower regime for crisis prevention and management.

(1) Both superpowers were involved in attempts to find a peace settlement formula in the wake of the Six-Day War. The Johnson–Kosygin Glassboro talks in late June 1967, while laying bare the divergences between the American and Soviet positions, heralded a formula combining Arab recognition of Israel with Israeli withdrawal (Whetten, 1981: 56). This formula was included in Security Council Resolution 242, which was endorsed by both superpowers and unanimously adopted on November 22, 1967. However, as the wording was sufficiently ambiguous to allow varying interpretations and neither of the regional protagonists wanted to take the first step, the situation remained frozen. And when the United States in late 1969 unilaterally presented its proposal for a peace settlement in the so-called Rogers Plan, it was promptly rejected first by Israel and then also by the Soviet Union, presumably under Egyptian pressure (cf. Whetten, 1981: 58-9; Quandt, 1977: 89-92).

(2) The Soviet resupply of military equipment to Egypt on the heels of the 1967 War followed the pre-war policy of providing Egypt with a limited strategic deterrent to reduce its vulnerability to Israeli attack, but not with a weapons supply sufficient to succeed in attacking Israeli forces and reconquering the occupied territories (Glassman, 1975: 104-8).

In 1969–70, during the so-called War of Attrition, the Soviet Union dramatically built up the Egyptian air defense to counter the devastating Israeli air attacks on the Egyptian forces and interior. In an unprecedented move, SAM-3 surface-to-air missiles (which had not even been provided to North Vietnam) and Soviet fighting personnel — SAM-3 operators and combat pilots — were dispatched to Egypt (cf. Pajak, 1975: 167; Glassman, 1975: 75-7).

Yet Soviet deliveries fell short of Egyptian demands. The Soviet refusal to provide the Egyptians with up-to-date equipment for offensive action was a cause of persistent friction, and in July 1972 President Anwar Sadat requested the withdrawal of Soviet military experts and the transfer of all military installations and equipment to Egyptian control. The Soviets promptly withdrew virtually all their personnel along with most Soviet-controlled equipment (Pajak, 1975: 169; Glassman, 1975: 94-6).

In early 1973 a reconciliation was reached, and Egypt's supply of tactical arms was selectively augmented, at the same time as the Soviet Union for the first time provided Egypt with an 'offensive' weapon (the SCUD surface-to-surface medium-range missiles) capable of striking at the interior of Israel. Moreover, the weapon was placed under Egyptian, not Soviet, operational control. In addition to the increased strategic threat to Israel represented by the SCUD delivery, the stepped-up Soviet supply of anti-aircraft and anti-tank weaponry enhanced Egypt's tactical offensive capabilities. The Soviets also apparently abandoned or modified earlier restrictions on certain uses of Soviet-supplied weapons (Glassman, 1975: 112-17).

In the wake of the Six-Day War the situation of America's Middle East client *vis-à-vis* its superpower protector differed significantly from that of the Soviet client.

> They won the 1967 war and needed less shoring up than the Arabs. They had no technological and military problems comparable to those of the Arabs and consequently no need to bring into Israel great numbers of American instructors and technicians. They held the occupied territories and needed no American help to defend them, while the Arabs wanted Soviet support to regain them. [Hottinger, 1975: 155]

Hence, the United States could afford a more 'even-handed' approach to the continuing Arab–Israeli conflict. Its military support to Israel was restricted by the desire to maintain American interests and retain leverage in the Arab world. Yet after the Jordan crisis of 1970 US–Israeli military relations were brought to an unprecedented high level. Military credits increased nearly tenfold, American arms were arriving in Israel in large quantities, and Washington for the first time agreed to the transfer of military technology (cf. Quandt, 1977: 163; Mangold, 1978: 149-50). Thus, on the eve of the 1973 crisis both superpowers had established themselves as indispensable arms suppliers to the regional protagonists.

(3) The Jordan crisis of September 1970 was precipitated by King Hussein's move against armed Palestinian groups which suffered a crushing defeat. Syria moved tanks into Jordan in an abortive attempt to support the Palestinians, and Israel mobilized forces on the Syrian border. The crisis involved active signaling and crisis management on

the part of the superpowers. The United States ostentatiously reinforced the Sixth Fleet and ordered it to move farther east, placed forces on high alert, established close military liaison with Israel, authorized stepped-up military aid to Israel, and warned the Soviets that both Israel and the United States might be forced to intervene unless the Syrians pulled back (cf. Quandt, 1977: 113-18). The presence of Soviet military advisers in the Syrian armed forces raised the specter of a superpower confrontation. The Soviet leadership, however, was 'conspicuous by its inaction' (Freedman, 1975: 33).

In Washington there was a tendency to overemphasize the global US–Soviet dimension of the Jordan crisis. American decision-makers inferred from the crisis first, that the Soviet lack of assertiveness was primarily a function of the strong American position and, second, that Soviet pressures significantly influenced Syria's behavior. No firm evidence can be adduced to support either of these 'lessons' which, however, came to influence US Middle East policy in the years ahead (cf. Quandt, 1977: 124-7).

(4) Another development of great significance for subsequent superpower behavior in the Middle East was the incipient crisis prevention and crisis management regime as one aspect of nascent US–Soviet *détente*. At their summit meeting in Moscow in June 1972, Nixon and Brezhnev signed a Joint Declaration of Basic Principles of Relations between the United States of America and the Union of Soviet Socialist Republics. Defining the basis for *détente*, the agreement included a set of general principles by which the superpowers were to regulate their rivalry in third areas and avoid military confrontation.

The United States and the Soviet Union agreed to collaborate in 'preventing the development of situations capable of causing a dangerous exacerbation of their relations.' They declared themselves prepared to 'do their utmost to avoid military confrontations and to prevent the outbreak of nuclear war' and 'to do everything in their power so that conflicts or situations will not arise which would serve to increase international tensions' (Keesing, 1972: 25313-14). At the same time, an Agreement on Prevention of Incidents at Sea was concluded. Aimed at ensuring safety of navigation by American and Soviet warships operating in proximity to each other, this agreement can be seen as a symbolic mutual recognition of the importance of naval forces for crisis management.

Among the superpowers' Middle East clients, these manifestations of US–Soviet concert gave the impression that the superpowers were forming a condominium to prevent the outbreak of war in the region. Both the Israelis and the Egyptians feared that the Moscow summit might lead to an imposed US–Soviet Middle East settlement injurious to their interests (Freedman, 1975: 74). The reaction was most violent in Cairo. During his April visit to Moscow, Sadat had apprised the Soviet leaders of his apprehensions regarding a possible superpower deal on the Middle East made behind his back (Freedman, 1975: 74; Dawisha, 1979: 62-3; Glassman, 1975: 103); and the summit agreement, Sadat records retrospectively, came as a 'violent shock' to Egypt (George, 1980b: 11).

At their second summit meeting in the United States in June 1973, Nixon and Brezhnev signed an Agreement on the Prevention of Nuclear War which, in some respects, completed the 1972 Joint Declaration. Besides reiterating the US–Soviet commitment to co-operate in crisis prevention, it included a significant additional provision concerning the requirement of consultations. Article 4 of the 1973 agreement reads as follows:

> If at any time relations between the parties or between either party and other countries appear to involve the risk of a nuclear conflict, or if relations between countries not parties to this agreement appear to involve the risk of nuclear war between the U.S.A. and the U.S.S.R. or between either party and other countries, the United States and the Soviet Union, acting in accordance with the provisions of this agreement, shall immediately enter into urgent consultations with each other and make every effort to avert this risk. [Keesing, 1973: 25999)]

A Soviet proposal to include a provision calling for joint Soviet–American intervention in a conflict if it threatened world peace — a virtual superpower condominium — was rejected by the United States (Caldwell, 1981: 6). The final agreement was to be tested during the events leading to the Yom Kippur War less than four months later.

Pre-Crisis Signaling

To pinpoint any one precipitant of the 1973 crisis is hardly possible. If, as suggested above, the whole 1967–73 period is viewed as a prelude to the Yom Kippur War, then the outcome of the Six-Day War can, in fact, be considered the precipitant of the 1973 War. Ever since the defeat in the 1967 War, Arab leaders had been clamoring for the reconquest of occupied territories. President Sadat had proclaimed

1971 as the 'year of decision' in the conflict with Israel. As both 1971 and the 1972 'year of inevitable battle' passed without any decisive turn of events, Sadat's bellicose rhetoric lost most of its credibility (cf. Hottinger, 1975: 163-4; Kissinger, 1982: 459). As Coral Bell (1974: 533-4) has observed:

> Therefore, when he again told the Egyptian armed forces in December 1972 to be ready for war in six months, neither the Israelis nor the Americans nor perhaps even the Russians seem to have taken the declaration entirely seriously. In effect, the stance of one "willing to wound but afraid to strike" seems to have provided a successful camouflage for the actual seriousness of Sadat's intentions as they developed in 1973.

Again, the Soviet Union, by virtue of being the protector of the frustrated, anti-status quo protagonist in the Arab–Israeli conflict, held the initiative in pre-crisis signaling between the superpowers. And, as in 1967, Soviet signaling was highly ambiguous. Until early 1973 the Soviet Union did not — either publicly or privately — back the recurrent Egyptian calls for an armed struggle against Israel but instead emphasized the desirability of a political settlement.

The Soviet posture changed in early 1973. On the one hand, there were signs of enduring restraint. Moscow continued to advise caution and urge a political settlement (cf. Quandt, 1976: 7). There are also indications that the Soviets, in the months preceding the Yom Kippur War, urged the Arabs to postpone their war plans another two to three years (Glassman, 1975: 118).

On the other hand, indications of a Soviet shift toward support of Cairo's political and military aims accumulated (cf. Kohler *et al.*, 1974: 36-55). The Soviet Union began to give full public support to Arab maximum demands and Egypt's rejection of the concept of a 'partial' settlement.' Of still greater significance were the recurrent references in Soviet commentaries to the right of the Arabs to use 'other' or 'every means of struggle' to regain lost territories in the face of Israeli intransigence. Asked about Soviet arms deliveries to Egypt at a press conference in Stockholm on April 5, Soviet Premier Kosygin replied: 'We believe that Egypt has a right to possess a powerful army now in order to defend itself against the aggressor and to *liberate its own lands*' (Kohler *et al.*, 1974: 36). The reference to the use of force to 'liberate' lost territories, rather than merely to defend against aggression, contrasted with earlier Soviet statements.

By September 1973, following a portentous chain of events, the notes of restraint waned in Soviet statements. First, the overthrow of the Allende regime in Chile in early September caused bitter disappointment in Moscow. The 'Popular Unity' government of Salvador Allende had been exploited in Soviet propaganda as an example proving that the Soviet policy of *détente* was working, and its overthrow — which was depicted by the Soviets as the product of a conspiracy between local 'reactionaries' and aggressive foreign 'imperialists' — seemed to indicate the opposite, particularly to already suspicious leaders in the Middle East, and heightened Soviet anxiety that the forces of 'imperialism' would use *détente* as a means to undermine the 'progressive' movement (cf. Glassman, 1975: 118-19; Freedman, 1975: 118-19).

Second, in 'a remarkable repetition of history' (Whetten, 1981: 70), the Israeli air force on September 13 drew Syrian MIGs into an air battle over the Mediterranean with humiliating losses to the Syrians. The battle was used by the Soviets as justification for increasingly open support for Arab military action against Israel (cf. Kohler *et al.*, 1974: 46-7). In addition, the Soviet media began repeating false reports from the Arab press of Israeli troop concentrations on the Syrian border in preparation for an attack on Syria. The false warnings were indeed reminiscent of Soviet pre-crisis signaling in 1967, the main difference being that now, unlike in 1967, the Soviets were echoing rather than generating the misinformation (cf. Kohler *et al.*, 1974: 47-8; Glassman, 1975: 120-1).

In assessing Soviet pre-crisis behavior in 1973, two questions stand out as crucial: (1) Did the Soviet leaders endorse, or at least have advance knowledge of, the Arab attack on Israel? (2) Did they fulfil their obligations under the 1972 and 1973 agreements to warn the* United States?

Most observers agree that, whereas the war was clearly the result of an Egyptian and not a Soviet decision, Moscow was indeed fully aware of Arab intentions to launch a war and unwilling to oppose the Arab plans for fear of jeopardizing its prestige and influence in the Arab world. The Egyptian insistence on war no doubt placed the Soviet Union on the horns of a dilemma. Whereas the initiation of hostilities might jeopardize the cherished US–Soviet *détente*, resistance to the Egyptian plans could lead to a repetition of the July 1972 breakdown of Soviet–Egyptian relations (cf. Glassman, 1975: 100; Golan, 1974: 107-8). Soviet policy prior to the Yom Kippur War can be understood as 'a continuing series of capitulations in the face of Egyptian insistence on the renewal of war with Israel' (Glassman, 1975: 104). As a result of its fear of losing hard-earned Soviet gains among 'progressive' nationalists in the Arab world and elsewhere, the Soviet Union 'had no choice but to go along' with the Arab war plans (Golan, 1974: 108).

There are several indications of Moscow's advance knowledge of, and tacit consent to, the Egyptian decision to launch hostilities. It seems unlikely that the several thousand Soviet military advisers in Egypt and Syria would have been unaware of Arab war preparations (Kohler *et al.*, 1974: 90). Moreover, the Arabs would hardly have launched their attack without some assurances of Soviet arms resupplies, and the efficacy of the large-scale Soviet airlift of weapons and ammunition which was initiated on the fifth day of the war suggested advance planning. Hungary was the principal staging area for these shipments, and in late September there were reports in the Soviet press of unusual military exercises and activities in Hungary and in the Soviet Military District bordering on Hungary which, in retrospect, might be interpreted as preparations for the airlift (Glassman, 1975: 122). In sum, the available evidence suggests that the Soviet Union did have advance knowledge of Arab plans but probably did not know of the exact timing of the attack until relatively late (Whetten, 1981: 70; Kohler *et al.*, 1974: 90).

The question as to whether the Soviet leaders, who apparently knew that war was imminent, gave the United States advance warning is a matter of controversy. While American officials assert that the Soviet Union never issued any explicit warning, the Soviet Union claims to have repeatedly warned the United States about the explosive situation in the Middle East.

The Soviet Union could obviously not have given the United States an explicit and unequivocal warning without openly acknowledging its complicity in the Arab military preparations and betraying their Arab clients (Whetten, 1981: 70; George, 1980b: 14). Secretary of State Kissinger admitted as much in his circumscribed answer to a question about advance Soviet warning at an October 12 press conference:

> In an ideal world, one would expect closer consultation but, given the particular volatility of the Middle East, it would have been a heavy responsibility to make known certain advance information. [quoted in Kohler *et al.*, 1974: 89]

If the Soviet Union did not provide what intelligence specialists refer to as 'tactical' warning (giving specific information, such as the date and place of a possible attack), there are indications of Soviet attempts at less specific 'strategic warning' (cf. George, 1980b: 12). At the second Nixon–Brezhnev summit in Washington and San Clemente in June 1973, Brezhnev 'warned that the Egyptians and Syrians were intent upon going to war and that the Soviet Union could not stop them' (Quandt, 1977: 159). According to Nixon's (1978: 885) own account, Brezhnev kept hammering at the need for American diplomatic pressure on Israel to bring about a Middle East settlement and avert the danger of war. The Soviet Union claims to have tried repeatedly in the months following the June summit to warn American officials, including Kissinger, that unless Israel withdrew from occupied territories, a new war in the Middle East could not be prevented (cf. Glassman, 1975: 122).

Three days before the war started Soviet dependants and civilian personnel were hurriedly evacuated from Syria and Egypt. Though unaccompanied by any verbal communication, the seemingly unnecessary evacuation may well have been intended as a tacit warning of the impending attack (cf. Glassman, 1975: 123; George, 1980b: 13-14). A Soviet specialist on United States affairs has indicated in private that the evacuation was done in a deliberately conspicuous manner precisely for that purpose (George, 1980b: 26). At the same time, this Soviet move can be seen as a signal to Washington that the USSR was not involved in the final decision to go to war, and a reminder to Egypt and Syria not to expect direct Soviet intervention (Quandt, 1976: 12). Also, on October 3 the Soviet Union started to launch observation satellites (Bell, 1974: 534; Sella, 1981: 94-5), and low-ranking Soviet diplomats made calls at certain Western chanceries inquiring whether the respective countries had any information concerning Egyptian and Israeli military preparations (Glassman, 1975: 224).

According to several sources, the Soviets were informed of the exact date of the Arab attack only on, or shortly before, October 3 (cf. Hottinger, 1975: 168; Glassman, 1975: 224; Golan, 1974: 107). The combination of Soviet moves that day can therefore be interpreted as a tacit and ambiguous 'tactical' warning to the United States which was probably as far as the Soviets could go without betraying their Arab clients.

At any rate, the United States failed to take the Soviet warnings, if such they were, seriously. In general, the United States remained remarkably passive prior to the outbreak of war in October 1973.

Henry Kissinger, who took over as Secretary of State on August 22, 1973, was highly critical of the Middle East policy of his predecessor, William Rogers, characterizing the publicized American peace initiatives as 'disastrous' (Quandt, 1977: 160). Kissinger's aim was 'to produce a stalemate until Moscow urged compromise or until, even better, some moderate Arab regime decided that the route to progress was through Washington' (Kissinger, 1979: 1279). He calculated that 'the longer the process went on, the more likely Sadat would seek to deal with us directly' (Kissinger, 1979: 1290). And things seemed to be going his way. At the 1972 Moscow summit the Soviets, much to his own surprise (cf. Kissinger, 1979: 1247-8, 1294), agreed to a bland communiqué on the Middle East conflict and a vague set of 'general principles' for a settlement, the practical consequence of which was to confirm the deadlock and contribute to the Soviet–Egyptian rift. And in early April 1972 Egypt opened a secret channel to the White House (Kissinger, 1979: 1292-1300). Besides, among all the urgent problems facing US decision-makers at home and abroad, the Middle East did not seem the most pressing.

Crisis Management

On the afternoon of October 6, 1973, massive Egyptian and Syrian forces launched a simultaneous attack on under-manned Israeli positions along the Suez Canal and on the Golan Heights. Both Israel and the United States were taken by surprise. Whereas Israeli intelligence apparently had adequate tactical military warning, the Arabs were not felt to be prepared politically or militarily to risk a new war. The United States saw the events leading up to the war as indications of a possible Israeli assault on the Arabs and repeatedly warned Israel not to pre-empt (Whetten, 1981: 71-2; Kalb and Kalb, 1974: 456-7). The initial course of the war proved to be an even greater surprise, apparently to both superpowers. Previous armed confrontations in the Middle East had created expectations of Israeli military preponderance. However, this time the initial Egyptian and Syrian penetration of Israeli forces in Sinai and on the Golan Heights proceeded smoothly, and unlike in 1967 the Soviet-equipped Arab air defense proved able to restrain Israeli air superiority.

Desiring to maintain a low military profile and expecting an early end to the fighting, the United States discreetly denied Israeli requests for large-scale arms shipments (Quandt, 1977: 175; Golan, 1976: 45-6). There are indications that the Soviet Union, too, initially expected an eventual Israeli victory. One puzzling aspect of Soviet behavior on the first day of the war was Ambassador Vinogradov's *démarche* to Sadat a few hours after hostilities began, claiming that Syria had accepted an early ceasefire and urging the Egyptians to do likewise. Sadat was incredulous and queried Syrian President Assad, who denied that any ceasefire proposal had been made. When Vinogradov returned the following day with the same request, he was angrily rebuffed by Sadat. Several interpretations can be made of this incident. Misunderstanding and misinterpretation are probably part of the story which we know only through Sadat's own account. Yet Moscow's expectations of Israeli military superiority and its desire not to become militarily involved may well account for the early unilateral Soviet ceasefire efforts (Quandt, 1976: 14-15).

As in 1967, the two superpowers opened direct communications at the outbreak of war. Kissinger met with Soviet Ambassador Dobrynin in Washington several times in the first days of the war. On October 7 he gave him a personal letter from President Nixon to Brezhnev, urging mutual restraint and calling for a Security Council meeting to consider a ceasefire. At the same time, Nixon alluded to the 1972 and 1973 US–Soviet agreements on crisis conduct. Brezhnev's reply that same day was conciliatory and encouraging (cf. Kalb and Kalb, 1974: 463; Quandt, 1977: 173; Glassman, 1975: 143). The first official Soviet government statement on the war, released in the evening of October 7, was relatively reserved, making no reference to the United States but blaming the outbreak of fighting on Israeli intransigence (Quandt, 1976: 15; Glassman, 1975: 143).

These verbal exchanges were underscored by naval movements. Before the initiation of hostilities both Soviet and American naval units were in normal deployments with substantial parts in port. On October 6 Soviet ships in Egyptian and Syrian ports moved away from the zone of combat. The Soviet Mediterranean fleet remained spread out and continued to carry out its normal peacetime surveillance of the Sixth Fleet (cf. Quandt, 1976: 13; Roberts, 1979: 196; Caldwell, 1981: 35). On the evening of October 6 the Commander of the US Sixth Fleet was ordered to move a taskforce consisting of the aircraft carrier *Independence* and three destroyers from Athens to a 'holding position' off Crete, half a day's sailing time from the Suez Canal (Kalb and Kalb, 1974: 462; Caldwell, 1981: 35). A major increase in the Soviet fleet occurred on October 10. However, two of the three vessels that entered the Mediterranean that day were on their way to pre-scheduled port calls in Italy which were carried out despite the crisis (Roberts, 1979: 193). All in all, the naval movements of both seemed to signal a 'wait and see' posture in the first week of the war.

As the possibility of a swift and conclusive Israeli military victory on both fronts faded, the initial superpower restraint began to erode. Confronted with the urgent need for replenishments of Arab weapons and ammunition, the Soviet Union on October 10 initiated a large-scale airlift of military supplies. This unprecedented Soviet involvement in a Middle East crisis was an event of great politic al and military significance.

Concurrently, the Soviet Union made certain military preparedness moves. On October 10 the United States received intelligence reports that the Soviet Union had put three airborne divisions on alert. The immediate purpose was apparently to signal Soviet readiness to come to the defense of Syria if Israel were to carry out its threats to march on Damascus. It was subsequently reported that advance Soviet staff had been transferred to Syrian military headquarters (cf. Roberts, 1979: 202; Quandt, 1976: 21, 28n; Mangold, 1978: 128-9; Kalb and Kalb, 1974: 470-1). On October 12 Soviet naval units moved into the active war zone off the Syrian coast. The force was probably intended to ensure the maintenance of Soviet air and sea lines of communication to Syria (Caldwell, 1981: 35).

Meanwhile Israeli pressure on the United States to replace lost arms and military equipment was mounting. Until the launching of an unsuccessful counterattack on the Egyptian front on October 8, Israel had not requested massive aid from the United States but asked only for certain items on a relatively short list of arms (Aronson, 1978: 184; cf. Kissinger, 1982: 485). On October 9 President Nixon approved the replacement of early Israeli losses. The resupply effort was, however, slow in coming into effect. Only on October 13, after the massive proportion of the Soviet resupply effort had become evident, did the United States initiate a full-scale airlift to Israel. The main considerations underlying the decision to relinquish the previous restraint were, first, to demonstrate to Moscow that the United States was capable of matching Soviet deliveries and that American power in the Middle East was still considerable; and, second, to convince the Arabs that they could never win a victory with Soviet arms and that, in order to achieve their aims, they would have to deal with the United States (cf. Quandt, 1977: 184; Kalb and Kalb, 1974: 471).

The initiation of the American airlift was accompanied by naval movements. The aircraft carrier *John F. Kennedy*, based in a British port following an exercise, was ordered south to augment the two carriers already in the Mediterranean. The *Franklin D. Roosevelt*, a carrier stationed in the western Mediterranean, moved to a position east of Sicily. The three US carriers were to provide navigation assistance and refueling for the transiting aircraft engaged in the US resupply effort to Israel (Caldwell, 1981: 36).

Parallel to rearming their clients, the two superpowers were probing a ceasefire resolution in the UN. As the superpower efforts were unsuccessful, the regional actors were left temporarily free to influence the outcome of the conflict. By October 15 the war was beginning to turn in Israel's favor. In control of most of the Golan Heights and with forces rapidly penetrating halfway down the road to Damascus, Israel shifted the focus of her efforts to the Sinai front. Having repulsed an Egyptian offensive toward the Mitla and Gidda passes, Israeli forces crossed to the west bank of the Suez Canal and gradually encircled the Egyptian Second and Third Armies. Faced with setbacks on the battlefield, the Arabs turned to the oil weapon.

Against this rather unpropitious background, the superpowers resumed their efforts to induce their respective clients to accept a ceasefire. As the tide was turning against the Arabs on the battlefield, the Soviet Union did so with greater urgency. On October 16 Soviet Premier Kosygin traveled to Cairo for three days of consultations with Sadat in which he tried to convince the Egyptian leader of the advisability of an early ceasefire. After intensive negotiations, Kosygin managed to get Egyptian agreement to a ceasefire formula which reportedly included Israeli withdrawal to the 1967 lines and either joint superpower or unilateral Soviet guarantees of its implementation (Glassman, 1975: 153).

At the same time as Kosygin tried to convince his clients in Cairo of the advantages of a ceasefire, Soviet Ambassador Dobrynin echoed the same line in long talks with Kissinger in Washington (Kalb and Kalb, 1974: 481). When Kosygin left Cairo late on October 18, Dobrynin handed Kissinger a draft of a Soviet ceasefire proposal. The official American response was noncommittal, merely stressing the importance of continued US–Soviet consultations and joint efforts to end hostilities. The United States was again stalling (cf. Nixon, 1978: 931; Kissinger, 1982: 540).

Israel was no doubt perceived by both superpowers to be the main obstacle to a ceasefire at this juncture. Increasingly successful in the war and assured of continuing American supplies, the Israelis showed little interest in a ceasefire. As the Soviets must have realized, only strong American pressure might induce Israel to accept a ceasefire.

Shortly after Kosygin's return to Moscow from Cairo, Brezhnev sent a message to Nixon requesting that Kissinger should immediately come to Moscow — or, alternatively, Gromyko fly to Washington — for urgent consultations on the Middle East crisis. After conferring with Nixon, Kissinger informed the Soviets that he would depart for Moscow that very evening. During the day, Kissinger deliberated with Israeli Ambassador Simcha Dinitz about a ceasefire scenario. Dinitz reminded Kissinger of Israel's desire to buy time in order to improve its military position, and Kissinger assured that the anticipated drawn-out negotiations in Moscow would accomplish precisely that. The Israeli Ambassador also repeated that a ceasefire linked to Israeli withdrawal to the 1967 lines or any mention of Resolution 242 would be unacceptable. He recommended instead a ceasefire linked to direct negotiations for peace between the two sides (cf. Kalb and Kalb, 1974: 483; Golan, 1976: 75-6; Kissinger, 1982: 542-4).

While Kissinger was preparing for his journey, President Nixon sent Congress a request for $2.2 billion in emergency military aid for Israel. This move represented a signal to Moscow that the United States was standing firmly behind its client and was no doubt designed to enhance Kissinger's bargaining position (Kalb and Kalb, 1974: 483). Furthermore, Nixon, on the morning of October 20, sent a 'stern' letter to Brezhnev, adding a handwritten note with personal regards. Nixon (1978: 933) has explained the idea behind the message thus:

> Brezhnev, I knew, would understand what this mixture conveyed: if he was willing to get behind a serious peace effort, I would not consider that the Soviet airlift had affected our personal relationship or deflected the course of *détente*.

Kissinger (1982: 547), for his part, claims that Nixon's message formed no part of a co-ordinated strategy and was in fact counter-productive to Kissinger's intended bargaining tactics. By explicitly granting Kissinger 'full authority' in the Moscow talks, Nixon's letter deprived Kissinger of the capacity to stall by referring any tentative agreement to the President for his approval.

In the days immediately preceding the negotiations in Moscow, the Soviet press expounded the advisability of accepting a ceasefire rather than stepping up the efforts to assist the Arabs. The political–military advantages that Israel had derived from its victory in the 1967 war had definitely been lost, it was argued. The initial Arab military gains, coupled with the global energy shortage, had strengthened the Arab cause, whereas American support for Israel was weakening. Thus, by the time of Kissinger's arrival in Moscow, the ground seemed to be well prepared for a ceasefire agreement (Glassman, 1975: 154-6).

Indeed, Kissinger and Brezhnev already reached an agreement by October 21. Brezhnev, who initially tried to link a ceasefire to a call for Israeli withdrawal to the 1967 lines, soon backed down and ultimately agreed to a simple ceasefire in place, together with a call to start the implementation of Resolution 242 and, at Kissinger's insistence, negotiations between the parties (cf. Quandt, 1977: 192-3; Kalb and Kalb, 1974: 485; Kissinger, 1982: 553-4). The UN Security Council was convened on October 22 and unanimously adopted the US–Soviet ceasefire agreement as Resolution 338. The Israelis, irritated that they had not been consulted in advance but confronted with a *fait accompli*, tried to delay the ceasefire and only shortly before the Security Council was to convene decided to accept the ceasefire resolution (Quandt, 1977: 193).

The superpowers now found themselves with the problem of enforcing the ceasefire on their reluctant clients. On October 22, just before the ceasefire was to go into effect, Egypt fired several Soviet-operated, Egyptian-controlled SCUD missiles at Israeli troops in the west bank salient. This was probably intended to demonstrate 'that strategic rockets were indeed present in Egypt, that they were functioning, and that the next time they could be used against the Israeli heartland' (Glassman, 1975: 137).

The ceasefire did not hold. Apparently taking advantage of an attempt by the trapped Egyptian Third Army to break out of the Israeli stranglehold, the Israelis intensified their military pressure on both sides of the canal and tightened the encirclement of the Third Army. This situation was intolerable to both superpowers. The Americans realized that the Israelis had to be stopped. An Israeli victory would not entail peace but rather create tensions that might trigger another war. It would also encourage a new wave of anti-Americanism in the Middle East and perpetuate the oil embargo. In a series of conversations with Israeli Ambassador Dinitz, Kissinger 'cajoled, pressured, urged, implored, warned, threatened and pleaded with the Israeli envoy to understand his logic and accept his policy' (Kalb and Kalb, 1974: 487). Dinitz was reportedly told that Israel would be unable to count on American military aid, if the war were to continue as a result of Israeli actions (Golan, 1976: 88).

Both Kissinger and Nixon received messages from the Soviets blaming the Israelis for the breakdown of the ceasefire and implying that the Americans might have colluded in Israel's action (Nixon, 1978: 936; Kissinger, 1982: 570-2). Through joint US–Soviet diplomatic efforts a second Security Council resolution was arranged on October 23 calling for a ceasefire monitored by UN observers which, however, did not end the fighting.

The Soviets must have revived memories of 1967, when Israel conquered the Golan Heights after the Syrians had agreed to a ceasefire (cf. Quandt, 1976: 31). And in the days immediately before and after the October 22 ceasefire, the Soviet Union took steps to strengthen its position and demonstrate its commitment to save Egypt and Syria from the imminent danger of defeat. Soviet supply flights to the Middle East eased off on October 22 and ceased the next day, creating suspicions in the United States that the aircraft were withdrawn to prepare transportation of the alerted airborne troops to the Middle East (Glassman, 1975: 161). There were also intelligence reports of a Soviet request to Yugoslavia to overfly its territory and the establishment of an airborne command post in the south of the Soviet Union (Caldwell, 1981: 31). Already in the early days of the war three Soviet airborne divisions had been put on alert. On October 24, four more airborne divisions were put on high alert, bringing the total to seven divisions or some 50,000 combat troops (Kalb and Kalb, 1974: 488; Caldwell, 1981: 31).

Another chain of events that gave rise to apprehensions among United States decision-makers started with the October 22 Egyptian–Soviet firing of SCUD missiles at Israeli forces. This was the first instance of direct Soviet participation in offensive actions against the Israelis. While the fired SCUDs were armed with conventional warheads, American fears that the Soviets might next turn to nuclear warheads were raised when a Soviet freighter, transiting the Bosporus on October 22 en route for Alexandria, gave off neutron emissions, indicating the possible presence of nuclear weapons on board. As it turned out, however, no nuclear weapons were delivered to Egypt, and after the crisis neutron emissions were recorded for the same ship returning from Alexandria to the Black Sea. It remains unknown whether this episode was intended as a signal, 'a demonstrative gesture of deterrence' (Glassman, 1975: 163), directed at the United States.

If the Soviets intended to send nuclear warheads to Egypt, they presumably would not send them by ship. If, however, they were engaging in a dangerous form of psychological warfare aimed at making the Americans worry about the possibility of nuclear weapons in the area, they might have chosen to send such weapons through the heavily monitored Turkish strait. [Quandt, 1977: 198n]

It was against the background of all these Soviet preparedness moves that the American decision-makers interpreted Soviet–Egyptian signaling on October 24. That afternoon Sadat publicly appealed to Nixon and Brezhnev to send a joint US–Soviet peacekeeping force to the Middle East. The Sadat initiative was received extremely negatively in Washington, and Nixon sent Sadat a message unequivocally opposing such a plan which 'would introduce an extremely dangerous potential for direct great-power rivalry in the area' (Nixon, 1978: 937-8; Glassman, 1975: 158). Yet the same theme was reiterated later that day in the Security Council by Soviet UN representative Malik and in two messages from Brezhnev to Nixon. The second Brezhnev note, described as 'very urgent' and delivered in a phone call from Dobrynin to Kissinger, also contained a threat of unilateral Soviet action. After charging Israel with 'drastically' violating the ceasefire and echoing the proposal for a joint US–Soviet contingent 'to compel observance of the ceasefire without delay,' Brezhnev added:

> I will say it straight, that if you find it impossible to act with us in this matter, we should be faced with the necessity urgently to consider the question of taking appropriate steps unilaterally. Israel cannot be permitted to get away with the violation. [Kalb and Kalb, 1974: 490; Quandt, 1976: 32; Glassman, 1975: 160]

Brezhnev's note, combined with the concurrent Soviet military moves, caused much alarm in Washington. According to Nixon (1978: 938), 'this message represented perhaps the most serious threat to US–Soviet relations since the Cuban missile crisis eleven years before.' It was unmistakably clear that the Soviet Union was determined not to let Israel destroy the Egyptian Third Army. In light of the Soviet military buildup in the preceding days, American experts had also to conclude that there was a high probability of some kind of unilateral Soviet move. Moreover, at the time of the delivery of Brezhnev's note several Soviet combat ships, including amphibious landing craft, began to move from their anchorage east of Crete toward the Egyptian coastline (cf. Quandt, 1976: 33; Glassman, 1975: 163; Kissinger, 1982: 584).

Within hours of receiving Brezhnev's message, the United States responded by ordering a worldwide alert of American military forces, both conventional and nuclear. The alert was designed to convey to the Soviets that they should not send troops into Egypt and that the Americans were determined to respond to any move they might make (cf. Caldwell, 1981: 31-2; Quandt, 1977: 197). To underscore the meaning of the alert, Nixon sent a letter to Brezhnev in which he said that unilateral Soviet action would be regarded as 'a matter of the gravest concern involving incalculable consequences' (Nixon, 1978: 939) and would be considered a violation of the 1973 agreement on the prevention of nuclear war (Quandt, 1977: 197). The letter was sent by messenger to avoid any softening by means of an explanation (Kissinger, 1982: 591).

Accompanying the alert, the Sixth Fleet was ordered to concentrate in the eastern Mediterranean. The aircraft carrier *John F. Kennedy* left its holding position just west of Gibraltar and entered the Mediterranean; the *Franklin D. Roosevelt* left Sicily to join the *Independence* south-east of Crete; and the helicopter carrier *Iwo Jima* carrying 1,800 marines entered the Mediterranean (Caldwell, 1981: 36).

Another response to the Soviet threat was direct American pressure on Israel. Kissinger told the Israelis in no uncertain terms that the United States would not permit the destruction of the Egyptian Third Army and apparently threatened that the United States would either allow Soviet intervention to save the encircled Egyptians or itself supply the humanitarian needs of the Third Army unless Israel accepted a ceasefire (Quandt, 1977: 198; Whetten, 1981: 75; Glassman, 1975: 164-5; Kissinger, 1982: 602-4, 608-9).

The Israelis acquiesced in supplying the Third Army with food and water. In the morning of October 25 Nixon received a conciliatory message from Sadat who now spoke of an international peacekeeping force under the auspices of the UN, and some hours later a message from Brezhnev arrived, announcing that the Soviet Union was going to send seventy individual 'observers' to the Middle East (Nixon, 1978: 940). At the UN, Soviet representative Malik yielded to American insistence that the superpowers be excluded from the UN peace-keeping force. The Security Council could therefore on October 25 pass a resolution establishing a UN emergency force 'composed of personnel drawn from state members of the United Nations except permanent members of the Security Council' (Kalb and Kalb, 1974:

496-7). On October 26 the United States started to lift its alert, and Brezhnev in a speech to the World Peace Congress in Moscow accused 'certain circles of the NATO countries' of 'an artificial fanning of passions through some kind of fantastic conjectures about the intentions of the Soviet Union in the Near East' (Glassman, 1975: 165). Brezhnev's implication that accusations of an imminent Soviet intervention were false seemed to indicate that the Soviet Union no longer saw any need to prolong or defend the intervention threat. The acute stage of the crisis was at an end.

The alert episode involved 'some rather loud signaling' (Bell, 1974: 537) on the part of the superpowers. The Americans were accused of over-reaction at home and abroad. There were widespread beliefs that the dramatic gesture of altering American forces worldwide was undertaken out of domestic political considerations, to turn the attention away from Watergate. Yet it can be argued that the signals needed to be loud 'in order to carry over certain background noises and to reach other ears than those of the American and Russian policy-makers concerned, who are, of course, perfectly well able to communicate in whispers, unless it is useful that others should hear' (Bell, 1974: 537).

Soviet signals — the military preparedness moves, the bid for a superpower condominium, and the threat of unilateral intervention — seem to have been designed primarily to prevail upon the United States to pressure the Israelis into observing the ceasefire (cf. Golan, 1974: 110-11; Glassman, 1975: 164). At the same time, the signals had to be forceful enough to convince the Arabs that the Soviet Union was honoring its commitments to them, and threatening enough to impress the victorious Israelis. The signals did, in fact, bring about American pressure on the Israelis, and it was this direct pressure that had the desired effect of inducing Israel's acceptance of a ceasefire (cf. Whetten, 1981: 75).

Summary

The 1973 Middle East crisis confirmed and amplified some of the patterns of superpower crisis management emerging from the 1967 Six-Day War. First, prospective superpower condominium was again thwarted. The 1972 and 1973 US–Soviet agreements had raised anew the specter of condominium, and at the height of the crisis the Soviet Union made a bid for condominium which was reminiscent of a similar Soviet proposal for joint superpower military intervention in 1956. But now, as in 1956, the United States categorically rejected the

Soviet probe, and the American response to Brezhnev's October 24 message made it unequivocally clear that *détente* could not be transformed into condominium.

Yet the Yom Kippur War involved an unprecedented degree of tacit superpower co-ordination. Arms supplies in the midst of hostilities was a novel component among Soviet and American crisis management instruments; and it is remarkable that the airlifts of both, conducted at the same time and through the same crowded airspace, proceeded without disturbances by the rival superpower or regional combatant (cf. Bell, 1978: 56; Glassman, 1975: 130).

Another illustration of the widening repertoire of signaling instruments was provided by the 1973 crisis, insofar as preparedness moves included an American nuclear alert and the possible Soviet introduction of a nuclear warhead into the region. These moves were clearly interpreted precisely as signals on both sides and did not cause undue alarm. Far from disrupting the US–Soviet dialogue, the brandishing of nuclear weapons in the 1973 crisis can be seen as an indication of its effectiveness (d'Encausse, 1975: 272).

The power asymmetries between the United States and the Soviet Union were laid bare during and, in particular, after the Yom Kippur War. To be sure, the Soviet Union had come considerably closer to military parity with the United States in the region as compared to 1967. Its naval presence in the Mediterranean was considered sufficient to counter the Sixth Fleet in regional crises (Jabber and Kolkowicz, 1981: 441). Unlike in 1967, the threat of Soviet military intervention was fully credible. And in contrast to the American airlift to Israel, the Soviet resupply effort encountered little difficulty in eliciting third-country transit co-operation or acquiescence (Jabber and Kolkowicz, 1981: 452). Yet increased Soviet military strength did not translate into improved control over crisis outcomes. Again it was demonstrated that only the United States could 'deliver' Israel. Arab leaders were graphically reminded of Moscow's inability to extract any concessions from Israel. Concomitantly, the United States became acutely aware of its vulnerability *vis-à-vis* the oil-producing Arab states. The 1973 crisis thus created strong mutual incentives for a US–Arab rapprochement. As Kissinger devoted his diplomatic talent to mediating a settlement and was able to exploit American economic strength to extend 'carrots' to the Arabs, the Soviet Union was relegated to the background and its position in the Arab world was gradually eroding. Yet, whereas the 1973 War revealed overall power asymmetries in favor of the United States, it also accentuated the shared problems of influencing recalcitrant clients. Especially in the initial stages of the crisis, both superpowers found themselves at the mercy of regional clients over whom neither had sufficient unilateral control.

Superpower Crisis Management: Conclusions

Superpower crisis management must be seen as learned behavior. In other words, it has evolved through a mutual learning process (cf. Bell, 1971b: 30; Neuhold, 1978: 4). The importance of signaling has gradually been recognized by the two superpowers as an essential part of crisis management. The superpowers have learned to back their words by deeds, their repertoire of signaling instruments has progressively widened, and there has been a gradual improvement in the ability of both to signal their own intentions and understand each other's signals. Both the United States and the Soviet Union have come a long way since the rather unsophisticated attempts at crisis management of 1956.

It is, for instance, instructive to compare the near panic caused by the rather hollow Soviet nuclear threats in 1956 with the restrained reaction to the far more substantial American nuclear alert in 1973, not only among decision-makers but also among the general public. Whereas the non-committal Soviet references to the possible use of nuclear weapons in 1956 raised the specter of nuclear war, the American move to actually raise its preparedness for a nuclear exchange in 1973 was more readily perceived to be a signal in crisis bargaining with the other superpower.

Partly by accident and partly by design (cf. Bell, 1971b: 1; Williams, 1976: 199), the superpowers seem to have arrived at a tacit understanding of principles guiding their crisis interaction. Between crises they may be willing to play poker; but once the crisis comes to a head they play chess. According to one observer (Williams, 1976: 200), 'one of the most remarkable features of superpower crises is the extent to which the proprieties, conventions and norms have been adhered to almost without deviation.' The 'rules of the game' appear to include the following (cf. Holbraad, 1979: 110-11; Neuhold, 1978: 7-13; Bell, 1978: 52-6; Evron, 1979: 34-41):

(1) Prefer conflict by proxy and avoid direct confrontation. As noted by Ian Smart (1974: 11), the avoidance of direct superpower confrontation, from being a 'prudential aspiration,' has come to be 'something close

to an assumption of international politics.' The importance attached to non-intervention was illustrated during the Six-Day War of 1967. When the Arabs claimed that American aircraft had taken part in air attacks on Egypt, the United States took great pains to demonstrate to the Soviets that the charges were unfounded. Similarly, the US President used the hot line to avoid the Soviets misinterpreting the dispatch of American aircraft to investigate the *Liberty* incident, as an indication of American intervention in the war.

To be sure, threats of intervention recurred in the three Middle Eastern crises. 'At or near the conclusion of every conflict the Soviet Union threatened military intervention' (Glassman, 1975: 177). Both in 1967 and 1973 these threats were obviously intended to make the United States pressure the Israelis into more scrupulous observance of the agreed ceasefires. Pardoxically, the threats were 'designed specifically to ensure that intervention would be unnecessary' (Williams, 1976: 109). In 1973 the verbal Soviet threat was supplemented by visible preparations for direct military intervention. Yet, in all likelihood these represented improved Soviet commitment techniques rather than increased willingness to risk a superpower confrontation, and 'what appeared as vigorous preparation for military action was probably intended as a substitute for it' (Williams, 1976: 109).

(2) Encourage your clients only up to the point where the danger of major war becomes acute; then check them. Such reversals in the relationships with the regional protagonists occurred in each Middle Eastern crisis. Pre-crisis signaling has typically been ambiguous, vacillating between encouragement and restraint, but as the crisis threshold has been passed, signals of restraint have in the end come to dominate.

(3) Urge your rival to restrain his clients as well. This corollary of the second principle has guided superpower behavior in the 1967 and 1973 crises. Messages to this effect were exchanged immediately after the outbreak of hostilities and repeated throughout the crises.

(4) Do not undertake moves which might make the rival feel compelled to intervene militarily. In Coral Bell's (1978: 54) formulation, 'one should not seek to win too much, since the other side cannot afford to lose too much.' The superpowers have gradually come to recognize certain 'red lines,' the trespassing of which has to be halted. One such 'red line' which emerges from the Middle Eastern crises is the situation

when a superpower client is facing military collapse (cf. Evron, 1979: 38-9). Then the protector of the victor will be reluctant to encourage its client for fear of military intervention by the rival superpower. American pressures to halt Israel's advance in 1967 and 1973 are cases in point.

(5) Urge your rival to refrain from moves which might make you feel compelled to intervene militarily. This corollary of the fourth principle is central to the identification and reinforcement of 'red lines.' In addition to pressuring their respective clients to avoid crossing 'red lines,' the superpower will spell out what moves they conceive to constitute trespassing of 'red lines' through threats of military intervention. As noted by Yair Evron (1979: 39), threats to intervene in order to deter the victor from completely defeating one's client will be more credible than the other superpower's deterrent counterthreats. Soviet threats to intervene on behalf of Syria in 1967 and on behalf of Egypt in 1973 are examples of this.

(6) Exercise self-restraint and allow a retreating rival to 'save face.' One must, in Bell's (1978: 54) words, 'build golden bridges behind the adversary, to facilitate his retreat.' The usefulness of face-saving devices has been well recognized ever since the Cuban missile crisis. And this principle was operative in the 1967 and 1973 crises in the Middle East. In both cases the United States seems to have perceived the need for — and did not overreact to — Soviet moves to save face internationally and regain its prestige with the Arabs in the wake of military defeat. Thus Kissinger (1982: 595), commenting on American behavior in the 1973 crisis, notes that 'if crisis management requires cold and even brutal measures to show determination, it also imposes the need to show the opponent a way out.'

Unbroken links of communication are obviously a prerequisite for these 'rules of the game' to be effective. Both in 1967 and in 1973 the superpowers opened a variety of direct communication channels immediately after the outbreak of hostilities which were maintained throughout the crises. Furthermore, these principles of crisis management dictate an emphasis on preserving options rather than incurring strong commitments and minimizing rather than manipulating shared risk.

The signaling of the superpowers in the Middle Eastern crises has been sufficiently ambiguous to retain flexibility and not create any irrevocable commitments. Both have started and remained low on the escalation ladder, relying heavily — in 1967 and 1973 — on displays of force and preparedness moves. Immediately after the outbreak of hostilities in 1967 and 1973 both superpowers resorted to direct communication to minimize shared risk. Neither superpower has been prepared to engage in 'brinkmanship.' Kissinger's assessments during the tense concluding phase of the 1973 crisis are illuminative in this regard. In a press conference of October 25 he said: 'as of now the Soviet Union has not yet taken any irrevocable action. . . . We are not asking the Soviet Union to pull back from anything that it has done.' And the American alert he explained thus: 'The alert that has been ordered is of a precautionary nature . . . it is not in any sense irrevocable' (Williams, 1976: 178, 179).

It is thus possible to detect certain similarities in American and Soviet crisis management, epitomized in tacit agreement on some minimal 'rules of the game.' Behind these similarities one can discern the hypothesized pattern of Soviet emulation of the United States in achieving equal superpower status. The Middle East region has been crucial to the assertion of the Soviet global role (cf. Lederer, 1974: 3; Campbell, 1974: 12).

> Throughout all the convolutions of Moscow's Middle East policy since 1955, the one common theme that emerges is the Kremlin's quest for full superpower status and consequent recognition that its interests must be considered in whatever regional arrangements are reached. [Smolansky, 1978: 105]

In this quest the Soviet Union has tended to imitate American crisis management techniques. Specifically with respect to naval diplomacy and signaling the USSR has modeled itself after the United States.

Similar 'currents' seem to have dominated decision-making in Washington and Moscow during crises in the Middle East. While superpower involvement in the crises clearly is an expression of globalism, their behavior during the 1967 and 1973 crises has reflected the tension between enemy and dual images. Kissinger (1982: 202), for example, describes American decision-making before and during the 1973 crisis in terms of a choice between his own 'recommendation of stonewalling radical pressures or State's view of defusing them by offering compromise solutions.' And one study of the perceptions of American Middle East policy officials before and after the Yom Kippur War (Bonham *et al.*, 1979) finds significant differences between those officials who were pessimistic and those who were optimistic about the role of the Soviet Union in a military conflict. In her analysis of the attitudes of different Soviet press organs toward Soviet involvement in the Middle East in the period 1966–73, Ilana Kass (1978) discerns a cleavage between those who depicted the Arab–Israeli conflict as an integral part of the global confrontation between imperialism and socialism and viewed the United States as the principal actor in the Middle East with Israel as a American proxy, on the one hand; and those who described the conflict as essentially a dispute between extremist governments with the United States 'encouraging' or 'supporting' Israeli aggression, on the other hand. The former current (globalism/enemy image), which seemed to represent the view of the military–industrial complex, considered the prospects for a political settlement slight and recommended unequivocal Soviet support for the Arab cause. The latter current (globalism/dual image), which apparently found expression within the party, argued that the Soviet Union ought to take an active part, along with the United States, in bringing about a peaceful settlement.

Similarities in behavior notwithstanding, no superpower condominium or 'crisis prevention regime' (George, 1980b) was ever established in the Middle East. Expectations of emerging condominium, created by the US–Soviet collusion in the Suez crisis and again by the 1972 and 1973 superpower agreements, were never borne out by subsequent events. To be sure, the Soviet Union made bids for condominium both in the 1956 and the 1973 crises. However, in each instance, the Soviet probe was categorically rejected by the United States. Persistent US–Soviet rivalry as well as the imperfect control of both over their regional clients have precluded the emergence of a superpower condominium in the Middle East.

'Controlled instability' (Campbell, 1974) is a term that better catches the predicament of the superpowers in the region. Bell (1974: 538-9) proposes the simile of a dual-control car of the type used by driving schools,

> except that the vehicle is an enormous bus with the rest of the society of states willy-nilly in the passenger seats, though not sitting quietly. The two powers that share the driver's seat are agreed that they want the brakes and steering to work, and that they should keep the bus away from the precipice, but they are not agreed about much else, certainly not about the direction in which the bus should go. And the passengers in the back are all intent on diverting it down roads that lead to their respective national destinations.

Many of them are in a position to grab the arms or chew the ear of one of the drivers, to get where they want to go. They are practically all conscious that too great a level of agreement between the drivers will permit them to overawe their fellow travellers and make the choices for them.

Though powerful, the superpowers do not possess the omnipotence needed to establish a condominium. Their shared lack of control over regional clients has been a common denominator of the crises in the Middle East. The United States and the Soviet Union have been consistently unable to prevent the outbreak of hostilities in the region. And in 1967 as well as 1973 even superpower consensus on ceasefire initiatives proved insufficient to terminate hostilities. It has been said of superpower performance in these two crises that 'it is only a slight exaggeration to say that the United States and the Soviet Union were better managed than managers' (Stein, 1980: 515).

However, the Middle East crises have also revealed persistent power asymmetries between the two superpowers. As the junior superpower, the USSR has sought official American recognition of equal status in the Middle East. The repeated Soviet bids for condominium and the importance attached by the Soviets to the 1972 and 1973 accords must be seen in this light.

Soviet influence in the Middle East has rested heavily on its military relations with regional clients. And, as pointed out by Galia Golan (1979: 50),

> if she is unwilling to provide the war option, she is virtually unable to provide anything else. She cannot play a role as potentially effective as the American one in bringing about a settlement, for she has no leverage over Israel. Nor can she compete significantly with the United States in the peaceful area of economic assistance.

In addition to arms, the United States has been able to offer its influence over Israel, economic benefits and, due to America's oil needs, relations based on interdependence and *mutual* influence. Therefore the United States alone was eventually able to play the role of mediator between the conflicting parties.

6 Nuclear Nonproliferation

Introduction

The nuclear proliferation issue goes to the very heart of superpower status and 'superpower politics.' To arrest the spread of nuclear weapons would be to perpetuate the international hierarchy with the United States and the Soviet Union at the top while denying superpower status to other states. The common US–Soviet interest in nonproliferation has become manifested in several ways, most notably in the Non-Proliferation Treaty of 1968 (NPT); and this is an issue-area where allegations of superpower 'condominium,' 'duopoly,' or 'hegemony' have been legion (cf. e.g., Millar, 1971; D. Keohane, 1981).

Nonproliferation is frequently analyzed in terms of existing and/or desirable regimes. In this chapter I shall look at the American and Soviet part in the different nonproliferation regimes that have existed. Have the two superpowers behaved in similar ways in their attempts to prevent nuclear proliferation? Have they been equally powerful in shaping and maintaining the nonproliferation regimes? Has a superpower 'condominium' been established in the field of nuclear nonproliferation?

Before identifying the nonproliferation regimes and scrutinizing superpower behavior, a brief digression into the constituent components of a nonproliferation regime seems warranted. Three crucial aspects may be distinguished. International regimes differ in their emphasis on (1) the significance of *military* vs. *civilian* technology for proliferation; (2) preventing proliferation by *reducing the inventives* vs. *limiting the capabilities* of non-nuclear weapon states (NNWS) to 'go nuclear;' and (3) *unilateral, bilateral,* or *multilateral* institutional arrangements.

(1) Nuclear fission has a dual nature. The explosive component of nuclear fission weapons and the fuel used in nuclear power plants are derived from the same substances. Moreover, civilian nuclear technology inevitably gives its possessors some of the knowledge needed to produce nuclear weapons. In short, 'there are no two atomic

energies' (Ernst Bergmann, as quoted in SIPRI, 1979: 2). Hence, nuclear weapons can be obtained either directly, through a program specifically manufacturing a military nuclear explosive, or indirectly, as a by-product of a civilian nuclear program. Whereas the present nuclear weapons states (NWS) have followed the first, direct path, the possibility of acquiring a nuclear weapons capability by diverting civil nuclear energy facilities to military purposes has been a matter of international concern since nuclear fission was first exploited as a source of energy.

A comprehensive nonproliferation regime therefore needs to prevent both avenues. From a nonproliferation viewpoint certain aspects of civil nuclear energy technology are especially 'sensitive:' enrichment at the front end, and reprocessing at the back end of the nuclear fuel cycle. Enrichment, the process of raising the percentage of the fissionable isotope U-235 in natural uranium to the level required for reactor fuel, is sensitive because the processes used to enrich uranium to 3–4 percent of U-235 — the level necessary to generate energy — are identical to those necessary to enrich to 90 percent or more — the level required to produce a nuclear explosion. Reprocessing, the process of recovering plutonium and residual uranium from spent fuel, is controversial because the extracted plutonium can be used in nuclear weapons.

(2) In the pursuit of nonproliferation two kinds of measures are available: those designed to limit capabilities to make nuclear weapons and those designed to reduce incentives (or increase disincentives) to acquire such weapons. Of course, capabilities and incentives are interrelated and not entirely separable factors. For instance, a very tight technical arrangement to impede proliferation, rather than increase disincentives, may reduce the legitimacy of the nonproliferation regime among NNWS. On the other hand, a loose technical arrangement makes it likely that NNWS will keep the nuclear weapons option to hedge against the possibility of widespread proliferation (cf. Greenwood *et al.*, 1977: 7).

As discussed above, limiting the capabilities of NNWS requires both blocking the construction of facilities specifically dedicated to the production of nuclear weapons and preventing the diversion of civil nuclear energy facilities to military purposes. The latter objective can be attained in various ways. One obvious approach is *technological denial*, precluding transfers of 'sensitive' facilities that require, produce, or are capable of producing weapons-grade materials. *Regulated transfer* represents an alternative approach, according to which the transfer of nuclear technology is permitted only if accompanied by a combination of political pledges by recipient states that it will not be used for military purposes, and safeguards to control the obedience of recipient states (cf. Greenwood *et al.*, 1977: 82-3).

(3) Nonproliferation measures may involve a combination of unilateral action, bilateral agreements, and multilateral arrangements. Although international regimes presuppose a certain degree of multilateralism, they may vary in their emphasis on individual vs. joint action.

Against this background, let us now proceed to a review of three consecutive nonproliferation regimes — the secrecy regime, the Atoms for Peace regime, and the NPT regime — and the part played by the superpowers in shaping and maintaining these regimes.

The Secrecy Regime

The development of the first atomic bomb was shrouded in secrecy. The Manhattan Project was surrounded by strict security measures. 'Compartmentalization' — dictating that the flow of information among the engaged scientists be regulated on a 'need to know' basis — was adopted as a counter-espionage measure. Designed to keep the project secret from the German enemy, it was soon transformed into a means for controlling the flow of information to American allies as well (Sherwin, 1975: 63). The American collaboration with Britain and Canada — masquerading as a joint effort in the field of tube alloys — was based on restricted interchange rather than full co-operation. In the choice between a policy of partnership in order to develop an atomic bomb as quickly as possible, and a policy of ensuring a post-war American atomic monopoly at the possible cost of delaying the bomb's production, the Americans opted for the latter (Sherwin, 1975: 76; Nieburg, 1964: 58-9).

In the words of George Quester (1973: 14), 'a proliferation problem could have been defined from the day the first atomic device was exploded, since Americans might naturally have wanted to keep the weapon for themselves.' In effect, worries about proliferation preceded the atomic explosions.

The secret Quebec agreement of September 1943 which defined the Anglo–American collaboration in nuclear research and development can be considered the first nonproliferation agreement (Goldschmidt, 1977: 70). First, the allies agreed not to communicate any information to third parties without mutual consent. In addition, the agreement stated that the United States, in view of its heavier investment in the project, would enjoy 'any post-war advantages of an industrial or commercial character.' From then on, British and Canadian participation was strictly limited to a 'need to know' basis. A curtain of secrecy was gradually drawn between the United States and its partners. As a result, at the end of the war the United States had a virtual monopoly of nuclear know-how and technology (cf. Nieburg, 1964: 57-60; Sherwin, 1975: 85-6).

After the tragic revelation of the awesome power of the atomic bomb in August 1945, the United States, as its sole possessor, was in a position to define the future of nuclear weapons. Even if American post-war policy in atomic energy matters included spectacular proposals for international control, unilateral efforts to retain the nuclear monopoly eventually took precedence.

The Acheson–Lilienthal report and the Baruch Plan of 1946 proposed internationalization of ownership and management of 'all intrinsically dangerous operations' in the field of atomic energy. The Soviets interpreted the Baruch Plan as an attempt to consolidate and extend the American atomic monopoly and interfere with Soviet efforts to develop atomic weapons (cf. Nogee, 1961: 64-5, 250-1). As the USSR submitted its counterproposal, the incompatibility of American and Soviet objectives was revealed (Nogee, 1961: 36-8). Whereas the United States was determined to preserve and extend its atomic weapons supply and not divulge any atomic secrets until a foolproof control system was in operation, the Soviet Union sought the elimination — or at least neutralization — of the American atomic monopoly and full revelation of nuclear secrets before considering international control. Underlying these divergences was the irreconcilable conflict between the Soviet resolve to develop its own atomic weapon as rapidly as possible and the American desire to prevent this development. Negotiations were soon deadlocked, and the grandiose schemes for internationalizing the atom, whether sincerely meant or not, never came to form the basis of a nonproliferation regime.

Instead, unilateral American measures to retain the secrets of atomic weapons manufacture laid the foundation of the immediate post-war regime. The Atomic Energy Act of 1946 (the McMahon Act) proscribed the release of sensitive data on the design of atomic weapons, classified as secret all information regarding the use of nuclear power for industrial purposes, and prohibited the transfer of fissionable materials to allies and non-allies alike. Secrecy was facilitated by strict government control over all nuclear facilities and fissionable materials (cf. Ebinger, 1978: 10; Skogmar, 1979: 50-1).

The Atomic Energy Act 'slammed the door of atomic co-operation' (Nieburg, 1964: 57). A number of tripartite conferences on declassification were held to maintain consistent secrecy practices among the United States, Britain and Canada. They involved asymmetrical information exchanges. Through these conferences, the Americans kept informed of British–Canadian programs, while carefully avoiding disclosure of any information that would expedite the weapons progress of their wartime collaborators (see Nieburg, 1964: 63-7).

The United States policy of secrecy was complemented by an effort, already begun in early 1943, to gain as complete control as possible over the uranium resources of the world (cf. Skogmar, 1979: 40-2; Sherwin, 1975: 105). By monopolizing and blocking the transfer to other countries of the two indispensible technical ingredients of any nuclear effort — know-how and uranium — the United States seemed to be pursuing the perfect nonproliferation policy. Yet the regime built upon unilateral American secrecy and control did not succeed in preventing proliferation. The Soviet Union exploded its first atomic bomb in September 1949, considerably earlier than expected in the West.

The 1949 Soviet explosion 'paradoxically terminated much of any anxiety about proliferation, since the worst damage had seemingly been done' (Quester, 1973: 15). Concerns about proliferation abated once 'each bloc' had the bomb. And in 1951 the US Atomic Energy Act was amended to permit limited information exchange. It was made clear that the new legislation was intended to apply only to Britain and Canada. Even if the 1951 amendments apparently did not entail any significant releases of information, they did provoke intensified pressures against secrecy (cf. Nieburg, 1964: 41, 72-3; Skogmar, 1979: 52-3).

By far the most potent external pressure came from Britain. Incensed by the fact that they had originally possessed the most advanced nuclear program but had had to move it to America during the war, the British in response to the American post-war policy of secrecy embarked on a dual-purpose nuclear program emphasizing the weapons aspect. In October 1952 Britain exploded its first atomic bomb.

Other factors contributed to the erosion of the secrecy regime. The organization of NATO in 1949 and the chronic weakness of its ground forces led to pressures for nuclear sharing. American scientists requested greater scientific communication and greater candor about the effects of nuclear weapons. With the enticing prospects for commercial applications American industry pushed for the abolition of the government monopoly and for greater private participation in the atomic industry. And the independent development of nuclear power reactor technology by Britain, Canada, France and the Soviet Union intensified fears that American commercial interests would fall behind in winning this new world market (cf. Nieburg, 1964: 73-7). The first Soviet thermonuclear explosion in August 1953 of a type not yet tested by the United States heralded the demise of the secrecy regime.

In sum, the secrecy regime rested on unilateralism, emphasized the military aspect of atomic energy, and concentrated on technological denial while neglecting other countries' incentives and disincentives to go nuclear. The regime amounted to an effort by the United States to exploit and extend its 'issue-specific power.' The rapid development of a Soviet nuclear weapons capability represented the primary failure of the regime and served as a catalyst for further proliferation pressures. The United States and the Soviet Union followed separate and opposite paths. Only after the Soviet entry into the 'nuclear club' was the foundation laid for possible future superpower collaboration or parallel action on the proliferation issue. Nor can the Baruch Plan be viewed as an invitation to US–Soviet condominium, since it was so patently unacceptable to the Soviets and the United States showed no willingness whatsoever to make any concessions to the Soviet viewpoints in subsequent negotiations.

The Atoms for Peace Regime

If the Soviet thermonuclear explosion in August 1953 marked the end of the early nonproliferation regime, President Eisenhower's famous 'Atoms for Peace' address before the UN General Assembly on December 8, 1953, heralded a new regime. Eisenhower proposed that governments with a nuclear capability should diminish their stockpiles of fissionable military materials by making joint contributions to a pool administered by an international agency under the aegis of the UN. This fissionable material was to be distributed for use in national civilian programs, in particular 'to provide abundant electrical energy to the power-starved areas of the world.' The proposed agency would be responsible for the impounding, storage and protection of the contributed materials and for their distribution and peaceful uses. However, unlike the Baruch Plan, Eisenhower's proposal did not foresee international ownership of nuclear materials (cf. e.g., Nieburg, 1964: 80-1; Ebinger, 1978: 12; Mabry, 1981a: 149).

The Atoms for Peace plan entailed a reversal of earlier United States policy in several respects. (1) In contrast to the initial one-sided stress on the military aspects of nuclear power, priority was now assigned to its civilian uses.

(2) The American policy emphasis shifted from technological denial to regulated transfer and active promotion of the peaceful uses of atomic energy. In 1954 the restrictive Atomic Energy Act was amended to allow expanded international co-operation. Specifically, the AEC (Atomic Energy Commission) was authorized to provide enrichment services to foreign nations under bilaterally negotiated nuclear co-operation agreements (cf. Mabry, 1981b: 174).

(3) The early policy of utmost secrecy gradually gave way to information sharing. Nuclear information was made available to other nations via three principal routes (cf. Nieburg, 1964: 84). First, data concerning the peaceful uses of the atom were progressively declassified. Second, the United States entered into bilateral agreements for both research and power reactor development (cf. Nieburg, 1964: 103-9). Third, in bilateral agreements with selected military allies the United States transferred information on nuclear defense plans and on certain characteristics of nuclear weapons (cf. Bader, 1968: 28-9).

(4) Previous American attempts at controlling raw materials were abandoned. The discovery of significant uranium resources in the United States led to overproduction, falling prices and, in the early 1960s, the termination of American purchases of uranium from Canada and South Africa, and an American embargo on foreign uranium imports to protect the domestic mining industry. As a result, a uranium 'world market' developed, and large amounts of nuclear material were made available (cf. Goldschmidt, 1977: 72-3; Skogmar, 1979: 110).

These shifts in American policy reflected a tendency to play down the relationship between the peaceful and the military atom, and to de-emphasize the dangers of nuclear proliferation. The safeguards against military diversion, upon which all American nuclear co-operation agreements were conditioned, were the only remnant of the early American preoccupation with proliferation. How, then, did the Soviet Union — the primary target of earlier American nonproliferation measures and a nascent nuclear rival — respond to this new American policy?

The immediate Soviet reaction to the Atoms for Peace program was negative. The entire concept of international co-operation in the peaceful uses of nuclear energy was rejected until nuclear disarmament was achieved, and the Soviet Union refused to participate in discussions about an international atomic energy agency. In a dramatic reversal of policy, the USSR in late 1954 agreed to discuss the issue of an international agency separate from disarmament, and its behavior in the subsequent negotiations was unusually co-operative (cf. Nogee, 1961: 224-7). The Soviets, rather than being outsiders, decided to enter the competition, as the United States launched its international program of co-operation in the peaceful uses of the atom.

The USSR in 1955 initiated its own 'Atom for Peace' program, as it were. Soviet nuclear co-operation and promotion of the peaceful atom took forms similar to those of the American program. Like the United States, the Soviet Union entered bilateral transfer agreements. The Soviet nuclear export program was, however, limited to countries within its orbit. In January 1955 Moscow promised 'scientific and technical assistance,' including research reactors and the 'necessary amount of fissionable materials for research purposes,' to China and other communist countries (Clemens, 1968: 15). Bilateral agreements were signed with Czechoslovakia, East Germany, Poland, Rumania and China in 1955, and with Bulgaria and Hungary in 1956 (Duffy, 1978: 85).

In addition, the Soviet Union accepted the American challenge in making nuclear information available to other countries. A new kind of 'atomic warfare' or 'World Atomic Olympics' ensued, as 'by gradual degree the nuclear giants lifted their skirts of secrecy, each challenging the other to reveal more evidence of dedication to the peaceful atom' (Nieburg, 1964: 92-3).

One area where the American and Soviet Atoms for Peace programs initially differed was that of controls and safeguards. Whereas all American exports of nuclear materials were conditioned on safeguards, the Soviet Union failed to apply safeguards to its early transfers to China and East European countries (Duffy, 1978: 84). Moreover, in the negotiations leading to the creation of the International Atomic Energy Agency (IAEA), the Soviet Union sided with the Third World countries in objecting to international safeguards, stressing the need to observe the sovereign rights of states (Nogee, 1961: 226-7).

The initial divergence in American and Soviet postures was, however, gradually blurred. In late 1956 the Soviet Union accepted a compromise on safeguards, paving the way for the establishment of the IAEA (Nogee, 1961: 227). The Soviets now at least paid lipservice to the principle of IAEA inspection, even if they continued to join Third World nations in attacking American insistence on control whenever this was politically profitable (cf. Nieburg, 1964: 86-7). There was an evident cutback in the Soviet nuclear energy program around 1957 (see Kramish, 1959: 145, 151), and after 1958 the Soviet Union slowed down nuclear transfers to its allies while at the same time adding safeguards. Many nuclear commitments were drawn out, renegotiated, or simply not fulfilled. The Soviets insisted that all countries receiving reactors from them should obtain the enriched fuel from the USSR and return all spent fuel rods to them for reprocessing. In that way, no raw material for nuclear weapons was allowed to rest outside the Soviet Union (Duffy, 1978: 86-7).

Concomitant with the growing Soviet concern about safeguards, the United States was compelled by alliance considerations to relax its own control objectives in bilateral agreements with Britain and Canada — which were already atomic powers — and, more significantly, in the 1957 agreement with Euratom which left inspection of American supplies to supranational European reactor programs to Euratom personnel (see Kramish, 1965: 176; Nieburg, 1964: 87; Skogmar, 1979: 131). In brief, the principle of safeguards came to be accepted by the United States and the Soviet Union, yet half-heartedly applied by both.

What, then, were the effects of the emergent consensus around an Atoms for Peace regime? First, the original visions and expectations concerning the role of the peaceful atom in transforming under-developed areas of the world proved to be vastly exaggerated, and disillusionment soon set in. The realization grew that nuclear power would neither be cheap for a long time to come nor directly applicable, except for countries with a highly developed industrial base.

Consequently, Atoms for Peace tended to widen rather than close the gulf between the 'haves' and the 'have-nots.' Nor was the nonprolifera-tion of nuclear weapons necessarily furthered by the unfulfilled promises of the peaceful atom. Many LDCs chose to embark on smaller-scale nuclear research project which tended to enhance the proliferation risks, since weapons-grade materials can be diverted from some of the larger research reactors (Ebinger, 1978: 17).

If the flow of nuclear materials was only a trickle, nuclear information virtually flooded the world. After the Second Geneva Conference on the Peaceful Uses of Atomic Energy in 1958 'practically all of the fences were down surrounding the peaceful atom' (Nieburg,

1964: 101). This disclosure contributed significantly to letting the 'nuclear genie' out of the bottle and making future nonproliferation schemes less feasible.

The emergent nuclear co-operation was, by and large, bilateral. To be sure, the International Atomic Energy Agency was established in 1957, but its role fell short of that envisaged in Eisenhower's Atoms for Peace address. Gone was the original conception of the IAEA as a custodian and sole transfer agent for fissionable materials. The new organization was merely to arrange and supervise transactions among its members. The atomic powers wanted to choose the countries to which they would transfer nuclear materials and prescribe the conditions of such transfers.

In terms of nonproliferation, France and China represented obvious failures of the American and Soviet Atoms for Peace programs respectively. Caught in a dilemma between alliance commitments and nonproliferation considerations, both superpowers had made feeble attempts to limit the nuclear capabilities of their allies while failing to address their incentives to go nuclear.

To summarize, the Atoms for Peace regime rested on bilateralism. In fact, it was hardly one regime but rather two parallel regimes, the American and the Soviet. The two potential proliferators followed similar paths. One leading Soviet spokesman on nuclear issues, V.S. Emelyanov, in 1963 suggested to a European nuclear energy official that nonproliferation would be best served if 'each take care of its own' (Duffy, 1978: 90; Goldschmidt, 1977: 84). And after the Chinese episode the Soviets did indeed 'take care of their own' client states, insisting on safeguards against military diversion in the same way as did the United States.

Again, an American proposal envisaging a multilateral framework with certain elements of superpower condominium proved unfeasible. Instead, the Atoms for Peace regime(s), by promoting civilian nuclear power and releasing nuclear 'secrets' while denying NNWS nuclear weapons technology and neglecting their incentives to go nuclear, underlined the limited ability of the superpowers to prevent proliferation. To be sure, parallel American and Soviet policies meant that many NNWS keen to acquire nuclear aid accepted safeguards which they would not otherwise have accepted. But once other nuclear nations decided to follow the American lead and disseminate their nuclear technologies, and international competition ensued to win the valuable future market of nuclear export sales, the floodgates for the potential proliferation of nuclear weapons were opened.

The NPT Regime

On July 1, 1968, the Treaty on the Non-Proliferation of Nuclear Weapons (NPT) was opened for signature. President Johnson labeled it 'the most important international agreement limiting nuclear arms since the nuclear age began' (Willrich, 1969: 3), and Premier Kosygin termed it a 'major success for the cause of peace' (Clemens, 1968: 168). Other observers have characterized the treaty in much less grandiose and positive terms. In the view of one American analyst (Bader, 1968: 102), the NPT merely exposes 'the fact that the United States and the Soviet Union can be equally pious when obliging themselves to refrain from doing something they would not have done in any event.' Alva Myrdal (1976: 168-9) calls the NPT 'a grossly discriminatory treaty' functioning as 'a seal on the superpowers' hegemonic world policy.' The purpose of a nonproliferation accord, according to one French minister, was to 'castrate the impotent' (Young, 1972: 58). And the Chinese greeted the treaty in these words (quoted in Willrich, 1969: 174):

> Obviously, the U.S. imperialists and Soviet revisionists concocted the treaty to put all non-nuclear countries in a subordinate position, that of being 'protectorates,' so that they may maintain their special status as big nuclear powers and remain 'nuclear overlords.'

Before going into the content of the NPT and addressing the question of possible superpower condominium or 'dual hegemony,' let us briefly recapitulate the developments that led up to this controversial treaty and the ensuing regime change.

In the late 1950s two new approaches to the proliferation problem appeared. From 1956 on, the Soviet Union began to advocate the idea of nuclear-free zones, and a 1957 American package of partial disarmament proposals included an undertaking on the part of the NWS not to transfer out of its control any nuclear weapons. The first draft resolution addressing nonproliferation as a separate measure was submitted by Ireland to the UN General Assembly in 1958 (UN, 1967: 185-6). From then on, nonproliferation was a recurrent agenda item in successive General Assemblies.

The partial nuclear test ban of July 1963 was the first manifestation of the growing superpower interest in joint nonproliferation measures. By prohibiting testing, a crucial intermediary stage between research and the production of nuclear weapons, the 1963 Moscow Treaty can be — and was indeed — interpreted as a non-proliferation measure.

In 1964–65 a US–Soviet consensus emerged that nonproliferation was to be accorded highest priority on the multilateral negotiating agenda. From the spring of 1965 the Eighteen-Nation Committee on Disarmament (ENDC) became the principal forum for negotiations on a nonproliferation treaty. During three years of negotiation certain issues divided the superpowers, other issues set the NWS apart from the NNWS, and other issues still proved divisive along both dimensions.

Among those causing controversy between the United States and the Soviet Union as well as between the nuclear 'haves' and 'have-nots,' the question of safeguards and controls was most prominent. The NNWS demanded that safeguards should apply to civilian as well as military nuclear activities in NNWS and NWS alike. India, for example, pointed out that 'institution of international controls on peaceful reactors and power stations is like an attempt to maintain law and order in a society by placing all its law-abiding citizens in custody while leaving its law-breaking elements free to roam the streets' (Willrich, 1969: 124). And several industrialized states expressed concern that if safeguards were applied to NNWS only, they would risk disclosure of industrial secrets, while their NWS competitors would not (Willrich, 1969: 102-3). Whereas the United States was willing to subject its civilian nuclear industry to safeguards, the Soviet Union refused to accept international inspection of any of its nuclear activities.

The question of indirect dissemination of nuclear weapons tended to split the two superpowers from the outset of negotiations. At issue was whether the NNWS were to be denied 'control over' (the American position) or 'access to' (the Soviet position) nuclear weapons (cf. Willrich, 1969: 84). The wording reflected divergent attitudes to nuclear sharing arrangements, the United States seeking to keep open the options for nuclear sharing within NATO, the Soviet Union trying to close them. In essence, the discussion revolved around the question of West German access to nuclear weapons, directly or indirectly. The initial disagreement concerned the American plans for a NATO Multilateral Nuclear Force (MLF), including Germany. One rationalization for the MLF proposal was that it would satisfy whatever nuclear aspirations Germany might have while precluding an independent German nuclear force. However, the mere idea of a West German finger on the nuclear trigger caused grave concerns in Moscow. In fact, the Soviets made it quite clear that to them the veto of any West German 'access to nuclear weapons' was the very essence of nonproliferation (cf. e.g., Wettig, 1969: 1082; Kolkowicz *et al.*, 1970: 95-6).

Issues dividing the NWS and the NNWS included links between a nonproliferation agreement and other arms limitation measures, security guarantees, and provisions for review, duration and withdrawal. First, neither the United States nor the Soviet Union wanted to incorporate in the body of a nonproliferation treaty any other arms control measures. The NNWS, on the other hand, consistently pointed to the link between 'vertical' proliferation — the accumulation of nuclear weapons by the NWS — and 'horizontal' proliferation — the spread of nuclear weapons to NNWS. Since, in their view, vertical proliferation generated horizontal proliferation, the treaty should constrain horizontal proliferation as well (cf. SIPRI, 1979: 77-99). The NNWS demanded arms reduction measures on the part of the NWS as a quid pro quo for forgoing their own nuclear weapon option and were not satisfied with the general noncommittal preambular references to such measures, as proposed by the superpowers. In the words of the Indian delegate, 'there is no balance . . . between a platitude on the one hand and a prohibition on the other' (SIPRI, 1979: 89).

Furthermore, nonaligned NNWS in particular demanded security guarantees from the NWS. Both 'positive' guarantees (in the form of commitments to protect the NNWS against attack by other NWS) and 'negative' guarantees (in the form of pledges not to attack the NNWS) were discussed. Originally neither superpower included any type of security guarantee in their draft treaties.

Finally, the procedural issues of review. duration and withdrawal caused disagreements between the NWS and the NNWS. The United States and the Soviet Union originally proposed that the treaty be of indefinite or unlimited duration. As the NNWS gradually realized that the NWS were unwilling to incorporate specific arms control measures and specific security guarantees in the treaty, they became increasingly insistent that the treaty contain review procedures and conditions of duration and withdrawal linking the NPT with progress in other arms control areas (SIPRI, 1979: 118-26).

Against the background of these and other divergences, it is evident that the final treaty had to be a compromise. The NPT commits NNWS not to manufacture, accept the transfer of, or otherwise acquire nuclear weapons and requires them to accept IAEA safeguards on their peaceful nuclear activities. In contrast to safeguards under the Atoms for Peace regime, the NPT regime places *all* peaceful nuclear activities of signatory NNWS, whether imported or indigenous, under safeguards (cf. Ebinger, 1978: 36; Mabry, 1981a: 162).

Owing to the persistent Soviet opposition to inspection, the NPT does not prescribe safeguards on the peaceful nuclear activities of the NWS. In return for their concession in this regard, the NNWS obtained the inclusion in the NPT of an undertaking by all parties 'to pursue negotiations in good faith on effective measures relating to cessation of the nuclear arms race at an early date' as well as two articles (a) asserting the 'inalienable right' of all parties to peaceful nuclear energy and (b) establishing an obligation for international sharing, on a nondiscriminatory basis, of any potential benefits that may be derived from peaceful applications of nuclear explosions. Apart from an article committing the signatories to the principle of nuclear-free zones, the NPT included no provision for security guarantees. However, in March 1968 the United States, the USSR and Britain jointly sponsored a Security Council resolution providing positive guarantees of assistance to NNWS parties to a nonproliferation treaty in case of aggression or the threat of aggression with nuclear weapons by a NWS. Many NNWS considered these guarantees inadequate and criticized the NWS for not providing any negative security guarantees (SIPRI, 1979: 108-17). Finally, the NNWS were instrumental in incorporating in the NPT a provision for periodic review conferences and made it quite clear that, in their view, the viability and duration of the treaty would hinge on the NWS fulfilling their obligation to negotiate effective arms control measures (SIPRI, 1979: 125-6).

Yet critics of the NPT have been decrying it as discriminatory or even the 'first unequal treaty of the twentieth century' (cf. Quester, 1981b: 214). What is regarded as discriminatory is not primarily the differentiation of states into the two classes of NWS and NNWS which is inherent in any attempt to control proliferation, but rather the asymmetrical distribution of obligations, risks and privileges under the treaty. Whereas strict and legally binding obligations and prohibitions are imposed upon the NNWS, the obligations incumbent upon the NWS are 'hortatory, putative, contingent and subject to fulfilment only at some unspecified future point in time' (SIPRI, 1979: 127).

It is also true that the negotiations leading to the NPT displayed an unprecedented degree of open collaboration and tactit understanding between the United States and the Soviet Union. As co-chairmen of the ENDC, the two superpowers held the initiative throughout the negotiations. Once the American MLF plans were abandoned, they were able to resolve their principal bilateral issues. In 1967, and again in 1968, the United States and the Soviet Union submitted identical draft treaties to the ENDC. In the assessment of one observer (Quester, 1981b: 227-8), 'the handling of the NPT negotiations from 1967 to 1968, and the handling of proliferation matters since then, might substantively and procedurally be viewed as almost the ideal of how smoothly Soviet–American dealings could run.' The superpowers also collaborated in inducing the NNWS to sign the NPT (cf. Clemens, 1968: 168-9).

Such visible signs of US–Soviet collaboration in combination with the discriminatory nature of the NPT have naturally fostered allegations of superpower hegemony or condominium. There are, however, a number of factors contradicting — or at least modifying — the characterization of the NPT regime as a US–Soviet condominium (cf. D. Keohane, 1981: 11-14). First, nonproliferation was — and is — not an exclusive superpower interest. In fact, negotiations on the NPT were in large measure the result of initiatives taken by other countries, such as Ireland, Sweden and Mexico. And, as we have seen, the superpowers had to make certain concessions to the NNWS in the course of negotiations. The characterization of the NPT as a US–Soviet imposition is further undermined by the refusal of a high proportion of 'threshold' states to join it. In effect, the two superpowers were less successful in obtaining adherence to the NPT than they were for the limited test ban treaty (cf. Goldschmidt, 1977: 76). Finally, the treaty does not appear to shackle the NNWS in permanent deprivation. On the contrary, it has been argued that under the NPT regime 'a nonweapon state can come closer to exploding a plutonium weapon today without violating an agreement not to make a bomb than the United States was in the spring of 1947' (Wohlstetter, 1977: 88).

Hence, in the overall assessment of Daniel Keohane (1981: 14), 'it is difficult to claim that a Treaty which does not place formidable obstacles in the way of resolute proliferators, does not embrace a number of would-be nuclear weapon States, allows comparatively easy withdrawal and formally provides for the supply of nuclear aid, constitutes an effective instrument of nuclear hegemony.'

In the years since the signing of the NPT the United States and the Soviet Union have not consistently followed the same or parallel paths, nor have they proved to be equally powerful in maintaining or altering the regime. There have, in short, been certain developments casting doubt on any potential or actual superpower condominium and eroding the NPT regime. Let us now turn our attention to these developments.

Erosion of the NPT Regime

A sequence of events in the mid-1970s tended to undermine confidence in the NPT regime. First, the 1973–74 oil embargo and the attendant fourfold increase in oil prices expanded the nuclear debate into the larger context of energy supply security and induced oil-dependent countries to renew their interest in nuclear technology. Emergent fears of impending uranium shortage accelerated plans for early commercial use of plutonium fuel (cf. Ebinger, 1978: 41-2, 49; Nye, 1981: 19).

Second, the Indian nuclear detonation in May 1974 dramatically demonstrated the dangers inherent in nuclear exports and the limitations of the NPT regime. Not a signatory to the NPT, India did not violate the letter of any agreement by exploding its 'peaceful' nuclear device. The plutonium used was extracted in a nationally-built reprocessing plant and derived from a research reactor imported from Canada in the mid-1950s, before international safeguards were introduced (cf. Goldschmidt, 1977: 78).

Third, the issue of nuclear exports and safeguards was further accentuated by controversial nuclear deals signed in 1975–76 by France and Germany, involving the transfer of 'sensitive facilities' (enrichment and reprocessing plants) to South Korea, Pakistan and Brazil.

Whereas these events were visible catalysts, longer-term trends in the international nuclear energy market contributed to the erosion of the NPT regime. To summarize: (1) the number of exporting countries grew, making the market increasingly competitive; (2) not only power reactors and fuel but the full range of nuclear fuel cycle facilities came to be exported; and (3) the competition sharpened as a result of a world-wide paralysis of nuclear energy growth since the mid-1970s.

The growing number of exporting countries implied the gradual loss of control by the superpowers. The United States, in particular, was deprived of its predominant position in the enrichment, reactor and reprocessing markets (cf. Joskow, 1976; Neff and Jacoby, 1979).

Widespread commitments to new nuclear power technologies and a 'plutonium economy' threatened to give many countries quick access to weapons-usable material, and this prospect brought the control of power-cycle technology into focus. Yet at the same time, the increasing number of nuclear suppliers, together with flagging demand in the mid-1970s, resulted in hardening competition among nuclear exporters which tended to erode political controls. As the domestic nuclear programs of several industrialized nations were paralyzed, their nuclear industries turned to the export market, each attempting 'to undercut the others in terms of safeguards and political conditions attached to exports in order not to lose lucrative export markets' (Baker, 1976: 205).

These developments in the international nuclear market challenged the conception of nonproliferation on which the NPT regime rested. The prevalent assumption had been that nuclear weapons development would always require long and costly programs and would most probably involve clandestine diversions of fissionable materials. The NPT safeguards system was geared to detect and deter such developments. However, as the Indian case demonstrated, the easiest and cheapest way of acquiring a bomb is via a small plutonium-producing reactor and an unsophisticated, pilot-scale reprocessing facility dedicated to a weapons program (Ebinger, 1978: 43; Greenwood *et al.*, 1977: 33). In addition, the spread of enrichment and reprocessing facilities had opened up the prospect of a complete and sudden reversal of a nuclear program from a peaceful to a military project. There is then, in Albert Wohlstetter's (1977: 149) words, 'a kind of Damoclean overhang of countries increasingly near the edge of making bombs.' The availability of a weapons option from commercial programs had permitted states to guard their intentions and still exploit their quasi-nuclear status. States can move closer to weapons 'without quite breaking the rules' (Wohlstetter, 1977) and without having to make, or acknowledge, explicit decisions to go nuclear. In short, a major new problem is that of 'latent proliferation' — a process whereby states 'simply refuse to foreclose or abjure the possibility of manufacturing weapons, while accumulating the resources and shortening the time required to do so' (Greenwood *et al.*, 1977: 7).

How, then, have the superpowers reacted to these events and developments? The immediate American and Soviet public responses to the 1974 Indian detonation were muted. Yet in the longer run the Indian nuclear explosion precipitated a profound American reassessment of the proliferation issue while bringing only marginal changes in Soviet nuclear policy. It has been suggested that India in 1974 provided the United States with a 'learning experience' or 'eye-opener' comparable to the lesson China had earlier taught the Soviet Union (Potter, 1982: 298).

In October 1976 President Ford, announcing that 'avoidance of proliferation must take precedence over economic interests,' recommended that reprocessing be deferred until 'there is sound reason to conclude that the world community can effectively overcome the associated risks of proliferation' (Gilinsky, 1978: 377-8). The Carter administration carried these intentions into effect by proclaiming an indefinite domestic deferral of both reprocessing and the introduction of fast breeder reactors into commercial use. The new nonproliferation policy was promulgated in the Nuclear Non-Proliferation Act (NNPA) of March 1978. Constituting a major amendment to the Atomic Energy Act of 1954, the NNPA established tighter rules for nuclear exports and called for the renegotiation of bilateral agreements to increase American controls (cf. e.g., Neff and Jacoby, 1979: 1127-30; Potter, 1982: 300-1; Skogmar, 1980: 227; Mabry, 1981b: 176-9).

Concomitant with these internal reassessments, Washington took steps to create a broader international consensus on the relationship between civil nuclear energy and proliferation. The American initiative led to the formation of a new multilateral body, the so-called London Suppliers Group, consisting of representatives of nuclear exporting countries. This body, which began meeting secretly in London during 1975, in 1978 published agreement on a set of guidelines for nuclear transfers which made the nonproliferation responsibilities of nuclear suppliers more explicit. In October 1977 the United States launched the International Nuclear Fuel Cycle Evaluation (INFCE) in an attempt 'to convince the international community that U.S. opposition to the plutonium economy was technically and economically sound' (Lellouche, 1980: 338).

However, having initiated these multilateral efforts, the United States in 1978 went ahead and passed the Nuclear Non-Proliferation Act without waiting for the results of the INFCE. Hence, the new American nonproliferation policy represented a marked shift in two respects. First, the previous policy of regulated transfer was superseded by technological denial. 'After having promoted full nuclear cooperation under its Atoms for Peace Plan of 1953, the United States was reverting to the policy of denial of the immediate post-war period' (Lellouche, 1981: 45). Second, unilateralism took precedence over multilateral efforts to prevent proliferation. All in all, the 1978 NNPA was 'a unilateral step toward revision of the worldwide nonproliferation regime' (Neff and Jacoby, 1979: 1123).

The American policy shift caused considerable alarm and irritation around the world. The NNPA appeared to compromise fuel supply security even for those nations that shared the American concern about nonproliferation, and to threaten the future viability of several major nuclear programs abroad. The Americans were therefore suspected of being less interested in nonproliferation than in perpetuating their commercial advantage.

The profound American reassessment in the mid-1970s had no counterpart in the Soviet Union. But although no major policy shift occurred, Soviet nuclear policy underwent certain modifications in the mid-1970s. First, Moscow's role in international nuclear trade expanded. The Soviet Union stepped in as a new enrichment supplier for those wishing to reduce their dependency on the United States. After 1975 the Soviet Union also allowed sales of nuclear reactors and equipment outside the bloc (Duffy, 1978: 91). Worth noting is the Soviet agreement to supply reactors to Libya.

> Political leverage added to technical control has served the USSR well in the past 18 years as a nonproliferation strategy, but only where leverage has been strong and direct. Libya, like China in 1959, is a country over which political leverage is far from secure. [Duffy, 1980: 41]

At the same time, Moscow became more articulate in its support of the NPT and IAEA safeguards. Signing the NPT was made a condition for Soviet nuclear exports outside the bloc, and the Soviet Union began to make active contributions to IAEA research on inspection techniques (Duffy, 1978: 95-9). The ensuing combination of expanded commercial activity and tightened controls revealed 'the contradictions inherent in simultaneously promoting an ambitious domestic nuclear development program (including breeder reactors and plutonium recycling) while retaining a commitment to the promotion of a strong international nuclear nonproliferation regime' (Potter, 1982: 305).

In short, whereas the United States appeared to be groping toward the creation of a new nonproliferation regime, the Soviet policy modifications took place within the framework of the NPT regime. The effects of these new superpower efforts upon proliferation are less than clear. Observers have tended to emphasize the following four discernible effects:

(1) The concentration on reprocessing and breeder reactors, created by the American policy shift and the INFCE, has, in large measure, been dysfunctional. It has resulted in 'a quarrel among the few industrialized countries able to develop such installations, whereas future proliferators, following Pakistan's example, will most likely follow the route of building small-scale clandestine facilities' (Lellouche, 1980: 342-3). Paradoxically, the immediate effect of the new American nonproliferation policy which was clearly aimed at unstable Third World countries was an acrimonious controversy among Western allies which tended to overshadow the original proliferation concern.

(2) The disruption of American enrichment and reprocessing supplies, by creating widespread mistrust and uncertainty, proved detrimental to the objective of nonproliferation.

(3) With the major nuclear suppliers collaborating and the London Suppliers Group apparently backing the American nonproliferation policy, many of the more industrially advanced Third World countries have resorted to co-operative self-help in their nuclear development (Ebinger, 1978: 76).

(4) On the positive side, the American policy shift triggered growing awareness in Europe and elsewhere of the proliferation implications of nuclear power development and a rapprochement of attitudes. As one French official told the Americans privately toward the end of the INFCE, 'we may encroach on your markets, but somehow we seem to have inherited your nonproliferation policy in the process' (Nye, 1981: 37; cf. Lellouche, 1981: 43).

In sum, while the picture is mixed, the net effect seems rather negative. By not addressing the most likely proliferation route in the Third World, the unilateral American nonproliferation initiatives have not prevented potential proliferators from coming closer to nuclear weapons. Nor have the Americans been able to convince the rest of the world to forgo the 'plutonium economy.' It was a combination of societal, economic, technical, and political reasons rather than American pressures that caused the paralysis of nuclear growth around the world. The ensuing situation has notable proliferation risks. Not only does it create increased exportation pressures, as noted above.

The decline of nuclear power might have been good news on the weapons proliferation front if the nuclear projects had never been begun. What has been begun and would persist in a half-finished state might be much more a mixed commodity. [Quester, 1981a: 6]

Half-finished reactor ventures which could easily become bomb projects might lead to a 'worst of all possible' worlds, 'in which a mortally wounded technology makes only marginal, temporary, and expensive contributions to legitimate energy supply and energy security needs, while at the same time it effectively removes one of the most important technical and economic barriers to quite widespread nuclear weapons proliferation' (Bupp, 1981: 75).

The Superpowers and Nonproliferation: Conclusions

Let us return, in conclusion, to the questions posed initially. Have the two superpowers behaved in similar ways in their attempts to prevent nuclear proliferation? Have they been equally powerful in shaping and maintaining the nonproliferation regimes? Has a superpower 'condominium' been established in the field of nuclear nonproliferation?

(1) The nonproliferation policies of the two superpowers display marked parallels throughout the post-war era. After an initial period of exclusive emphasis on the military aspects of atomic energy followed by a period of active promotion of civilian, and presumably safe, nuclear technology with little regard for its military implications, the apprehensions of both superpowers have converged around the connection between civilian nuclear exports and nuclear weapons. And today Washington and Moscow share a desire to prevent the establishment of self-contained fuel cycles in NNWS. Hence, it may be concluded that 'the central dilemma in nuclear exports and nonproliferation policy is basically the same for the United States and the Soviet Union' (Duffy, 1978: 108).

Our hypothesized 'causal chain' may be discerned behind these similarities. The nonproliferation issue is obviously central to the superpower role, and the pattern of Soviet emulation of the United States recurs. The enemy image of the other superpower dominated decision-making in both Washington and Moscow during the secrecy regime. The dual image, which presupposes common superpower interests, gradually gained ground and was codified in the NPT. The tension between globalism and particularism has surfaced among both superpowers at different stages of the nonproliferation regime evolution: as a choice between global nonproliferation concerns, on the one hand, and narrow commercial interests in the early 1950s, alliance interests in the late 1950s and early 1960s. Since the NPT the dual image/globalism current has dominated, even if elements of the enemy image and particularism have entered the nonproliferation policies of both superpowers in recent years.

The nonproliferation strategies of both the United States and the Soviet Union have concentrated on denying NNWS the technical capability to go nuclear rather than focusing on their incentives to do so, with the result that American and Soviet initiatives have frequently been perceived by other states as self-serving attempts to protect the political and/or economic interests of the two superpowers (cf. Ebinger, 1978: 11). Yet, whereas 'technical fixes have been a recurrent theme in American thinking about nuclear weapons spread since 1945' (Lellouche, 1980: 338-9), the Soviets have relied on a combination of technological and political controls.

Another frequently noted difference is that between American 'universalistic' and Soviet 'selective' approaches to nonproliferation.

> The Nonproliferation Treaty, for example, was attractive to the United States because the spread of nuclear weapons anywhere, under any circumstances, seemed undesirable. Nonproliferation was for Americans a kind of international public good. The Soviets, by contrast, may have been moved not by a commitment to the general principle of nonproliferation but by the fear that the states likeliest to acquire nuclear weapons would promptly train them on the Soviet Union. [Mandelbaum, 1979: 211]

Forestalling a West German nuclear weapon was, as we have seen, a major consideration in Moscow's acceptance of the NPT. And today a majority of the most probable proliferators (such as South Korea, Taiwan, Pakistan, South Africa and Brazil) are friendly to the United States and hostile to Soviet client states (cf. Duffy, 1980: 18; Nacht, 1981: 210). Moreover, the only proliferation to have occurred outside the industrialized world has taken place in the Soviets' own backyard. China's and India's accession to nuclear status as well as the possible future acquisition of nuclear weapons by Pakistan and other Asian and Middle Eastern countries present the USSR with direct security challenges. To Moscow, unlike Washington, nuclear proliferation is therefore also a regional problem (Duffy, 1980: 18-19).

One major source of divergence between American and Soviet policies since the mid-1970s has been the enthusiastic Soviet support of nuclear energy in general and breeder development in particular which contrasts with American second thoughts about nuclear power and abnegation of the 'plutonium economy.' Current Soviet policy, which seems to be founded on forecasts of declining fossil fuel productivity and expanding power capacity needs along with perceptions of future uranium scarcity (cf. Potter, 1982: 306; Duffy, 1978: 105), puts the USSR in a somewhat contradictory and uncomfortable nonproliferation position. Unlike the United States, which has undertaken a series of exemplary policies domestically, the Soviet Union, in asking other countries to forego reprocessing and enrichment, cannot offer itself as an example (Duffy, 1978: 108).

In sum, whereas the historical survey of international regimes revealed parallels between American and Soviet nonproliferation policies, today the differences between the two superpowers seem to be no less significant than the similarities.

(2) The differences between the United States and the Soviet Union become even more pronounced when we turn to the question of relative influence over international nonproliferation regimes. The United States, by virtue of its diplomatic leverage abroad and its domination of the world nuclear market, has held the initiative and has been able to set international norms, whereas the Soviet Union has by and large followed suit. The secrecy regime was simply American policy writ large — a reflection of the American nuclear monopoly. As the Soviet Union broke that monopoly and thus necessitated a regime change, it was again the United States that took the initiative in establishing the Atoms for Peace regime. The USSR then picked up the American challenge and became a competitor in the field of peaceful nuclear aid. The NPT regime is exceptional in being the first multilaterally-negotiated international regime. Yet recently the United States has again made unilateral attempts to revise that regime.

If the historical record clearly indicates American preponderance and relegates the Soviet Union to a position of 'second in command,' the trend over time has, however, been toward overall decline in superpower leverage. The NNWS no longer accept being pawns in the hands of the superpowers.

> Thus, most of the nuclear 'have-not' nations reject the notion of superpower strategic nuclear parity as a stabilizing geopolitical force; they reject the concept of hierarchical ordering of 'responsible states'; they reject the argument that horizontal nuclear proliferation is more a threat to world stability than the vertical proliferation of nuclear weapons held by the superpowers; and they assert the right of all sovereign nations to foster their economic independence and strategic security. [Ebinger, 1978: 12]

While the two superpowers may still be equally willing and able to prevent transfers of nuclear weapons, their reduced leverage derives from the increasingly significant nexus between civil and military nuclear energy. Having lost their monopoly — either individually or jointly — over reactor technologies and fuel cycle processes, the superpowers are no longer in a position to control the spread of 'sensitive' technologies. And in opposing superpower efforts to restrict international nuclear trade, competitors and customers can fall back on the NPT which both Washington and Moscow have encouraged all countries to sign and whose Article IV guarantees 'the inalienable right of all the parties to the Treaty to develop research, production and use of nuclear energy for peaceful purposes without discrimination' (cf. Joskow, 1976: 800-1).

The United States, in particular, has been slow in realizing this loss of control. In the words of one observer (Lellouche, 1981: 42),

> the United States, which was accustomed to treating nonprolifera-
> tion unilaterally as its own 'special responsibility' (to be shared at
> best with the other superpower), took a very long time before
> realizing the magnitude of the changes that had taken place in
> international nuclear relations.

Even if the loss of control has affected both superpowers, the differentials in potential power remain. Specifically, the Soviet Union has comparatively less leverage over potential proliferators —through either export relationships or political influence — than has the United States. This is particularly true of the near-nuclear 'pariah' states, such as Israel, South Africa, Taiwan and South Korea (cf. Harkavy, 1981). We are thus left with the irony that the USSR, the superpower with greater immediate interests in preventing proliferation (which is likely to occur among hostile countries close to its own borders), also has considerably less leverage.

(3) The NPT may be as close to a superpower condominium as the world has ever come. Yet, as we have seen, it falls short of being an effective condominium. In establishing the NPT regime, the super-powers had to make concessions to other states, failed to achieve universal adherence to the NPT, and did not succeed in blocking all avenues to nuclear weapons. Moreover, the unprecedented degree of US–Soviet collaboration which has characterized the nonproliferation issue-area for more than a decade seems now to be in danger. Not only have the two superpowers come to be competitors in the international

nuclear energy market, but their divergent and contradictory attitudes to nuclear technology have assumed increasing significance. Today, paradoxically, the superpower with strong and unbroken faith in the blessings of nuclear power is less active in the export market, whereas the more active exporter is having second thoughts about nuclear technology. This ambiguity in combination with the previously noted decline in the individual or combined leverage of the superpowers makes any tightened condominium unlikely in the foreseeable future.

Conclusions

The main thesis of this book can now be summarized. There are conspicuous similarities in American and Soviet external conduct which derive in large measure from similar conceptions of the 'superpower role.' More specifically, the Soviet Union has tended to emulate American behavior in its ambition to enact the 'superpower role' and acquire equal status with the United States. Soviet–American congruence in role conceptions has, in turn, tended to reinforce and amplify those background factors which portend parallel behavior. In particular, historical, ideological, and bureaucratic factors interact to produce similar foreign policy outlooks and groupings. These similarities notwithstanding, significant dissimilarities can be discerned in American and Soviet foreign policy which are associated with power asymmetries. Differences in capabilities and socio-economic systems, in combination with differential impacts of changes in the international system, make for Soviet inferiority in comparison with the United States, with respect to potential leverage around the world. These power diffentials have, in turn, contributed to the failure to establish any effective superpower condominium.

In all three issue-areas analyzed in this book prominent similarities have been found between American and Soviet behavior which are in large measure attributable to Soviet emulation of American conduct. The United States was pioneer and policy initiator with regard to foreign aid, crisis management in the Middle East, and nonproliferation alike. In all three areas Moscow has picked up the American challenge, and all three areas have apparently been considered by Soviet policy-makers to be crucial to the superpower status of the USSR.

The degree of overt or tacit co-operation has varied between the issue-areas, from the almost complete lack of collaboration efforts in Third World aid, via the tacit understanding of certain 'rules of the game' governing crisis management in the Middle East, to the embryonic condominium to prevent the spread of nuclear weapons under the NPT regime. These issue-areas obviously typify varying degrees of common superpower interest. Aid relations with the Third

World are characterized by a relative lack of common interests, crisis management in the Middle East offers a complex mix of rivaling and common interests, and nuclear nonproliferation represents a predominant common interest. In neither issue-area has Soviet–American collaboration and joint influence been extensive enough to produce any effective and lasting condominium. The two superpowers may, in Zhou Enlai's famous formulation, 'lie in the same bed, but they do not dream the same dreams' (quoted in Hassner, 1977: 18).

The USSR — the junior superpower — has been more interested in condominium–like arrangements than the United States which has generally preferred unilateral action. While both superpowers may be likely to resort to condominium–like arrangements to avoid direct confrontation in a crisis, this is seen by the United States as a provisional device, by the Soviet Union as a step toward a more permanent structure. Coral Bell (1974: 535) even contends that the notion of condominium has deep roots in the Soviet view of the world from the Stalinist period on.

The lack of superpower collaboration and the lack of joint or individual control are obviously interrelated. The US–Soviet rivalry has limited the influence of either superpower. This rivalry has made it possible for Third World countries to play one superpower off against the other, for Middle East adversaries to draw the superpowers into confrontations that neither wanted, and for a series of NNWS to come considerably closer to the nuclear threshold under the Atoms for Peace regime. As suggested by the NPT regime, a condominium would require the mutual prevalence of dual images rather than enemy images, coupled with globalism.

Moreover, the leverage of the superpowers seems to have diminished over time, so that today both suffer from what Stanley Hoffmann (1978: 209-14) has labeled the 'great power blues' — the frustrations engendered by the disparity between might and achievements. Bargaining and compromises rather than supremacy and dictates have come to characterize the relations between the superpowers and the rest of the world.

At the same time, recent developments have tended to accentuate the Soviet inferiority in potential leverage as compared with the United States. Specifically, Moscow's economic weaknesses and relative absence from the games of interdependence have entailed eroding influence. Thus, the Soviet Union is unable to maintain the prestige it previously enjoyed in the Third World as a result of its exploitation of anti-Western sentiments and declared support of Third World aims, is losing its foothold in the Middle East as a consequence of its inability to offer anything but military support, and has little leverage over potential nuclear proliferators close to its own borders. More generally, it has been argued that the Soviet 'entry into globalism means entry into the politics of uncontrollable allies, where the inadequacy of her instruments for influence must make itself felt more and more' (Hassner, 1977: 28). This is consonant with a study of trends of Soviet influence around the world from 1945 to 1980 which concludes that 'Soviet world influence was at its height in the 1950s and there has been no significant Soviet geopolitical momentum in recent years' (Defense Monitor, 1980: 4).

What about the future, then? Although the trend over time seems to be toward increasing similarities in American and Soviet behavior, there is reason to question whether this trend will necessarily continue. In all three issue-areas investigated above there are mounting signs of prospective dissimilarities. To the extent that foreign aid takes the back seat to other aspects of the relations between rich and poor countries, the divergence between American and Soviet economic ties with the Third World becomes increasingly glaring. To the extent that oil supply security becomes an overriding concern for both superpowers in Middle East conflicts, it is doubtful that previously established tacit 'rules of the game' will hold. And to the extent that competition hardens and American and Soviet attitudes diverge in the realm of civil nuclear power, continued parallel superpower behavior on nonproliferation issues seems uncertain.

Nor does the convergence of American and Soviet role conceptions necessarily entail more co-operation. On the contrary, it might well be argued that 'the more the Soviets imitate the Americans' role as a great power, the greater the danger of a violent clash of the giants' (Barnet, 1977: 171). US–Soviet rivalry has persisted and is likely to continue, foreclosing any effective superpower condominium. In Stanley Hoffmann's (1968: 350–1) eloquent metaphor, 'Each superpower, torn between its stakes in the rivalry and the lure of the common interest, is like an acrobat who wants to leap from one trapeze to another but fears he will fall the moment he lets go.' In terms of the conceptualization of superpower suggested previously, rivalry with the other superpower looms large in the role conceptions of either giant. Each uses this rivalry to define its own identity and purpose. To enter a condominium arrangement would expose both to charges that 'the emperors had been shorn of their ideological clothes' (Steel, 1977: 45).

In other words, American and Soviet mutual enemy images are likely to remain the prevalent analytical filters through which global realities will be mediated.

In addition to continuing rivalry, the trend toward declining superpower leverage also bodes ill for any future condominium. US–Soviet relations have increasingly come to rest, not on joint control and combined power, but rather on a 'balance of mutual weakness' (Brandon, 1973: 345). There has been a tendency to exaggerate the power of the superpowers. Radical critics of American foreign policy at home and abroad as well as extreme advocates of American interventionism have succumbed to the myth of American omnipotence (cf. Bartlett, 1974: 180). Similarly, both leftist critics from China and conservative alarmists draw a picture of swelling Soviet might. This is not to suggest that the illusion of superpower omnipotence ought to give way to a no less misleading projection of impotence. The point of departure for any speculation about prospective superpower leverage must be the *limited* influence of the Big Two, either individually or jointly. Let me once again borrow a graphic metaphor from Stanley Hoffmann (1968: 70): 'The superpowers are like two giants who try to walk through a crowded room, in which they are not only slowed down by a pack of midgets but pushed aside by men of normal size,and cannot hit back.' There are signs that the superpowers have grudgingly come to accept these limitations in their global influence.

> A very important element of the informal 'code of conduct' for superpower behavior in the Third World is the willingness to live with failure. The Soviets in Egypt in 1972 and the Americans in Iran in 1979 could have used force to resist expulsion and did not. Acceptance of loss of influence without overreaction is necessary for both superpowers in the face of frequent setbacks. [Defense Monitor, 1980: 7]

Although their influence may be declining, the superpowers are not likely to drastically alter their global role. Each forces the other to maintain its 'superpower role.' Even if particularism has an ideological and bureaucratic foundation in both superpowers, rivalry with the other superpower has propelled globalist currents to pre-eminence in the United States as well as the Soviet Union throughout the post-war era. While particularist currents may temporarily come to the fore in either superpower, conincidental and persistent withdrawal of both does not seem likely. President Nixon in 1971 expressed his conviction that

> for the next twenty-five years the United States is destined to play this super-power role as both an economic and nuclear giant. We just have to do this. We cannot dodge our responsibilities. [quoted in Fulbright, 1972: 8]

This reasoning applies no less to the junior superpower. In Robert Wesson's (1974: 187-8) assessment,

> a world of four or five truly independent superpowers or near-superpowers is entirely contrary to the Russian way. The inspiration of Russia is no longer so outstanding in the global picture. The political utopia is plausible only for a self-engrossed empire or for a polity with hopes of overcoming competition, but only its utopia separates Communism from ordinary dictatorship. The Soviet Union must represent itself as harbinger of historical justice, the flood tide which must sweep over all, a position which becomes unsustainable in a multipolar world. The Communist parties likewise have no special role if the Soviet Union is only one of several counterbalancing powers. Russia is and must be unconditionally opposed to the open pluralistic state system.

In conclusion, the limited character of this endeavor bears repeating. My conclusions, as well as the preceding analyses are, in varying degrees, tentative. The chief purpose of this study has been to demonstrate the feasibility of comparative analysis of American and Soviet foreign policy, drawing on the existing two sets of specialized literature. This book does not offer conclusive 'proofs.' It does offer an interpretation of the extant literature on American and Soviet foreign policy and suggest a framework for the comparative analysis of superpower external conduct. To the extent that it may inspire more rigorous and technically sophisticated comparisons of American and Soviet foreign policy, my effort has been justified. For even though the United States and the Soviet Union have not been able to 'sway the destinies of half the globe,' as anticipated by de Tocqueville a century and a half ago, they remain the most important actors in contemporary international politics.

References

ACDA (1975), *World Military Expenditures and Arms Transfers 1965–74*, Washington, DC, US Arms Control and Disarmament Agency.

Adler, L.K. and T.G. Paterson (1970), 'Red Fascism: The Merger of Nazi Germany and Soviet Russia in the American Image of Totalitarianism, 1930s–1950s,' *American Historical Review*, LXXV (April), 1046–64.

Adomeit, H. (1973), 'Soviet Risk-Taking and Crisis Behaviour: From Confrontation to Coexistence?' *Adelphi Papers*, no. 101.

Agursky, M. and H. Adomeit (1979), 'The Soviet Military-Industrial Complex,' *Survey*, 24 (Spring), 106–24.

Alexander, A.J. (1979), 'Decision-Making in Soviet Weapons Procurement,' *Adelphi Papers*, no. 147/148.

Arbatov, G.A. (1970), 'American Foreign Policy on the Threshold of the 1970s,' *Soviet Law and Government*, 9, no. 1, reprinted in M.A. Kaplan (ed.) *Great Issues of International Politics*, 2nd ed., Chicago, Aldine, 1974.

Arbatov, G.A. (1973), 'O sovetsko-amerikanskikh otnosheniyakh' (On Soviet–American Relations), *Kommunist*, no. 3 (February).

Arbatov, G.A. (1974), 'United States Foreign Policy and Prospects for Soviet–American Relations,' in D.R. Lesh (ed.) *A Nation Observed: Perspectives on America's World Role*, Washington, DC, Potomac Associates, Inc.

Aron, R. (1967), *Peace and War: A Theory of International Relations*, New York, Praeger.

Aron, R. (1974), *The Imperial Republic: The United States and the World 1945–1973*, Englewood Cliffs, Prentice-Hall.

Aron, R. (1979), 'The 1978 Alastair Buchan Memorial Lecture,' *Survival*, XXI (January–February), 2–7.

Aronson, S. (1978), *Conflict and Bargaining in the Middle East*, Baltimore, Johns Hopkins University Press.

Aspaturian, V.V. (1971), *Process and Power in Soviet Foreign Policy*, Boston, Little, Brown.

Aspaturian, V.V. (1972), 'The Soviet Military–Industrial Complex — Does It Exist?,' *Journal of International Affairs*, 26 (1), 1–28.

Aspaturian, V.V. (1980a), 'Soviet Global Power and the Correlation of Forces,' *Problems of Communism*, XXIX (May–June), 1–18.

Aspaturian, V.V. (1980b), 'Vulnerabilities and Strengths of the Soviet Union in a Changing International Environment: The Internal Dimension,' in E.P. Hoffmann and F.J. Fleron, Jr. (eds) *The Conduct of Soviet Foreign Policy*, 2nd ed., New York, Aldine.

Bader, W.B. (1968), *The United States and the Spread of Nuclear Weapons*, New York, Pegasus.

Bailey, T.A. (1950), *America Faces Russia: Russian–American Relations from Early Times to Our Own Day*, Ithaca, NY, Cornell University Press.

Baker, S.J. (1976), 'Monopoly or Cartel?,' *Foreign Policy*, no. 23, 202–20.

Barghoorn, F.C. (1950), *The Soviet Image of the United States*, New York, Harcourt, Brace and Co.

Barghoorn, F.C. (1971), 'The Security Police,' in H.G. Skilling and F. Griffiths (eds) *Interest Groups in Soviet Politics*, Princeton, Princeton University Press.

Barnet, R.J. (1973), *Roots of War*, New York, Penguin.

Barnet, R.J. (1977), *The Giants: Russia and America*, New York, Simon and Schuster.

Barron, J. (1974), *KGB: The Secret Work of Soviet Secret Agents*, New York, Bantam.

Bartlett, C.J. (1974), *The Rise and Fall of the Pax Americana: United States Foreign Policy in the Twentieth Century*, London, Paul Elek.

Bell, C. (1971a), 'The Adverse Partnership,' in C. Holbraad (ed.) *Super Powers and World Order*, Canberra, Australian National University Press.

Bell, C. (1971b), *The Conventions of Crisis: A Study in Diplomatic Management*, Oxford, Oxford University Press.

Bell, C. (1974), 'The October Middle East War: A Case Study in Crisis Management During Detente,' *International Affairs*, 50 (October), 531–43.

Bell, C. (1978), 'Decision-Making by Governments in Crisis Situations,' in D. Frei (ed.) *International Crises and Crisis Management*, Farnborough, Saxon House.

Bell, D. (1962), *The End of Ideology*, 2nd rev. ed., New York, Collier.

Bell, D. (1970), 'Ideology and Soviet Politics,' in R. Cornell (ed.) *The Soviet Political System: A Book of Readings*, Englewood Cliffs, Prentice-Hall.

Bell, D. (1973), *The Coming of Post-Industrial Society*, New York, Basic Books.

Bergson, A. (1981), 'Soviet Economic Slowdown and the 1981–85 Plan,' *Problems of Communism*, XXX (May–June), 24–36.

Bertelman, T. (1983), *De sovjetiska rustningarnas drivkrafter* (Motive forces of Soviet armaments), Stockholm, SSLP.

Bialer, S. (1978) 'Succession and Turnover of Soviet Elites,' *Journal of International Affairs*, 32 (2), 181–200.

Biddle, B.J. (1979), *Role Theory: Expectations, Identities, and Behaviors*, New York, Academic Press.

Blake, D.H. and R.S. Walters (1976), *The Politics of Global Economic Relations*, Englewood Cliffs, Prentice-Hall.

Bloomfield, L.P. (1974), *In Search of American Foreign Policy*, New York, Oxford University Press.

Bonham, G.M., M.J. Shapiro and T.L. Trumble (1979), 'The October War: Changes in Cognitive Orientation Toward the Middle East Conflict,' *International Studies Quarterly*, 23 (March), 3–44.

Brandon, H. (1973), *The Retreat of American Power*, Garden City, NY, Doubleday.

Brecher, M., B. Steinberg and J. Stein (1969), 'A Framework for Research on Foreign Policy Behavior,' *Journal of Conflict Resolution*, 13 (1): 75–101.

Brown, S. (1974), *New Forces in World Politics*, Washington, DC, Brookings Institution.

Brzezinski, Z.K. (1956), *The Permanent Purge*, Cambridge, Mass., Harvard University Press.

Brzezinski Z.K. (1967), *Ideology and Power in Soviet Politics*, rev. ed., New York, Praeger.

Brzezinski (1976), *Between Two Ages: America's Role in the Technetronic Era*, Harmondsworth, Penguin.

Brzezinski, Z.K. and S.P. Huntington (1964), *Political Power: USA/USSR*, New York, Viking Press.

Bull, H. (1971), 'World Order and the Super Powers,' in C. Holbraad (ed.) *Super Powers and World Order*, Canberra, Australian National University Press.

Bull, H. (1977), *The Anarchical Society: A Study of Order in World Politics*, London, Macmillan.

Bupp, I.C. (1981), 'The Actual Growth and Probable Future of the Worldwide Nuclear Industry,' *International Organization*, 35 (1), 59–76.

Burns, A.L. (1971), 'Introduction,' in C. Holbraad (ed.) *Super Powers and World Order*, Canberra, Australian National University Press.

Burns, E.M. (1957), *The American Idea of Mission*, New Brunswick, Rutgers University Press.

Burton, J.W. (1972), *World Society*, Cambridge, Cambridge University Press.

Cahn, A.H. (1979), 'United States Arms to the Middle East 1967–76: A Critical Examination,' in M. Leitenberg and G. Sheffer (eds) *Great Power Intervention in the Middle East,* New York, Pergamon.

Cahn, A.H. (1980), 'The Economics of Arms Transfers,' in S.G. Neuman and R.E. Harkavy (eds) *Arms Transfers in the Modern World,* New York, Praeger.

Caldwell, D. (1981), *Soviet–American Crisis Management in the Cuban Missile Crisis and the October War,* Santa Monica, Ca., California Seminar on International Security and Foreign Policy Discussion Paper, no. 96.

Campbell, J.C. (1974), 'The Continuing Crisis,' in I. Lederer and W.S. Vucinich (eds) *The Soviet Union and the Middle East: The Post World War II Era,* Stanford, Hoover Institution Press.

Carral, J. (1971), *La prise du pouvoir mondial: Vers la domination americano–soviétique de la planète,* Paris, Denoël.

CDSP (1963), Gromyko's Speech in Supreme Soviet Discussion (*Pravda,* December 14), *Current Digest of the Soviet Press,* 15 (1), 11–12.

CDSP (1971), Kosygin's Report on the Five-Year Plan — II (*Pravda,* April 7), *Current Digest of the Soviet Press,* 23 (16), 1–11.

CIA (1977), *Communist Aid to the Less Developed Countries of the Free World, 1976* Washington, DC, US Central Intelligence Agency.

CIA (1980), *Communist Aid Activities in Non-Communist Less Developed Countries, 1979 and 1954–79,* Washington, DC, US Central Intelligence Agency.

Clark, P.G. (1972), *American Aid for Development,* New York, Praeger.

Clemens, W.C., Jr. (1968), *The Arms Race and Sino-Soviet Relations,* Stanford, Hoover Institution Press.

Clemens, W.C., Jr. (1978), *The U.S.S.R. and Global Interdependence: Alternative Futures,* Washington, DC, American Enterprise for Public Policy Research.

Cline, R.S. (1975), *World Power Assessment: A Calculus of Strategic Drift,* Washington, Center for Strategic and International Studies, Georgetown University.

Cohen, R. (1980), 'Rules of the Game in International Politics,' *International Studies Quarterly,* 24 (March), 129–49.

Cohen, R. (1981), *International Politics: The Rules of the Game,* London, Longman.

Cooper, O. (1970), 'Soviet Economic Assistance to the Less Developed Countries of the Free World,' in *Economic Performance and the Military Burden in the Soviet Union,* a compendium of papers submitted to the Sub-committee on Foreign Policy of the Joint Economic Committee, US Congress, Washington, DC, US Government Printing Office.

Crabb, C.V. (1976), *Policy-Makers and Critics: Conflicting Theories of American Foreign Policy,* New York, Praeger.

Crozier, B. (1969), *The Masters of Power,* London, Eyre & Spottiswoode.

Dahl, R.A. (1957), 'The Concept of Power,' *Behavioral Science,* 2 (July), 201–15.

Dallin, A. (1979), 'The United States in the Soviet Perspective,' *Adelphi Papers,* no. 151.

Dallin, A. (1980a), 'Soviet Perspectives on the U.S.–Soviet–Chinese Triangle,' paper prepared for Second World Congress for Soviet and East European Studies, Garmisch-Partenkirchen, September 30–October 4.

Dallin, A (1980b), 'The Road to Kabul: Soviet Perceptions of World Affairs and the Afghan Crisis,' in *The Soviet Invasion of Afghanistan: Three Perspectives,* Los Angeles, Center for International and Strategic Affairs Working Paper, no. 27.

Dallin, A. (1981), 'The Domestic Sources of Soviet Foreign Policy,' in S. Bialer (ed.) *The Domestic Context of Soviet Foreign Policy,* Boulder, Westview.

Dawisha, K. (1979), *Soviet Foreign Policy Towards Egypt,* London, Macmillan.

Defense Monitor (1980), 'Soviet Geopolitical Momentum: Myth or Menace?,' Washington, DC, Center for Defense Information.

Dinerstein, H.S. (1968), *Fifty Years of Soviet Foreign Policy*, Baltimore, Johns Hopkins Press.

Documents on International Affairs, 1956, Royal Institute of International Affairs, Oxford, Oxford University Press, 1959.

Donaldson, R.H. (1981), 'The Second World, the Third World, and the New International Economic Order,' in R.H. Donaldson (ed.) *The Soviet Union in the Third World: Successes and Failures*, Boulder, Westview.

Donovan, J.C. (1974), *The Cold Warriors: A Policy-Making Elite*, Lexington, Mass., D.C. Heath.

Doran, C.F. (1976), *Domestic Conflict in State Relations: The American Sphere of Influence*, Beverly Hills, Sage Professional Paper in International Studies, 02–037.

DuBoff, R.B. (1970), 'Pentagonism or Imperialism?' in H.I. Schiller and J.D. Phillips (eds) *Super-State: Readings in the Military-Industrial Complex*, Urbana, University of Illinois Press.

Duffy, G. (1978), 'Soviet Nuclear Exports,' *International Security*, 3 (Summer), 83–111.

Duffy, G. (1980), 'The Soviet Union and Nuclear Drift,' in W.R. Duncan (ed.) *Soviet Policy in the Third World*, New York, Pergamon.

Dukes, P. (1970), *The Emergence of the Super-Powers*, New York, Harper & Row.

Dunn, K.A. (1981), 'Soviet Involvement in the Third World: Implications of US Policy Assumptions,' in R.H. Donaldson (ed.) *The Soviet Union in the Third World: Successes and Failures*, Boulder, Westview.

Ebinger, C.K. (1978), 'International Politics of Nuclear Energy,' *Washington Papers*, no. 57, Beverly Hills, Sage.

Eden, A. (1960), *Full Circle*, London, Cassell.

d'Encausse, H.C. (1975), *La politique soviétique au Moyen-Orient 1955–1975*, Paris, Presses de la Fondation Nationale des Sciences Politiques.

d'Encausse, H.C. (1979), 'La puissance soviétique aujourd'hui,' *Relations internationales*, 17 (printemps), 29–48.

Eulau, H. (1963), *The Behavioral Persuasion in Politics*, New York, Random House.

Evron, Y. (1979), 'Great Powers' Military Intervention in the Middle East,' in M. Leitenberg and G. Sheffer (eds) *Great Power Intervention in the Middle East*, New York, Pergamon.

Fann, K.T. and D.C. Hodges (eds) (1971), *Readings in U.S. Imperialism*, Boston, Porter Sargent.

Farley, P.J., S.S. Kaplan, and W.H. Lewis (1978), *Arms Across the Sea*, Washington, DC, Brookings Institution.

Faurby, I. (1976), 'Premises, Promises, and Problems of Comparative Foreign Policy,' *Cooperation and Conflict*, XI (3), 139–62.

Fei, E.T. (1980), 'Understanding Arms Transfers and Military Expenditures: Data Problems,' in S.G. Neuman and R.E. Harkavy (eds) *Arms Transfers in the Modern World*, New York, Praeger.

Feshbach, M. (1978), 'The Structure and Composition of the Soviet Labor Force,' in *The USSR in the 1980s*, Brussels, NATO.

Feshbach, M. (1982), 'Between the Lines of the 1979 Soviet Census,' *Problems of Communism*, XXXI (January–February), 27–37.

Finer, H. (1964), *Dulles over Suez*, Chicago, Quadrangle.

Fisher, H.H. (1946), *America and Russia in the World Community*, Claremont, Ca., Claremont College.

Fox, W.T.R. (1944), *The Super-Powers*, New York, Harcourt, Brace and Co.

Fox, W.T.R. (1980), 'The Super-Powers Then and Now,' *International Journal*, XXXV (Summer), 417–36.

Franck, T.M. and E. Weisband (1972), *World Politics: Verbal Strategy Among the Superpowers*, New York, Oxford University Press.

Franck, T.M. and E. Weisband (1979), *Foreign Policy by Congress*, New York, Oxford University Press.

Frank, C.R., Jr. and M. Baird (1975), 'Foreign Aid: Its Speckled Past and Future Prospects,' in C.F. Bergsten and L.B. Krause (eds) *World Politics and International Economics*, Washington, DC, Brookings Institution.

Freedman, R.O. (1975), *Soviet Policy Toward the Middle East Since 1970*, New York, Praeger.

Fulbright, J.W. (1972), *The Crippled Giant: American Foreign Policy and Its Domestic Consequences*, New York, Random House.

Gaddis, J.L. (1972), *The United States and the Origins of the Cold War 1941–1947*, New York, Columbia University Press.

Gaddis, J.L. (1978), *Russia, the Soviet Union, and the United States: An Interpretive History*, New York, John Wiley.

Galbraith, J.K. (1973), *Economics and the Public Purpose*, Boston, Houghton Mifflin.

Galtung, J. (1966), 'East–West Interaction Patterns,' *Journal of Peace Research*, 3 (2), 146–76.

Geertz, C. (1964), 'Ideology as a Cultural System,' in D. Apter (ed.) *Ideology and Discontent*, New York, Free Press.

George, A.L. (1968), 'Some Comments on the Use of Role Theory for the Study of Political Leadership,' Stanford University, mimeo.

George, A.L. (1979), 'The Causal Nexus Between Cognitive Beliefs and Decision-Making Behavior: The "Operational Code" Belief System ,' in L .S. Falkowski (ed.) *Psychological Models in International Politics*, Boulder, Westview.

George, A.L. (1980a), 'Domestic Constraints on Regime Change in U.S. Foreign Policy: The Need for Policy Legitimacy,' in O.R. Holsti *et al.* (eds) *Change in the International System*, Boulder, Westview.

George, A.L. (1980b), *Towards a Soviet–American Crisis Prevention Regime: History and Prospects*, Los Angeles, Center for International and Strategic Affairs Working Paper, no. 28.

Gerner, K. (1980), 'Kazan and Manchu: Cultural Roots of Soviet Foreign Relations,' *Cooperation and Conflict*, XV (2), 57–70.

Gibert, S.P. (1970), 'Soviet–American Military Aid Competition in the Developing World,' *Orbis*, 13 (Winter), 1117–37.

Gilinsky, V. (1978), 'Plutonium, Proliferation and the Price of Reprocessing,' *Foreign Affairs*, 57 (Winter), 374–86.

Glassman, J.D. (1975), *Arms for the Arabs: The Soviet Union and War in the Middle East*, Baltimore, Johns Hopkins University Press.

Golan, G. (1974), 'Soviet Aims and the Middle East War,' *Survival* (May–June).

Golan, G. (1979), 'Soviet Power and Policies in the Third World: The Middle East,' *Adelphi Papers*, no. 152.

Golan, M. (1976), *The Secret Conversations of Henry Kissinger*, New York, Bantam.

Goldmann, K. (1975), *The Foreign Sources of Foreign Policy: Causes, Conditions, or Inputs?* Stockholm, Swedish Institute of International Affairs research report UI-75-2.

Goldmann, K. (1978), *Det internationella systemet: En teori och dess begränsningar* (The International System: A Theory and Its Limitations), Stockholm, Aldus.

Goldschmidt, B. (1977), 'A Historical Survey of Nonproliferation Policies,' *International Security*, 2 (1), 69–87.

Goldwin, R.A. *et al.* (eds) (1959), *Readings in Russian Foreign Policy*, New York, Oxford University Press.

Gouré, L. *et al.* (1973), *Convergence of Communism and Capitalism: The Soviet View*, Miami, Center for Advanced International Studies, University of Miami.

Gay, C.S. (1981), 'The Most Dangerous Decade: Historic Mission, Legitimacy, and Dynamics of the Soviet Empire in the 1980s,' *Orbis*, 25 (Spring), 13–28.

Greenwood, T. *et al.* (1977), *Nuclear Proliferation: Motivations, Capabilities, and Strategies for Control*, New York, McGraw-Hill.

Griffith, W.E. (1975), 'The World and the Great Power Triangles,' in W.E. Griffith (ed.) *The World and the Great Power Triangles*, Cambridge, Mass., MIT Press.

Griffiths, F. (1967), 'Inner Tensions in the Soviet Approach to "Disarmament," ' *International Journal*, 22 (4), 593–617.

Griffiths, F. (1971), 'A Tendency Analysis of Soviet Policy-Making,' in H.G. Skilling and F. Griffiths (eds) *Interest Groups in Soviet Politics*, Princeton, Princeton University Press.

Gupta, S. (1969), 'The Third World and the Great Powers,' *Annals of the American Academy of Political and Social Science*, 386, 54–63.

Gupta, S. (1971), 'Great Power Relations and the Third World,' in C. Holbraad (ed.) *Super Powers and World Order*, Canberra, Australian National University Press.

Haas, E.B. (1980), 'Why Collaborate? Issue-Linkage and International Regimes,' *World Politics*, 32 (April), 357–405.

Hansen, R. (1979), *Beyond the North–South Stalemate*, New York, McGraw-Hill.

Harkavy, R.E. (1979), 'Strategic Access, Bases, and Arms Transfers: The Major Powers' Evolving Geopolitical Competition in the Middle East,' in M. Leitenberg and G. Sheffer (eds) *Great Power Intervention in the Middle East*, New York, Pergamon.

Harkavy, R.E. (1980), 'The New Geopolitics: Arms Transfers and the Major Powers' Competition for Overseas Bases,' in S.G. Neuman and R.E. Harkavy (eds) *Arms Transfers in the Modern World*, New York, Praeger.

Harkavy, R.E. (1981), 'Pariah States and Nuclear Proliferation,' *International Organisation*, 35 (Winter), 135–163.

Hartz, L. (1955), *The Liberal Tradition in America*, New York, Harcourt, Brace and Co.

Hassner, P. (1977), 'Super-Power Rivalries, Conflicts and Co-operation,' *Adelphi Papers*, no. 134.

Hauslohner, P. (1981), 'Prefects as Senators: Soviet Regional Politicans Look to Foreign Policy,' *World Politics*, 33 (January), 197–233.

Hedlund, S. (1983), *Crisis in Soviet Agriculture?*, Lund, Studentlitteratur.

Hermann, C.F. (1969), 'International Crisis as a Situational Variable,' in J.N. Rosenau (ed.) *International Politics and Foreign Policy*, New York, Free Press.

Hermann, C.F. (1972a), 'Policy Classification: A Key to the Comparative Study of Foreign Policy,' in J.N. Rosenau, V. Davis and M.A. East (eds) *The Analysis of International Politics*, New York, Free Press.

Hermann, C.F. (1972b), 'Some Issues in the Study of International Crisis,' in C.F. Hermann (ed.) *International Crises*, New York, Free Press.

Hermens, F.A. (1959), 'Totalitarian Power Struggle and Russian Foreign Policy,' *Journal of Politics*, 21 (3), 434–54.

Hilsman, R. (1967), *To Move a Nation*, Garden City, NY, Doubleday.

Hoffmann, S. (1968), *Gulliver's Troubles, or the Setting of American Foreign Policy*, New York, McGraw-Hill.

Hoffmann, S. (1978), *Primacy or World Order: American Foreign Policy since the Cold War*, New York, McGraw-Hill.

Höhmann, H.-H. (1982), 'Die Kriese der sowjetischen Wirtschaft und ihre aussen-politische Bedeutung,' *Europa-Archiv*, 27 (14), 431–8.

Holbik, K. (1968), *The United States, the Soviet Union, and the Third World*, Hamburg, Verlag Weltarchiv.

Holbraad, C. (1971), 'Condominium and Concert,' in C. Holbraad (ed.) *Super Powers and World Order*, Canberra, Australian National University Press.

Holbraad, C. (1979), *Superpowers and International Conflict*, London, Macmillan.

Hollander, P. (1973), *Soviet and American Society: A Comparison*, New York, Oxford University Press.

Holsti, K.J. (1970), 'National Role Conceptions in the Study of Foreign Policy,' *International Studies Quarterly*, 14 (3), 233–309.

Holsti, O.R. (1979), 'The Three-Headed Eagle: The United States and System Change,' *International Studies Quarterly*, 23 (3), 339–59.

Holsti, O.R. and J.N. Rosenau (1979), 'Vietnam, Consensus, and the Belief Systems of American Leaders,' *World Politics*, 32 (1), 1–56.

Holsti, O.R. and J.N. Rosenau (1980), 'Cold War Axioms in the Post-Vietnam Era,' in O.R. Holsti, R.M. Siverson and A.L. George (eds) *Change in the International System*, Boulder, Westview.

Hölzle, E. (1953), *Russland und Amerika: Aufbruch und Begegnung zweier Weltmächte*, München, R. Oldenbourg.

Horelick, A.L. (1972), 'Soviet Policy in the Middle East: Policy from 1955 to 1969,' in P.Y. Hammond and S.S. Alexander (eds) *Political Dynamics in the Middle East*, New York, American Elsevier.

Horelick, A.L., A.R. Johnson and J.D. Steinbruner (1975), *The Study of Soviet Foreign Policy: Decision-Theory-Related Approaches*, Beverly Hills, Sage.

Horowitz, I.L. (1966), *Three Worlds of Development*, New York, Oxford University Press.

Horvath, J. (1970), 'Economic Aid Flow from the USSR: A Recount of the First Fifteen Years,' *Slavic Review* (December), 613–32.

Hottinger, A. (1975), 'The Great Powers and the Middle East,' in W. Griffith (ed.) *The World and the Great Power Triangles*, Cambridge, Mass., MIT Press.

Hough, J.L. (1980), *Soviet Leadership in Transition*, Washington, DC, Brookings Institution.

Howe, J.R. (1971), *Multicrises: Sea Power and Global Politics in the Missile Age*, Cambridge, Mass., MIT Press.

Hurewitz, J.C. (1969), 'Origin of the Rivalry,' in J.C. Hurewitz (ed.) *Soviet–American Rivalry in the Middle East*, New York, Academy of Political Science.

Husband, W.B. (1979), 'Soviet Perceptions of U.S. "Positions-of-Strength" Diplomacy,' *World Politics*, 31 (4), 495–517.

IISS (1981), *The Military Balance 1981–1982*, London, International Institute for Strategic Studies.

Jabber, P. and R. Kolkowicz (1981), 'The Arab-Israeli Wars of 1967 and 1973,' in S.S. Kaplan, *Diplomacy of Power*, Washington, DC, Brookings Institution.

Jaster, R.C. (1969), 'Foreign Aid and Economic Development: The Shifting Soviet View,' *International Affairs*, 45 (3), 452–64.

Jervis, R. (1982), 'Security Regimes,' *International Organization*, 36 (Spring), 357–78.

Johnson, L.B. (1971), *The Vantage Point: Perspectives on the Presidency 1963–1969*, New York, Holt, Rinehart and Winston.

Johnson, P. (1957), *The Suez War*, London, MacGibbon & Kee.

Jönsson, C. (1979a), *Soviet Bargaining Behavior: The Nuclear Test Ban Case*, New York, Columbia University Press.

Jönsson, C. (1979b), 'The Paradoxes of Superpower: Omnipotence or Impotence?' in K. Goldmann and G. Sjöstedt (eds) *Power, Capabilities, Interdependence*, London, Sage.

Jönsson, C. (1982a), 'Foreign Policy Ideas and Groupings in the Soviet Union,' in R.E. Kanet (ed.) *Soviet Foreign Policy and East–West Relations*, New York, Pergamon.

Jönsson, C. (1982b), 'The Ideology of Foreign Policy,' in C.W. Kegley and P. McGowan (eds) *Foreign Policy USA/USSR. Sage International Yearbook of Foreign Policy Studies, Volume 7*, Beverly Hills, Sage.

Jönsson, C. and U. Westerlund (1982), 'Role Theory in Foreign Policy Analysis,' in C. Jönsson (ed.) *Cognitive Dynamics and International Politics*, London, Frances Pinter.

Joshua, W. and S.P. Gibert (1969), *Arms for the Third World: Soviet Military Aid Policy*, Baltimore, Johns Hopkins Press.

Joskow, P.L. (1976), 'The International Nuclear Industry Today,' *Foreign Affairs*, 54 (4), 788–803.

Kalb, M. and B. Kalb (1974), *Kissinger*, London, Hutchinson.

Kaldor, M. (1979), 'Economic Aspects of Arms Supply Policies to the Middle East,' in M. Leitenberg and G. Sheffer (eds) *Great Power Intervention in the Middle East*, New York, Pergamon.

Kalleberg, A.L. (1966), 'The Logic of Comparison: A Methodological Note on the Comparative Study of Political Systems,' *World Politics*, 19 (1), 69–82.

Kanet, R.E. (1973), 'Soviet and American Behavior Toward the Developing Countries: A Comparison, *Canadian Slavonic Papers*, XV, 439–61.

Kanet, R.E. (1974a), 'The Soviet Union and the Colonial Question, 1917–1953,' in R.E. Kanet (ed.) *The Soviet Union and the Developing Nations*, Baltimore, Johns Hopkins University Press.

Kanet, R.E. (1974b), 'Soviet Attitudes toward Developing Nations since Stalin,' in R.E. Kanet (ed.) *The Soviet Union and the Developing Nations*, Baltimore, Johns Hopkins University Press.

Kanet, R.E. (1981), 'Soviet Policy toward the Developing World: The Role of Economic Assistance and Trade,' in R.H. Donaldson (ed.) *The Soviet Union in the Third World: Successes and Failures*, Boulder, Westview.

Kaplan, J.J. (1967), *The Challenge of Foreign Aid*, New York, Praeger.

Kass, I. (1978), *Soviet Involvement in the Middle East: Policy Formulation, 1966–1973*, Boulder, Westview.

Kaufman, E. (1976), *The Superpowers and Their Spheres of Influence*, London, Croom Helm.

Keesing (1972), 'Statement of Basic Principles of U.S.–Soviet Relations and Joint U.S.–Soviet Communiqué,' *Keesing's Contemporary Archives*, 25313–15.

Keesing (1973), 'The Soviet–American Agreements,' *Keesing's Contemporary Archives*, 25999–6001.

Kegley, C.W. (1980), *The Comparative Study of Foreign Policy: Paradigm Lost?*, Columbia, S.C., Institute of International Studies, University of South Carolina, Essay Series, no. 10.

Kegley, C.W. and P. McGowan (1982), 'Introduction: Comparing the Foreign Policy Behavior of the United States and the Soviet Union,' in C.W. Kegley and P. McGowan (eds) *Foreign Policy USA/USSR. Sage International Yearbook of Foreign Policy Studies, Volume 7*, Beverly Hills, Sage.

Kemp, G. *et al.* (1978), 'The Military Buildup in Less Industrial States: Policy Implications,' in U. Ra'anan, R.L. Pfaltzgraff, Jr., and G. Kemp (eds) *Arms Transfers to the Third World: The Military Buildup in Less Industrial Countries*, Boulder, Westview.

Kennan, G.F. (1982), 'Scholarship, Politics, and the East-West Relationship,' in R.E. Kanet (ed.) *Soviet Foreign Policy and East–West Relations*, New York, Pergamon.

Keohane, D. (1981), 'Hegemony and Nuclear Non-Proliferation,' in *The Year Book of World Affairs*, London, Stevens & Sons.

Keohane, R.O. (1969), 'Lilliputians' Dilemmas,' *International Organization*, 23 (Spring), 291–310.

Keohane, R.O. (1971), 'The Big Influence of Small Allies,' *Foreign Policy*, no. 2 (Spring), 161–82.

Keohane, R.O. (1980), 'The Theory of Hegemonic Stability and Changes in International Economic Regimes, 1967–1977,' in O.R. Holsti *et al.* (eds) *Change in the International System*, Boulder, Westview.

Keohane, R.O. and J.S. Nye (1977), *Power and Interdependence*, Boston, Little, Brown.

Khrushchev, N.S. (1974), *Khrushchev Remembers: The Last Testament*, London, André Deutsch.

Kissinger, H.A. (1969), *American Foreign Policy: Three Essays*, London, Weidenfeld and Nicolson.

Kissinger, H.A. (1979), *White House Years*, Boston, Little, Brown.

Kissinger, H.A. (1982), *Years of Upheaval*, Boston, Little, Brown.

Klinghoffer, A.J. (1974), 'The Soviet Union and Africa,' in R.E. Kanet (ed.) *The Soviet Union and the Developing Nations*, Baltimore, Johns Hopkins University Press.

Knorr, K. (1966), *On the Uses of Military Power in the Nuclear Age*, Princeton, Princeton University Press.

Knorr, K. (1975), *The Power of Nations*, New York, Basic Books.

Koestler, A. (1975), *The Act of Creation*, rev. ed., London, Picador.

Kohler, F.D., L. Gouré and M.L. Harvey (1974), *The Soviet Union and the October 1973 Middle East War*, Miami, Fla., Center for Advanced International Studies, University of Miami.

Kolko, G. (1969), *The Roots of American Foreign Policy*, Boston, Beacon Press.

Kolkowicz, R. *et al.* (1970), *The Soviet Union and Arms Control: A Superpower Dilemma*, Baltimore, Johns Hopkins Press.

Korey, W. (1969), 'The Comintern and the Geneology of the "Brezhnev Doctrine," ' *Problems of Communism*, XVIII (May–June), 52–8.

Kramish, A. (1959), *Atomic Energy in the Soviet Union*, Stanford, Stanford University Press.

Kramish, A. (1964), 'The Emergent Genie,' in R.N. Rosecrance (ed.) *The Dispersion of Nuclear Weapons*, New York, Columbia University Press.

Kramish, A. (1965), *The Peaceful Atom in Foreign Policy*, New York, Dell.

Krasner, S.D. (1982), 'Structural Causes and Regime Consequences: Regimes as Intervening Variables,' *International Organization*, 36 (Spring), 185–205.

Kratochwil, F.V. (1978), *International Order and Foreign Policy: A Theoretical Sketch of Post-War International Politics*, Boulder, Westview.

Kulski, W.W. (1973), *The Soviet Union in World Affairs: A Documented Analysis 1964–1972*, Syracuse, Syracuse University Press.

Laird, R.F. (1975), 'Post-Industrial Society: East and West,' *Survey*, 21 (4), 1–17.

Laird, R.F. and E.P. Hoffmann (1980), ' "The Scientific–Technological Revolution," "Developed Socialism," and Soviet International Behavior,' in E.P. Hoffmann and F.J. Fleron, Jr. (eds) *The Conduct of Soviet Foreign Policy*, 2nd ed., New York, Aldine.

Lampert, D.E., L.C. Falkowski, and R.W. Mansbach (1978), 'Is There an International System?' *International Studies Quarterly*, 22 (March), 143–66.

Laqueur, W.Z. (1959), *The Soviet Union and the Middle East*, London, Routledge & Kegan Paul.

Laqueur, W.Z. (1969), *The Road to War 1967*, 2nd ed., London, Weidenfeld and Nicolson.

Larson, T.B. (1978), *Soviet–American Rivalry*, New York, W.W. Norton & Co.

Laurance, E.J. and R.G. Sherwin (1978), 'Understanding Arms Transfers through Data Analysis,' in U. Ra'anan, R.L.Pfaltzgraff, Jr., and G. Kemp (eds) *Arms Transfers to the Third World: The Military Buildup in Less Industrial Countries*, Boulder, Westview.

Laux, J.K. (1981), 'Beyond Detente: Eastern Europe's Reintegration in the International Economic System,' paper prepared for ISA Convention, Philadelphia (March 18–21).

Lederer, I.J. (1974), 'Historical Introduction,' in I.J. Lederer and W.S. Vucinich (eds) *The Soviet Union and the Middle East: The Post World War II Era*, Stanford, Hoover Institution Press.

Lee, W.T. (1972), 'The "Politico-Military-Industrial Complex" of the U.S.S.R.,' *Journal of International Affairs*, 26 (1), 73–86.

Lefever, E.W. (1979), *Nuclear Arms in the Third World: U.S. Policy Dilemma*, Washington, DC, Brookings Institution.

Lefever, E.W. (1980), 'Arms Transfers, Military Training, and Domestic Politics,' in S.G. Neuman and R.E. Harkavy (eds) *Arms Transfers in the Modern World,* New York, Praeger.

Legvold R. (1977), 'The Nature of Soviet Power,' *Foreign Affairs,* 56 (1), 49–71.

Leiss, A.C. (1978), 'International Transfers of Armaments: Can Social Scientists Deal with Qualitative Issues?' in U. Ra'anan, R.L. Pfaltzgraff, Jr., and G. Kemp (eds) *Arms Transfers to the Third World: The Military Buildup in Less Industrial Countries,* Boulder, Westview.

Lellouche, P. (1980), 'International Nuclear Politics,' *Foreign Affairs,* 58 (2), 336–50.

Lellouche, P. (1981), 'Breaking the Rules Without Quite Stopping the Bomb: European Views,' *International Organization,* 35 (Winter), 39–58.

Lenin, V.I. (1967), *Selected Works, Volume 3,* Moscow, Progress Publishers.

Lerner, M. (1958), *America as a Civilization,* London, Jonathan Cape.

Lewis, B. (1969), 'The Great Powers, the Arabs, and the Israelis,' *Foreign Affairs,* 47 (4), 642–52.

Lewis, W.H. (1980), 'Political Influence: The Diminished Capacity,' in S.G. Neuman and R.E. Harkavy (eds) *Arms Transfers in the Modern World,* New York, Praeger.

Lieberman, J.I. (1970), *The Scorpion and the Tarantula: The Struggle to Control Atomic Weapons, 1945–1949,* Boston, Houghton Mifflin.

Lieberson, S. (1973), 'An Empirical Study of Military–Industrial Linkages,' in S. Rosen (ed.) *Testing the Theory of the Military–Industrial Complex,* Lexington, Mass., Lexington Books.

Lijphart, A. (1975), 'The Comparable-Cases Strategy in Comparative Research,' *Comparative Political Studies,* 8 (July), 158–77.

Liska, G. (1960), *The New Statecraft: Foreign Aid in American Foreign Policy,* Chicago, University of Chicago Press.

Liska, G. (1967), *Imperial America: The International Politics of Primacy,* Baltimore, Johns Hopkins Press.

Liska, G. (1980), *Russia & World Order: Strategic Choices and the Laws of Power in History,* Baltimore, Johns Hopkins University Press.

Lowenthal, R. (1977), *Model or Ally? The Communist Powers and the Developing Countries,* New York, Oxford University Press.

Mabry, R.T. (1981a), 'The Present International Nuclear Regime,' in J.A. Yager, *International Cooperation in Nuclear Energy,* Washington, DC, Brookings Institution.

Mabry, R.T. (1981b), 'The Export Policies of the Major Suppliers,' in *ibid.*

McGowan, P.J. (1975), 'Meaningful Comparisons in the Study of Foreign Policy: A Methodological Discussion of Objectives, Techniques, and Research Designs,' in C.W. Kegley *et al.* (eds) *International Events and the Comparative Analysis of Foreign Policy,* Columbia, S.C., University of South Carolina Press.

McGowan, P.J. and H.B. Shapiro (1973), *The Comparative Study of Foreign Policy: A Survey of Scientific Findings,* Beverly Hills, Sage.

McKinlay, R.D. and R. Little (1977), 'A Foreign Policy Model of U.S. Bilateral Aid Allocation,' *World Politics,* 30 (1), 58–86.

McKinlay, R.D. and R. Little (1979), 'The U.S. Aid Relationship: A Test of the Recipient Need and the Donor Interest Models, *Political Studies,* 27 (2), 236–50.

Magdoff, H. (1969), *The Age of Imperialism: The Economics of United States Foreign Policy,* New York, Monthly Review Press.

Mandelbaum, M. (1979), *The Nuclear Question: The United States and Nuclear Weapons, 1946–1976,* New York, Cambridge University Press.

Mangold, P. (1978), *Superpower Intervention in the Middle East,* London, Croom Helm.

Marchetti, V. and J.D. Marks (1974), *The CIA and the Cult of Intelligence,* New York, Dell.

Mason, E.S. (1964), *Foreign Aid and Foreign Policy*, New York, Harper and Row.

Mathias, C.McC., Jr. (1982), 'Ethnic Groups and Foreign Policy,' *Dialogue* (3), 30-3.

Matthews, M. (1978), *Privilege in the Soviet Union*, London, George Allen & Unwin.

May, E.R. (1968), 'The Cold War,' in C.V. Woodward (ed.) *The Comparative Approach to American History*, New York, Basic Books.

May, E.R. (1973), *'Lessons' of the Past: The Use and Misuse of History in American Foreign Policy*, New York, Oxford University Press.

Micunovic, V. (1980), *Moscow Diary*, Garden City, NY, Doubleday.

Mihalka, M. (1980), 'Supplier-Client Patterns in Arms Transfers: The Developing Countries, 1967–76,' in S.G. Neuman and R.E. Harkavy (eds) *Arms Transfers in the Modern World*, New York, Praeger.

Millar, J.R. (1977), 'The Prospects for Soviet Agriculture,' *Problems of Communism*, XXVI (May–June), 1-16.

Millar, T.B. (1971), 'The Nuclear Non-Proliferation Treaty and Super Power Condominium,' in C. Holbraad (ed) *Super Powers and World Order*, Canberra, Australian National University Press.

Mills, C.W. (1956), *The Power Elite*, New York, Oxford University Press.

Moodie, M. (1980), 'Defense Industries in the Third World: Problems and Promises,' in S.G. Neuman and R.E. Harkavy (eds) *Arms Transfers in the Modern World*, New York, Praeger.

Morgenthau, H.J. (1966), *Politics Among Nations*, 3rd ed., New York, Alfred A. Knopf.

Morison, D. (1970), 'The U.S.S.R. and the Middle East War of 1967,' in W.R. Duncan (ed) *Soviet Policy in Developing Countries*, Waltham, Mass., Ginn-Blaisdell.

Morozow, M. (1971), *Das sowjetische Establishment*, Stuttgart, Seewald.

Myrdal, A. (1976), *The Game of Disarmament*, New York, Pantheon.

Nacht, M. (1981), 'The Future Unlike the Past: Nuclear Proliferation and American Security Policy,' *International Organization*, 35 (Winter), 193-212.

Nash, H.T. (1975), *Nuclear Weapons and International Behavior*, Leyden, A.W. Sijthoff.

Neff, T.L. and H.D. Jacoby (1979), 'Nonproliferation Strategy in a Changing Nuclear Fuel Market,' *Foreign Affairs*, 57 (5), 1123-43.

Neuhold, H. (1978), 'Principles and Implementation of Crisis Management: Lessons from the Past,' in D. Frei (ed) *International Crises and Crisis Management*, Farnborough, Saxon House.

Newsweek (1983), 'A Portrait of America,' (January 17), 18-29.

Niebuhr, R. (1964), 'The Social Myths in the "Cold War," ' *Journal of International Affairs*, 21 (1), 40-56.

Nieburg, H.L. (1964), *Nuclear Secrecy and Foreign Policy*, Washington, DC, Public Affairs Press.

Nixon, R.M. (1971), *U.S. Foreign Policy for the 1970's: Building for Peace*, Washington, DC, US Government Printing Office.

Nixon, R.M. (1978), *The Memoirs of Richard Nixon*, London, Arrow.

Nogee, J.L. (1961), *Soviet Policy towards International Control of Atomic Energy*, Notre Dame, University of Notre Dame Press.

Nye, J.S. (1974), 'Transnational Relations and Interstate Conflicts: An Empirical Analysis,' *International Organization*, 28 (Autumn), 961-96.

Nye, J.S. (1981), 'Maintaining a Nonproliferation Regime,' *International Organization*, 35 (Winter), 15-38.

O'Connor, R. (1969), *Pacific Destiny*, Boston, Little, Brown.

OECD (1968), *Development Assistance, 1968 Review*, Paris, OECD Publications.

OECD, (1974), *Development Co-operation, 1974 Review*, Paris, OECD Publications.

OECD (1978), *Development Co-operation, 1978 Review*, Paris, OECD Publications.

OECD (1981), *Development Co-operation, 1981 Review*, Paris, OECD Publications.

Ojha, I.C. (1970), 'The Kremlin and Third World Leadership: Closing the Circle?' in

W.R. Duncan (ed) *Soviet Policy in Developing Countries*, Waltham, Mass., Ginn-Blaisdell.

Osgood, R.E. and R.W. Tucker (1967), *Force, Order and Justice*, Baltimore, Johns Hopkins Press.

Pajak, R.F. (1975), 'Soviet Arms and Egypt,' *Survival*, 17 (4), 165-73.

Pajak, R.F. (1979), 'West European and Soviet Arms Transfer Policies in the Middle East,' in M. Leitenberg and G. Sheffer (eds) *Great Power Intervention in the Middle East*, New York, Pergamon.

Pajak, R.F. (1981), 'The Effectiveness of Soviet Arms Aid Diplomacy in the Third World,' in R.H. Donaldson (ed) *The Soviet Union in the Third World: Successes and Failures*, Boulder, Westview.

Parenti, M. (ed) (1971), *Trends and Tragedies in American Foreign Policy*, Boston, Little, Brown.

Parker, W.H. (1972), *The Superpowers: The United States and the Soviet Union Compared*, London, Macmillan.

Parsons, T. (1951), *The Social System*, New York, Free Press.

Petersson, O. (1982), *Väljarna och världspolitiken* (Voters and World Politics), Stockholm, Norstedts.

Petrén, K. (1976), *Maktstrukturens huvuddrag: En kvantitativ analys av 20 maktindikatorer* (Principal Traits of the Power Structure: A Quantitative Analysis of 20 Indicators of Power), Stockholm, Swedish Institute of International Affairs research report UI-76-2.

Pick, O. (1981), 'Introduction: Political and Ideological Aspects,' in E.J. Feuchtwanger and P. Nailor (eds) *The Soviet Union and the Third World*, London, Macmillan.

Pierre, A.J. (1982), *The Global Politics of Arms Sales*, Princeton, Princeton University Press.

Potter, W.C. (1982), 'Nuclear Export Policy: A Soviet–American Comparison,' in C.W. Kegley and P. McGowan (eds) *Foreign Policy: USA/USSR. Sage International Yearbook of Foreign Policy Studies, Vol. 7*, Beverly Hills, Sage.

Przeworski, A. and H. Teune (1970), *The Logic of Comparative Social Inquiry*, New York, John Wiley.

Pye, L.W. (1960), 'Soviet and American Styles in Foreign Aid,' *Orbis*, 4 (Summer), 159-73.

Quandt, W.B. (1976), *Soviet Policy in the October 1973 War*, Santa Monica, Ca., Rand Report R-1864-ISA.

Quandt, W.B. (1977), *Decade of Decisions: American Policy Toward the Arab–Israeli Conflict, 1967–1976*, Berkeley, University of California Press.

Quandt, W.B. (1978), 'Influence through Arms Supply: The U.S. Experience in the Middle East,' in U. Ra'anan, R.L. Pfaltzgraff, Jr., and G. Kemp (eds) *Arms Transfers to the Third World: The Military Buildup in Less Industrial Countries*, Boulder, Westview.

Quester, G.H. (1970), *Nuclear Diplomacy: The First Twenty-Five Years*, New York, Dunellen.

Quester, G.H. (1973), *The Politics of Nuclear Proliferation*, Baltimore, Johns Hopkins University Press.

Quester, G.H. (1979a), 'The Middle East: Imposed Solutions or Imposed Problems?' in M. Leitenberg and G. Sheffer (eds) *Great Power Intervention in the Middle East*, New York, Pergamon.

Quester, G.H. (1979b), 'Nuclear Proliferation: Linkages and Solutions,' *International Organization*, 33 (Autumn), 541-66.

Quester, G.H. (1981a), 'Introduction: In Defense of Some Optimism,' *International Organization*, 35 (Winter), 1-14.

Quester, G.H. (1981b), 'Preventing Proliferation: The Impact on International Politics,' *International Organization*, 35 (Winter), 213-40.

Ra'anan, U. (1978), 'Soviet Arms Transfers and the Problem of Political Leverage,' in U. Ra'anan, R.L. Pfaltzgraff, Jr., and G. Kemp (eds) *Arms Transfers to the Third World: The Military Buildup in Less Industrial Countries*, Boulder, Westview.

Rakowska-Harmstone, T. (1976), 'Toward a Theory of Soviet Leadership Maintenance,' in P. Cocks, R.V. Daniels, and N.W. Heer (eds) *The Dynamics of Soviet Politics*, Cambridge, Mass., Harvard University Press.

Rapoport, A. (1971), *The Big Two: Soviet-American Perceptions of Foreign Policy*, Indianapolis, Pegasus.

de Riencourt, A. (1968), *The American Empire*, New York, Delta.

Roberts, H.L. (1962), 'Russia and America,' in I.J. Lederer (ed) *Russian Foreign Policy: Essays in Historical Perspective*, New Haven, Yale University Press.

Roberts, S.S. (1979), 'Superpower Naval Confrontations: The October 1973 Arab–Israeli War,' in B. Dismukes and J. McConnell (eds) *Soviet Naval Diplomacy*, New York, Pergamon.

Rohwer, J. (1975), 'Superpower Confrontation on the Seas,' *Washington Papers*, no. 26, Beverly Hills, Sage.

Ro'i, Y. (ed) (1974), *From Encroachment to Involvement: A Documentary Study of Soviet Policy in the Middle East, 1954–1973*, New York, Wiley.

Romagna, J.R. (1978), 'Beyond Status Discrepancy: The Next Stage in Status Theory,' paper prepared for ISA Convention, Washington, DC, February 22-25.

Ronfeldt, D.F. (1978), 'Superclients and Superpowers,' Santa Monica, Rand paper P-5945.

Rosen, S. (1973), 'Testing the Theory of the Military–Industrial Complex,' in S. Rosen (ed) *Testing the Theory of the Military–Industrial Complex*, Lexington, Mass., Lexington Books.

Rosenau, J.N. (1966), 'Pre-Theories and Theories of Foreign Policy,' in R.B. Farrell (ed) *Approaches to Comparative and International Politics*, Evanston, Ill., Northwestern University Press.

Rosenau, J.N. (1974), 'Comparing Foreign Policies: Why, What, How,' in J.N. Rosenau (ed) *Comparing Foreign Policies*, Beverly Hills, Sage.

Roskin, M. (1974), 'From Pearl Harbor to Vietnam: Shifting Generational Paradigms and Foreign Policy,' *Political Science Quarterly*, 89 (Fall), 563-88.

Rystad, G. (1975), *Ambiguous Imperialism: American Foreign Policy and Domestic Politics at the Turn of the Century*, Stockholm, Esselte Studium.

Rystad, G. (ed) (1981), *Congress and American Foreign Policy*, Stockholm, Esselte Studium.

Rywkin, M. (1970), 'Central Asia and Soviet Manpower.' *Problems of Communism*, XXVIII (January-February), 1-13.

Saivetz, C.R. (1980), 'The Soviet Perception of Military Intervention in Third World Countries,' in W.R. Duncan (ed) *Soviet Policy in the Third World*, New York, Pergamon.

Salmore, B.G. and S.A. Salmore (1978), 'Political Regimes and Foreign Policy,' in M.A. East, S.A. Salmore, and C.F. Hermann (eds) *Why Nations Act*, Beverly Hills, Sage.

Sarbin, T.R. (1968), 'Role: Psychological Aspects,' in *International Encyclopedia of the Social Sciences, Vol. 13*, New York, Macmillan/Free Press.

Sartori, G. (1969), 'Politics, Ideology, and Belief Systems,' *American Political Science Review*, 63 (June), 398-411.

Schechter, M.G. (1981), 'The Soviet Union and the New International Economic Order: The Case of the Common Fund,' paper prepared for ISA Convention, Philadelphia, March 18-21.

Schelling, T.C. (1963), *The Strategy of Conflict*, New York, Oxford University Press.

Schelling, T.C. (1966), *Arms and Influence*, New Haven, Yale University Press.

Schiller, H.I. and J.D. Phillips (1970), 'The Military–Industrial Establishment: Complex or System?' in H.I. Schiller and J.D. Phillips (eds) *Super-State: Readings in the Military–*

Industrial Complex, Urbana, University of Illinois Press.

Schlesinger, A.M., Jr. (1965), *A Thousand Days: John F. Kennedy in the White House*, Greenwich, Conn., Fawcett.

Schlesinger, A.M., Jr., (1974), *The Imperial Presidency*, New York, Popular Library.

Schroeder, G.E. (1970), 'Soviet Technology: System vs. Progress,' *Problems of Communism*, XIX (September-October), 19-30.

Schurmann, F. (1974), *The Logic of World Power*, New York, Pantheon.

Schwartz, M. (1973), 'The USSR and Leftist Regimes in Less-Developed Countries,' *Survey*, 19 (2), 209-44.

Schwartz, M. (1975), *The Foreign Policy of the USSR: Domestic Factors*, Encino, Ca., Dickenson.

Schwartz, M. (1978), *Soviet Perceptions of the United States*, Berkeley, University of California Press.

Schwartz, M. (1980), 'Shifting Soviet Images of U.S. Foreign Policy,' paper prepared for Second World Congress for Soviet and East European Studies, Garmisch-Partenkirchen, September 30–October 4.

Scott, A.M. (1970), 'Military Intervention by the Great Powers: The Rules of the Game,' in I.W. Zartman (ed) *Czechoslovakia: Intervention and Impact*, New York, New York University Press.

Sella, A. (1981), *Soviet Political and Military Conduct in the Middle East*, London, Macmillan.

Semmel, A.K. (1982), 'Security Assistance: U.S. and Soviet Patterns,' in C.W. Kegley and P. McGowan (eds) *Foreign Policy: USA/USSR. Sage International Yearbook of Foreign Policy Studies, Vol. 7.*, Beverly Hills, Sage.

Sherwin, M.J. (1975), *A World Destroyed: the Atomic Bomb and the Grand Alliance*, New York, Alfred A. Knopf.

Sherwin, R.G. and E.J. Laurance (1979), 'Arms Transfers and Military Capability: Measuring and Evaluating Conventional Arms Transfers,' *International Studies Quarterly*, 23 (3), 360-89.

Shils, E. (1968), 'The Concept and Function of Ideology,' in *International Encyclopedia of the Social Sciences, Vol. 7*, New York, Macmillan/Free Press.

SIPRI (1975), *The Arms Trade with the Third World*, Harmondsworth, Penguin.

SIPRI (1976), *Armaments and Disarmament in the Nuclear Age: A Handbook*, Stockholm, Almqvist & Wiksell International.

SIPRI (1977), *World Armaments and Disarmament: SIPRI Yearbook 1977*, Stockholm, Almqvist & Wiksell International.

SIPRI (1978), *World Armaments and Disarmament: SIPRI Yearbook 1978*, London, Taylor & Francis.

SIPRI (1979), *Postures for Non-Proliferation*, London, Taylor & Francis.

SIPRI (1982), *World Armaments and Disarmament: SIPRI Yearbook 1982*, London, Taylor & Francis.

Sivachev, N.V. and N.N. Yakovlev (1979), *Russia and the United States: U.S.–Soviet Relations from the Soviet Point of View*, Chicago, University of Chicago Press.

Skogmar, G. (1979), *Atompolitik*, Malmö, Frank Stenvalls Förlag.

Skogmar, G. (1980), 'Nuclear Energy and Dominance: Some Interrelationships between Military and Civil Aspects of Nuclear Energy in U.S. Foreign Policy since 1945,' *Cooperation and Conflict*, XV (4), 217-35.

Smart, I. (1974), 'The Superpowers and the Middle East,' *The World Today*, (January), 4-15.

Smith, H. (1976), *The Russians*, New York, Quadrangle.

Smith, W.S. (1971), 'Soviet Policy and Ideological Formulations for Latin America,' *Orbis*, 14 (Winter), 1122-46.

Smolansky, O.M. (1965), 'Moscow and the Suez Crisis, 1956: A Reappraisal,' *Political Science Quarterly*, 80 (4), 581-605.

Smolansky, O.M. (1978), 'The United States and the Soviet Union in the Middle East,' in

G. Kirk and N.H. Wessell (eds) *The Soviet Threat: Myths and Realities*, New York, Praeger.

Snider, L.W. (1976), 'From Arms to Influence: An Evaluation of Arms Transfers as an Instrument of Supplier Influence on the Political Action of Middle Eastern Recipients,' paper prepared for ISA Convention, Toronto, February 25-29.

Snyder, G.H. and P. Diesing (1977), *Conflict Among Nations: Bargaining, Decision Making, and System Structure in International Crises*, Princeton, Princeton University Press.

Sokloloff, G. (1979), 'Sources of Soviet Power: Economy, Population, Resources,' *Adelphi Papers*, no. 151.

Sonnenfeldt, H. and W.G. Hyland (1979), 'Soviet Perspectives on Security,' *Adelphi Papers*, no. 150.

Sorokin, P.A. (1944), *Russia and the United States*, New York, E.P. Dutton.

Speier, H. (1957), 'Soviet Atomic Blackmail and the North Atlantic Alliance,' *World Politics*, 9 (3), 307-28.

Spero, J.E. (1977), *The Politics of International Economic Relations*, London, George Allen & Unwin.

Spiegel, S.L. (1972), *Dominance and Diversity: The International Hierarchy*, Boston, Little, Brown.

Spiro, H.J. and B.R. Barber (1971), 'Counter-Ideological Uses of "Totalitarianism," ' in E.P. Hoffmann and F.J. Fleron, Jr. (eds) *The Conduct of Soviet Foreign Policy*, Chicago, Aldine-Atherton.

Steel, R. (1977), *Pax Americana*, rev. ed., Harmondsworth, Penguin.

Stein, J.G. (1980), 'Proxy Wars — How Superpowers End Them: The Diplomacy of War Termination in the Middle East,' *International Journal*, XXXV (Summer), 478-519.

Stenelo, L.-G. (1972), *Mediation in International Negotiations*, Lund, Studentlitteratur.

Stillman, E. and W. Pfaff (1966), *Power and Impotence: The Failure of America's Foreign Policy*, New York, Random House.

Stoessinger, J.G. (1977), *The United Nations and the Superpowers: China, Russia, and America*, 4th ed., New York, Random House.

Szeftel, M. (1964), 'The Historical Limits of the Question of Russia and the West,' in D.W. Treadgold (ed) *The Development of the USSR: An Exchange of Views*, Seattle, University of Washington Press.

Taubman, W. (1975), 'Political Power: USA/USSR Ten Years Later — Comparative Foreign Policy,' *Studies in Comparative Communism*, 8 (1/2), 192-203.

Thomas, E.J. and B.J. Biddle (1966a), 'The Nature and History of Role Theory,' in B.J. Biddle and E.J. Thomas (eds) *Role Theory: Concepts and Research*, New York, Wiley.

Thomas, E.J. and B.J. Biddle (1966b), 'Basic concepts for Classifying the Phenomena of Role,' in *ibid*.

Thorp, W.L. (1971), *The Reality of Foreign Aid*, New York, Praeger.

Triska, J.F. and D.D. Finley (1968), *Soviet Foreign Policy*, New York, Macmillan.

Trout, B.T. (1975), 'Rhetoric Revisited: Political Legitimation and the Cold War,' *International Studies Quarterly*, 19 (3), 251-84.

Tucker, R.W. (1968), *Nation or Empire: The Debate Over American Foreign Policy*, Baltimore, Johns Hopkins Press.

Tucker, R.W. (1971), *The Radical Left and American Foreign Policy*, Baltimore, Johns Hopkins Press.

Turner, R.H. (1968), 'Role: Sociological Aspects,' in *International Encyclopedia of the Social Sciences, Vol. 13*, New York, Macmillan/Free Press.

Ulam, A.B. (1962), 'Nationalism, Panslavism, Communism,' in I.J. Lederer (ed) *Russian Foreign Policy: Essays in Historical Perspective*, New Haven, Yale University Press.

Ulam, A.B. (1968), *Expansion and Coexistence: The History of Soviet Foreign Policy, 1917–67*, New York, Praeger.

Ulam, A.B. (1971), *The Rivals: American and Russia since World War II*, New York, Viking.

Ulam, A.B. (1974), 'The Destiny of Eastern Europe,' *Problems of Communism*, XXIII (January–February), 1-12.

Ulam, A.B. (1981), 'Russian Nationalism,' in S. Bialer (ed) *The Domestic Context of Soviet Foreign Policy*, Boulder, Westview.

UN (1967) *The United Nations and Disarmament 1945–1965*, New York, United Nations.

UN (1971), *Yearbook of the United Nations 1971*, New York, United Nations.

UN (1979a), *Demographic Yearbook 1979*, New York, United Nations.

UN (1979b), *Yearbook of International Trade Statistics 1979*, New York, United Nations.

US AID (1978), *US Overseas Loans and Grants and Assistance from International Organizations: Obligations and Loan Authorizations July 1, 1945–September 30, 1977*, Washington, DC, US Agency for International Development.

US Congress (1977), *The Soviet Union and the Third World: A Watershed in Great Power Policy?*, Report to the Committee on International Relations, House of Representatives, by the Senior Specialists Division, Congressional Research Service, Library of Congress, Washington, DC, US Government Printing Office.

US Department of Defense (1982), *Soviet Military Power*, Washington, DC, US Government Printing Office.

USSR Ministry of Defense (1982), *Whence the Threat to Peace*, Moscow, Military Publishing House.

Valenta, J. (1979), *Soviet Intervention in Czechoslovakia, 1968: Anatomy of a Decision*, Baltimore, Johns Hopkins University Press.

Valkenier, E.K. (1970a), 'New Trends in Soviet Economic Relations with the Third World,' *World Politics*, 22 (3), 415-32.

Valkenier, E.K. (1970b), 'Recent Trends in Soviet Research on the Developing Countries,' in W.R. Duncan (ed.) *Soviet Policy in Developing Countries*, Waltham, Mass, Ginn-Blaisdell.

Valkenier, E.K. (1974), 'Soviet Economic Relations with the Developing Nations,' in R.E. Kanet (ed) *The Soviet Union and the Developing Nations*, Baltimore, Johns Hopkins University Press.

Valkenier, E.K. (1979), 'The USSR, the Third World, and the Global Economy,' *Problems of Communism*, XXVIII (July-August), 17-33.

Valkenier, E.K. (1981), 'Great Power Economic Competition in Africa: Soviet Progress and Problems,' *Journal of International Affairs*, 34 (2), 259-68.

Valkov, V.A. (1965), *SSSR i SShA: ikh politicheskie i ekonomicheskie otnosheniya* (USSR and USA: Their political and economic relations), Moscow, Izdatelstvo Nauka.

Walker, S.G. (1979), 'National Role Conceptions and Systemic Outcomes,' in L.S. Falkowski (ed) *Psychological Models in International Politics*, Boulder, Westview.

Wallace, W. (1971), *Foreign Policy and the Political Process*, London, Macmillan.

Walters, R.S. (1970), *American and Soviet Aid: A Comparative Analysis*, Pittsburgh, University of Pittsburgh Press.

Weeks, A.L. (1970), *The Other Side of Coexistence: An Analysis of Russian Foreign Policy*, New York, Pitman.

Weinberg, A.K. (1958), *Manifest Destiny*, Gloucester, Mass., Peter Smith.

Weisband, E. (1973), *The Ideology of American Foreign Policy: A Paradigm of Lockian Liberalism*, Beverly Hills, Sage Professional Paper in International Studies 02-016.

Welch, W. (1970), *American Images of Soviet Foreign Policy*, New Haven, Yale University Press.

Wells, A.R. (1979), 'Superpower Naval Confrontations: The June 1967 Arab–Israeli War,' in B. Dismukes and J.M. McConnell (eds) *Soviet Naval Diplomacy*, New York, Pergamon.

Wesson, R.G. (1974), *The Russian Dilemma: A Political and Geopolitical View*, New Brunswick, NJ, Rutgers University Press.

Wettig, G. (1969), 'Soviet Policy on the Nonproliferation of Nuclear Weapons, 1966–1968,' *Orbis*, 12 (Winter), 1058-84.

Wheeler, H. (1960), 'The Role of Myth Systems in American–Soviet Relations,' *Journal of Conflict Resolution*, 4 (2), 179-84.

Whetten, L.L. (1981), 'The Arab–Israeli Dispute: Great Power Behaviour,' in G. Treverton (ed) *Crisis Management and the Super-Powers in the Middle East*, Farnborough, Gower.

Wilkinson, D.O. (1969), *Comparative Foreign Relations: Framework and Methods*, Belmont, Ca., Dickenson.

Williams, P. (1976), *Crisis Management: Confrontation and Diplomacy in the Nuclear Age*, New York, John Wiley.

Williams, W.A. (1952), *American–Russian Relations, 1781–1947*, New York, Rinehart.

Williams, W.A. (1972), *The Tragedy of American Diplomacy*, rev. ed., New York, Dell.

Williams, W.A. (1980), *Empire as a Way of Life*, New York, Oxford University Press.

Willrich, M. (1969), *Non-Proliferation Treaty: Framework for Nuclear Arms Control*, Charlottesville, Va., Michie.

Windsor, P. (1979), 'The Soviet Union in the International System of the 1980s,' *Adelphi Papers*, no. 152.

Wish, N.B. (1977), *Relationships between National Role Conceptions, National Attributes, and Foreign Policy Behavior*, unpublished Ph.D. dissertation, New Brunswick, NJ, Rutgers University.

Wish, N.B. (1978), 'Utilizing National Role Conceptions to Study Changes in the International System,' paper prepared for ISA Convention, Washington, DC, February 22-25.

Wish, N.B. (1980), 'Foreign Policy Makers and Their National Role Conceptions,' *International Studies Quarterly*, 24 (4), 532-54.

Wittkopf, E. (1975), 'Containment Versus Underdevelopment in the Distribution of United States Foreign Aid,' in W.D. Coplin and C.W. Kegley (eds) *Analyzing International Relations: A Multi-Method Introduction*, New York, Praeger.

Wohlstetter, A. (1977), 'Spreading the Bomb Without Quite Breaking the Rules,' *Foreign Policy*, no. 25, 88-96, 145-79.

Woodruff, W. (1974), *America's Impact on the World: A Study of the Role of the United States in the World Economy, 1750–1970*, London, Macmillan.

Wylie, J.C. (1969), 'The Sixth Fleet and American Diplomacy,' in J.C. Hurewitz (ed) *Soviet–American Rivalry in the Middle East*, New York, Academy of Political Science.

Yager, J.A. (1981), *International Cooperation in Nuclear Energy*, Washington, DC, Brookings Institution.

Yanov, A. (1977), *Détente after Brezhnev: The Domestic Roots of Soviet Policy*, Berkeley, Institute of International Studies, University of California.

Yearbook of International Organizations, 1981, Brussels, Union of International Associations.

Yellon, R.A. (1970), 'Shifts in Soviet Policies Towards Developing Areas 1964–1968,' in W.R. Duncan (ed) *Soviet Policy in Developing Countries*, Waltham, Mass., Ginn-Blaisdell.

Yergin, D. (1978), *Shattered Peace: The Origins of the Cold War and the National Security State*, Boston, Houghton Mifflin.

Young, E. (1972), *A Farewell to Arms Control?*, Harmondsworth, Penguin.

Young, O.R. (1967), 'Intermediaries and Interventionists: Third Parties in the Middle East Crisis,' *International Journal*, 23 (1), 52-73.

Young, O.R. (1968), *The Politics of Force: Bargaining During International Crises*, Princeton, Princeton University Press.

Young, O.R. (1980), 'International Regimes: Problems of Concept Formation,' *World Politics*, 32 (April), 331-56.

Zimmerman, W. (1969), *Soviet Perspectives on International Relations 1956–1967*, Princeton, Princeton University Press.

Index